D1800202

Germany, France and the Integration of Europe

Germany, France and the Integration of Europe

A realist interpretation

Thomas Pedersen

PINTER

London and New York

PINTER
A Cassell imprint
Wellington House, 125 Strand, London WC2R 0BB, England
370 Lexington Avenue, New York, NY 10017–6550, USA

First published 1998
© Thomas Pedersen 1998

British Library Cataloguing in Publication Data
A catalogue record for this book is available from the British Library.

ISBN 1–85567–537–4

Library of Congress Cataloging-in-Publication Data
Pedersen, Thomas.
    Germany, France and the integration of Europe : a realist interpretation/by Thomas
Pedersen.
        p.   cm.
    Includes bibliographical references and index.
    ISBN 1–85567–537–4 (hardcover)
    1. European federation.   2. European Union.   3. France—Foreign relations—
1981   4. Germany—Foreign relations—1945–   5. Realism.
I. Title.
JN15.P412 1998
341.242'2—dc21   97–52770
                                                                                                              CIP

Typeset by York House Typographic Ltd, London
Printed and bound in Great Britain by Biddles Ltd, Guildford and King's Lynn

Contents

Preface

When in 1982 I started taking an interest in European integration, the EC was not a popular subject. It could with some justification be said of those of my generation who dedicated ourselves to the study of European integration that, with a phrase borrowed from Churchill, our decision was one of the few cases in history where rats had been seen to jump on board a sinking ship. Only we were not rats, and the ship did not sink. In fact, only two years after the *Economist* had written its sombre obituary on the 25th anniversary of the EC in March 1982, the Community entered what was to become a long period of constitutive reform, the most recent expression of which is the Amsterdam Treaty. The excitement of being present at the creation, as it were, stimulated my academic interest in the constitutive politics of the EC, defined as the decisions on the basic rules and principles of European integration. This interest was soon translated into a theoretical interest – what made big nation-states accept transfers of sovereignty on a large scale to a regional decision centre? An early academic source of inspiration was William Riker's comparative-historical study of federal systems, in which he insisted on interpreting federalism from a power-politics perspective and, I thought, got away with it rather well.

In the late 1980s, I did a minor comparative study on the role of the UK, France and Germany in the EC. This, combined with my participation in some highly stimulating policy networks in the UK and Germany, drew my attention to the importance of informal coalition patterns in European integration. As time went by, I also grew increasingly concerned about the amount of wishful thinking in scholarly as well as political debate about European integration. Would it not be possible to separate ideology and wishful thinking from sober reasoning and naked facts? Although this book was written in less than two years, it does summarize, articulate and clarify a certain number of questions and conjectures which have been with me from the early days of my academic career.

I am indebted to a number of people for having helped me produce this book. A number of former politicians, higher civil servants and academic pundits in various member states generously set aside precious time to talk with me. I am deeply grateful for their willingness to discuss what must often have seemed rather arcane questions and ideosyncratic views with me. A special thanks should go to Dr Erling Bjøl, based in Paris, with whom I had some frank and very useful discussions and to my colleagues Professor Nikolaj Petersen and Professor Georg Sørensen, whose professionalism has been a constant source of inspiration. The Institute of Political Science at Aarhus University also provided valuable assistance in gathering source material for the book. Ms Kristine Kjærsgaard Nielsen served as my research assistant, carrying out her task competently and with a unique mixture of patience and dedication. I also had stimulating discussions with my students, whose capacity for independent and trenchant comment continues to surprise me. However, the responsibility for the book and for its various flaws remains my own.

Thomas Pedersen
Aarhus, 14 November 1997

For my father and in memory of my mother

1 Introduction

Although attempts have recently been made to create a synthesis between realism and pluralism, the two main competing paradigms within international relations theory, the two paradigms continue to disagree sharply, notably about the possibilities of international cooperation. It is fair to say that the case of Western Europe represents the biggest challenge to realism. In Western Europe, a number of states have ceded a considerable amount of sovereignty to an institutional system with supranational features. Given the centrality of international institutions in the European region, the theoretical battle between realism and pluralism is thus essentially fought on European ground. *Prima facie* the extraordinary institutional density of the European region lends credence to pluralist propositions about the existence of common interests and the tendency for states to concentrate on absolute gain. European integration is thus a hard case for realists.

This study sets out to explain the evolution of European integration from a realist point of view. Its aim is to examine how far a realist theory can take us in the direction of explaining central features of regionalism in the European region. In a sense, the book can be read as a rescue attempt. It is not a defence of neo-realist theory. Abandoning hard-core neo-realism, it suggests that the case of European integration can only be explained in realist terms by rediscovering and revising classical realism with its emphasis on ideas and historical learning. For lack of a more elaborate meta-theoretical framework, I offer the preliminary suggestion that an *ideational realism* centring on the concept of grand strategy is helpful in understanding central features of European politics in the post-war period.

1

A natural point of departure for a realist analysis of European integration is to concentrate on the major powers and their interests. Indeed, a recurring theme in many scholarly accounts of European integration has been the special role of France and Germany in fostering closer integration. The metaphors describing this role abound: from 'motor' to 'axis' to 'core'. Yet, notwithstanding some interesting recent contributions, it remains unclear what the theoretical basis and implications of these empirical observations are. The theoretical part of the book sketches out a set of concepts which might be helpful in understanding the behaviour of big states in relation to processes of regional integration. The empirical part of the study seeks to apply and illustrate the relevance of this conceptual framework.

The empirical section of the book tries to assess whether France and Germany do in fact play the leading role in EU politics and asks why and how France and Germany try to lead the process of European unification. It is argued that the experience of European integration has not, as yet, transcended *Realpolitik*, but that it has modified it in important respects. As indicator of Franco–German influence I focus on the constitutive negotiations on the Single European Act in 1985 and the negotiations on the Maastricht Treaty in 1991. However, I try to paint a full picture of the Franco–German role in the EU, including the shadow of the past and the horizon towards which the actors are moving.

Neo-realist theory, with its emphasis on international structure, has had difficulty explaining the demise of the bipolar system. The collapse of bipolarity, which Waltz claimed would be eminently stable, the peaceful transition to the post-Cold War era and the continuing Franco–German collaboration in the absence of a stabilizing bipolar overlay are all anomalies from the point of view of neo-realism. Neo-realists have attempted to rescue their theory by offering new interpretations of European politics, but characteristically their strongest defence has been to ask the court for a postponement. In Mearsheimer's words: 'since this systemic change is just beginning, we should not yet expect to find marked changes in patterns of state behaviour'.[1]

It would be hasty to interpret the major transformations of the European and international scene of the last seven years as confirmation of pluralist or neo-idealist theories. An ideational realism emphasizing historical evolution and the role of ideas is likely to generate more persuasive answers to the puzzles of European politics.

A central theoretical proposition in this study is that a realist behavioural logic is not incompatible with a high degree of regional institutionalization. I propose a new realist interpretation of European politics based on the view that region-building is one of several ideal-type strategies which big powers may pursue in order to maximize their influence. I try to show that Germany, in terms of population and economics the strongest power in Europe, has played a key role in the constitutive politics of the EU. Far from being a passive instrument in France's grand strategy, I argue that Germany has consistently pursued a grand strategy of cooperative hegemony in which France and European unification have played an essential role. A high degree of regional institutionalization is compatible with a soft hegemony provided at least two basic conditions are fulfilled: 1) that the aspiring hegemon can accept regional power-sharing and 2) that the state seeking institutionalized hegemony has sufficient negotiating power to enable it to shape the regional institutions to its advantage. Asymmetrical federation is one of the goals which cooperative hegemons may pursue.

The question of Franco–German leadership in the process of European integration is also of some relevance to the debate about the dynamics of regional integration. Neo-functionalists and their institutionalist successors have argued that processes of regional integration cannot be controlled by state actors. This study challenges that view, arguing that in the crucial area of constitutive politics, state actors do in fact 'rein in' supranational actors. Moreover, it will be argued that to the extent that spillover and institutionalist dynamics play a role in regional integration, they mainly do so as elements in state strategies. Realist and intergovernmentalist analyses of regional institutionalization are attentive to the role of informal leadership. A key question which has already been the subject of interesting contributions by realists such as Paul Taylor, Andrew Moravcsik and others is how France and Germany have managed to make progress towards European unification despite being confronted by considerable opposition and restrictive decision-making rules. This volume tries to elaborate on these reflections.

That the question of leadership in European integration deserves attention was recognized by second-generation neo-functionalists like Lindberg and Scheingold, who, in *Europe's Would-Be Polity* in 1971, included a leadership factor in their political system model of the EC.[2] Attempting to rescue neo-functionalist theory from the onslaught of reality they stressed that political factors were of crucial importance as activators of integration dynamics. They were of course mainly inspired by the experience of de Gaulle vetoing supranational reforms in the EC in the mid-1960s. Interestingly, however, the leadership factor was never discussed systematically, nor was it integrated into a more elaborate, theoretical model. Leadership was mainly discussed in negative terms as a disintegrative factor belonging to the national level. Neither were attempts made to introduce hegemonic perspectives in the debate on European politics when in the early 1980s realism emerged as a dominant theoretical perspective within international relations. There were, however, important solitary efforts to address the issue of leadership, such as de Schoutheete's concept of subsystems and William and Helen Wallace's insistence on the importance of informal negotiation dynamics.[3]

This book is not the product of a revelation. It is inspired by the approach adopted by other realist scholars such as Stanley Hoffmann, Alan Milward and Andrew Moravcsik, the latter having shown in his seminal article on the Single European Act how the outcome of the intergovernmental conference negotiations can essentially be explained by looking only at the positions of the three largest member states.[4] The weakness of Moravcsik's approach, which comes out most clearly in his more recent works, is that it combines realist and pluralist assumptions. Thus in his important article from 1993, *Preferences and Power in the European Community*, he in fact endorses a central tenet of neo-functionalism, arguing that 'other premises, particularly the focus on economic interests, may still be viable. It remains plausible, for example, to argue that integration is a distinctive policy response of modern welfare states to rising economic interdependence'.[5] This study has a sharper theoretical focus seeking to explain a central feature of European politics from the perspective of realism, pure and simple.

This study also stands on the shoulders of some perceptive analysts of German foreign policy. As Günther Hellmann rightly points out: 'with regard to *Einbindungspolitik* ... little systematic research has thus far been carried out as to why German leaders have chosen to pursue this approach'.[6] In a more recent article, Hellmann points out the striking difference between the assumptions of German and non-German (mostly American) studies of German foreign policy after unification, the realist paradigm being much more influential outside Germany. In his discussion of contemporary German foreign policy he also makes a welcome plea for a rediscovery of the concept of grand strategy adding that '(such studies) ... must not leave out a rethinking of the theoretical foundations underlying the study of grand strategy'.[7]

Some recent studies challenge conventional pluralist interpretations of Germany's integration policy, implicitly or explicitly adopting a hegemonic approach.[8] For instance Thomas O. Hueglin argues in his discussion of 'Europe's ambiguous federalism' that 'it is a tool of political organization that can be used or abused for whatever purpose the dominant powers may decide'. And elsewhere: 'Germany succeeded in implementing a hegemonic regime of monetary stabilization at the behest of its own export industries'.[9] Hueglin goes on to pose the highly pertinent question 'Why has a dominant or even hegemonic Germany become the most ardent promoter of a supranational European Union and of increased use of qualified majority voting in particular?'.[10] Other analysts have made valuable attempts to address this question from a basically realist perspective.[11] Stanley Hoffmann remains in a category of his own, having produced numerous perspicacious and elegant essays on the intricacies of European politics. It is not surprising, therefore, that it is in Hoffmann's writings more than perhaps anywhere else that one finds a detached and balanced assessment of contemporary German EU policy. In 1993 Hoffmann wrote that 'especially after unification increased the relative weight of Germany among the Twelve, the Federal Republic's economic and financial might has made the EC an instrument of German influence'.[12]

What is lacking in all of these studies, however, is an attempt to fit the analysis of German policy into a general discussion of the role of big powers in processes of regionalization.

As indicated above, to the extent that Germany exercises a kind of leadership, in the EU this leadership has throughout been exercised in close collaboration with France. Another central aspect of this study is thus the special problems relating to dual leadership and the interaction between intra-hegemonic relations and relations between the hegemonic leadership and balancing and secondary states in a region. The literature on the Franco–German relationship is huge and mainly empirical. Roy Willis wrote his classical study on France, Germany and the new Europe in the 1960s in which he stressed the process of learning and the emergence of new norms after the Second World War.[13] Important studies have since been made of the more recent period in Franco–German relations, prominent examples being Haig Simonean's *The Privileged Partnership* and Patrick Mccarthy's *France–Germany 1983–1993. The Struggle to Cooperate.*[14] Picht and Wessels have published a valuable collection of analyses, *Motor für Europa?*, addressing both constitutive and sectoral issues.[15]

A common feature of these and other important studies of the relationship is the absence of any attempt to interpret the relationship theoretically. Even from a chronological point of view the available literature is not complete. What is lacking is an analysis of the most recent period in Franco–German relations and particularly an analysis of the role played by France and Germany in the 'history-making decisions' leading to the Single European Act, the Maastricht Treaty and the Amsterdam Treaty.[16] At the empirical level, this study can thus be read as a successor to Haig Simonean's volume, which traces Franco–German EU policy into the early 1980s.

In my attempt to theorize about the role of big powers in processes of regional integration I to a certain extent rely on reasoning by analogy. As Wallace and Wallace point out in a comment on political science research into European integration, 'this unavoidable absence of historical perspective perhaps made it too tempting for the contemporary social scientists to over-emphasize the specificity and novelty of the EC integration model'. They add correctly that 'as records from the 1950s and 1960s have become available, the gap is being filled, often disconcertingly'.[17]Obviously, historical parallels should be used with great care. As pointed out by King, Keohane and Verba, a comparative approach is always at least as good and usually better than an analogy. The reason is that comparative analyses involve more observations, which allows stochastic factors to be averaged out.[18] Analogies cannot be used as confirmation of propositions. At the most, they may be used as illustrations. They are most useful as sources of inspiration for constructing ideal-types. Theory-building will thus often develop as an interplay between deductive reasoning and historical ideal-types.

The topic of France and Germany's role in European integration raises at least two major questions. First, there is the question of power. In theoretical terms, the key question is how big powers may safeguard their national interests within the confines of regional institutionalization. In empirical terms, the question is to what extent one can say that some member states in the EU integration system have a privileged position and benefit disproportionately from the process of integration. Here one may examine the extent to which Germany, France and the UK, representing the West European big powers in the narrow sense, have been able to control the outcome of constitutive negotiations. We posit that France and Germany have in fact so far been able to control those negotiations. They have managed to do so by pursuing a particular great power strategy, that of cooperative hegemony. Cooperative hegemony can be expected to have a particular attraction for comparatively 'weak' (or declining) big powers which for geopolitical, historical or other

6

reasons are unable and/or unwilling to use military coercion (cf. Chapter 5). Assuming that the strategy of cooperative hegemony is of special relevance to Germany, we shall be particularly interested in Germany's ability to control the outcomes of constitutive bargains in the EU.

Second, there is the question of how what could be called subsystemic leadership affects integration dynamics at the level of the regional system. Here one will have to examine what forms subsystemic leadership may assume, and look at reactions to gestures of subsystemic leadership in other member states. It could be hypothesized that the two questions are closely related. The reason why France and Germany have consistently been pressing for closer European integration is basically that closer integration has been regarded as a national asset for each of the two states, 'closer integration' having become largely synonymous with 'extension of national power'.

How does one test the proposition that France and Germany together have played a leading role in European integration and that they have benefited disproportionately from European integration? First of all, it seems important to examine to what extent the duo has been the initiating force prior to treaty changes. Linked to this is the more specific question of the extent to which the two have been able to set the agenda prior to the intergovernmental conferences (IGCs) on European Union. Secondly, as regards the negotiating process, it seems reasonable to make it a minimum requirement of effective leadership that France and Germany should play a more important leadership role at the IGCs than the presidency and the Commission. The presidency is especially important here. The presidency is the formal leader of the IGCs and as such reflects the hierarchical (as opposed to the anarchical) element in the EU system.

Thirdly, it must be shown that France and Germany have to a significant degree been able to control the outcome of the negotiations at the IGCs, thereby satisfying their specific interests. I deliberately use the term significant control, because it is implied in the notion of cooperative hegemony that the would-be hegemon is willing to share power. An important indicator of a cooperative hegemonic approach to regional integration would be willingness on the part of the hegemon to grant major side-payments and share power (cf. Chapter 5). 'Significant control' is obviously a vague concept especially as there is no generally accepted ranking of sectors in terms of their integrative value. The question of French and German influence will therefore have to be answered in relative terms as well. Comparing the French and German

7

negotiating score with that of the UK will give us a clearer picture of French and German influence. Given the structural similarities between the UK and France, a comparison between these two states is particularly revealing. An assessment of a member state's control of negotiating outcomes can be undertaken at various levels. The ideal approach would be to compare the outcomes of all of the written proposals submitted by the member states in the course of negotiations with amendments. I have refrained from doing so, first of all because I doubt whether such a comprehensive analysis is necessary to answer the questions I have raised and secondly, because it would have made this book much less readable.[19] What I have done in most cases is to compare outcomes with more general summaries of French and German nego- tiating positions. I have subsequently taken a closer look at French and German (as well as certain other) positions in selected areas of partic- ular importance to the state in question.

European constitutive politics involve a range of different actors at various levels. Statesmen, civil servants and, less visibly, a range of institutions, personalities and interest groups try to influence the nego- tiations. In this study the actors in European constitutive politics are defined narrowly in keeping with the realist premises of the study.[20] I am basically examining statements and actions of ministers and heads of state, whilst dealing with the preparatory work of civil servants in more summary terms. However, the foreign policy advisors to the French president and German chancellor are assumed to be very useful sources of information about negotiations between political leaders.

It is important not to define the outcome of EU constitutive negoti- ations too narrowly. EU decisions, especially at IGCs, are often broad statements of intent which need to be ratified by national parliaments and interpreted and implemented by Union and national authorities. Moreover, concessions at IGCs often consist of promises to the effect that an issue will be decided upon or reexamined at a later stage, as is evident in the case of the Maastricht Treaty.[21] IGC outcomes ought therefore to be interpreted within an extended time-horizon.

It should also be said that we cannot draw very firm conclusions regarding the overall distribution of influence within the Union on the basis of analyses of the outcomes of constitutive negotiations. Such analyses can be used as rough indicators of power distribution in the EU. But the negotiating 'score' at IGCs must be seen within the context of normal politics and the pattern of implementation of decisions in various member states, which is known to be quite uneven.

I use the outcome of constitutive negotiations as an indicator of Franco–German influence. For realist theory this is obviously a soft measure. Ideally, one ought to analyse the influence of big powers in normal politics as well. This could be done by means of case studies. If it could be shown that France and Germany exercise a disproportionate influence in normal politics this would constitute a particularly strong confirmation of realist claims. For practical reasons, however, I have refrained from doing so.

The empirical focus of this volume is on the role of two of the big countries in one particular type of EU politics, that of constitutive politics, here defined as decisions at intergovernmental conferences (IGCs) on treaty changes. This roughly corresponds to what Anderson terms 'big-bang studies' and what Peterson calls 'history-making decisions'.[22] Clearly, to define 'history-making decisions' is not a straightforward matter. It could be argued that only with the benefit of hindsight can one see what was 'history-making'. 'Constitutive' therefore seems a more useful expression. To concentrate on constitutive decisions implies that change through deliberate political decisions constitutes important change. Against this view it can be argued that in some cases 'normal politics' can be highly significant, e.g. in being able to socialize actors and create expectations among societal groups. I do not totally reject that view, but claim that states exercise control when it comes to decisions at the EU's IGC and that IGC decisions have a major impact on the power distribution in the EU. As Anderson points out: 'straightforward theoretical extrapolation from one big bang to the next is very risky', since past grand bargains may change the institutional framework within which future grand bargains emerge.[23] Apart from the fact that the European Parliament was officially associated with the IGC negotiations leading up to the Amsterdam Treaty, the institutional framework in the constitutive sphere has, however, remained quite stable.

This book does not cover France and Germany's EU policy during the entire period of European integration. I focus upon the period from 1983 to 1993 but stray back into history in order to point out some important continuities in European politics and to expand the number of 'cases' by considering instances over time.[24] The year 1983 is a chosen as the starting point as this was the year when the process of European integration was relaunched. 1993 is chosen as the cut-off point, because by December 1993 the Maastricht Treaty had been ratified in all member states. While the in-depth analysis concentrates on the period from

1983 to 1993, an overview of trends in the following years is added. The year 1994 thus saw several initiatives by France and Germany indicating the direction in which they wanted to take the Union in the following years.

European constitutive politics are not easy to study scientifically. We are dealing with sensitive decisions made at the highest level. A large number of key written sources on the topic of intergovernmental conferences will thus be classified. The traditional historian will therefore tend to define this topic as being beyond the reach of scientific analysis for several decades. Yet to leave contemporary and recent political history entirely in the hands of journalistic comment is not a happy solution. Faced with this inherent difficulty, I have chosen several indirect and second-best strategies. First of all, I rely quite heavily on written memoirs by politicians or higher civil servants. It seems to me that the value of memoirs and diaries as a source of knowledge for scholars has been underestimated. With due correction for bias such writings can be extremely useful. They take one to the centre of events and give the analyst a flavour of the unwritten conventions which are as important as they are difficult to pinpoint for the outside observer. In this case, the analysis has been facilitated by the fact that French politicians and civil servants have a highly developed tradition of publishing their thoughts, even in mid-career. The unevenness in the availability of such written sources involves the risk of giving the analysis a certain bias. This risk must be kept in mind.

It should be stressed that memoirs should of course always be attentive to the purpose and audience of the author. Inevitably, the author of memoirs will at times fall prey to the temptation to embellish his own or his country's contribution to the course of events. The timing of a publication is likely to be important for its credibility. Memoirs published while other witnesses are still alive must *ceteris paribus* be ascribed greater credibility than memoirs written in old age, when most of these witnesses may no longer be able to react to false claims. As for political diaries, in one sense they constitute valuable sources with a high degree of trustworthiness, as in most cases the author will have taken notes during or immediately after the events he describes. In other respects, however, political diaries have a more questionable credibility. At least in France, such publications are often used as a means of damaging political opponents. The role of the author at the time of writing is thus important. Any assertion in a political diary must be seen in context. With that proviso, such publications may be valuable, particularly as sources of information about that sphere of politics, high politics and constitutive EU politics, which is rarely described in other written sources.

Secondly, to a limited extent, I have relied on interviews with decision-makers and academic pundits. Given the sensitive nature of the topic, the interviewees have all been granted total anonymity. This obviously raises certain methodological problems, in that part of the book's empirical evidence cannot be controlled. However, account should be taken of the fact that the interviews only serve as supplementary evidence and that the main purpose of the book is to outline a theoretical framework and illustrate it in the case of Germany and France in the EU's constitutive politics.

Notes

1. John J. Mearsheimer, 'Reply', *International Security*, Vol. 15, no. 2, Fall 1990, p. 195.
2. Leon Lindberg and Stuart Scheingold, *Europe's Would-Be Polity*, New Jersey: Prentice-Hall, 1971. See also my own modest contribution to the revision of neo-functionalism in Thomas Pedersen, 'Political Change in the European Community: The Single European Act as a Case of System Transformation', *Cooperation & Conflict*, Vol. 1, 1992.
3. See e.g. William Wallace, *The Transformation of Western Europe*, London: Pinter, 1989; Helen Wallace, 'Institutionalized Bilateralism and Multilateral Relations: Axis, Motor or Detonator?', in Robert Picht and Wolfgang Wessels (eds), *Motor für Europa?*, Bonn: Europa Union Verlag, 1990, pp. 145–59.
4. See Andrew Moravcsik, 'Negotiating the Single European Act', in Robert O. Keohane and Stanley Hoffmann (eds), *The New European Community. Decision-making and Institutional Change*, Boulder: Westview, 1991.
5. Andrew Moravcsik, 'Preferences and Power in the European Community: A Liberal Intergovernmentalist Approach', *Journal of Common Market Studies*, Vol. 31, no. 4, December 1993, p. 476.
6. See Gunther Hellmann, *'Einbindungspolitik'. United Germany and the Promise of Foreign Policy Continuity*. Paper prepared for the 36th Annual Convention of the International Studies Association in Chicago, 21–25 February 1995, p. 25.
7. Gunther Hellmann, 'Goodbye Bismarck? The Foreign Policy of Contemporary Germany', *Mershon International Studies Review*, Vol. 40, Supplement 1, April 1996, pp. 27ff.
8. See Andrei S. Markovits and Simon Reich, *The New Face of Germany: Gramsci, Neo-Realism and Hegemony*, Graduate School of Public and International Affairs, University of Pittsburgh, Working Paper Series 28, and Jeffrey J. Anderson, *A United Germany in Europe: Hard Interests and Soft Power*. Paper delivered at the 1995 Annual Meeting of the American Political Science Association in Chicago,

31 August–3 September 1995. See also the empirically-based analysis in Jeffrey J. Anderson and John B. Goodman, 'Mars or Minerva? A United Germany in a Post-Cold War Europe', in R. Keohane, J. Nye and S. Hoffmann (eds), *After the Cold War. International Institutions and State Strategies in Europe 1989–1991*, Cambridge, Mass.: Harvard University Press, 1993.

9. Thomas O. Hueglin, 'Europe's Ambiguous Federalism: A Conceptual and Analytical Critique', in Alan W. Cafruny and Carl Lankowski (eds), *Europe's Ambiguous Unity*, London and Boulder: Lynne Rienner Publishers, 1997.

10. *Ibid.*, p. 56.

11. See in particular Daniel Hamilton, 'A More European Germany. A More German Europe', *Journal of International Affairs*, no. 45, Summer 1991, and Gary L. Geipel, 'The Nature and Limits of German Power', in Gary L. Geipel (ed.), *Germany in a New Era*, Indianapolis: Hudson Institute, 1993.

12. Reprinted from 'The New York Review of Books' in his brilliant *The European Sisyphus. Essays on Europe 1964–1994*, Boulder: Westview, 1995.

13. Roy F. Willis, *France, Germany and the New Europe 1945–1963*, Stanford: Stanford University Press, 1965.

14. Haig Simonean, *The Privileged Partnership*, Oxford: Clarendon, 1985, and Patrick McCarthy, *France–Germany 1983–1993. The Struggle to Cooperate*, London: Macmillan, 1993.

15. Picht and Wessels *op. cit.*

16. See John Peterson, 'Decision-Making in the European Union: Towards a Framework for Analysis', *Journal of European Public Policy*, Vol. 2, no. 1, 1995, pp. 69–93.

17. See Helen Wallace and William Wallace, *Policy-Making in the European Union*, Oxford: Oxford University Press, 1996, p. 10.

18. Gary King, Robert O. Keohane and Sidney Verba, *Designing Social Inquiry. Scientific Inference in Qualitative Research*, Princeton: Princeton University Press, 1994, p. 212.

19. Of course, one might consider placing a detailed analysis of this kind in an appendix, summarizing overall patterns in the text.

20. An alternative approach is adopted in Colette Mazzucelli, *France and Germany at Maastricht. Politics and Negotiations to Create the European Union*. New York: Garland Publishing, 1996. Mazzucelli's focus is broader and stresses the role of what she calls 'new politico-administrative actors' in the EU's constitutive politics.

21. The Maastricht Treaty contains several references to 1996 as the year in which certain parts of the treaty would be reviewed.

22. See Jeffrey J. Anderson, 'The State of the (European) Union': From the Single Market to Maastricht. From Singular Events to General Theories, *World Politics*, Vol. 47, no. 3, April 1995, and John Peterson, 1995, *op. cit.*

23. Anderson, 'The State of the (European) Union', *op. cit.*, p. 463.

24. King, Keohane and Verba, *op. cit.*, p. 221.

2 Structure or strategy?

In a recent article John Lewis Gaddis usefully distinguishes three methodological approaches to the study of international relations: the behavioural, the structural and the evolutionary.[1] The behavioural approach departs from the premises of classical empiricism; it looks for evidence in the form of observations; the method applied is quantification or simulation. The structural approach focuses on unobservable and unmeasurable structures which nevertheless have observable effects. The evolutionary approach assumes the interaction of behaviour and structure and is concerned with the effects of time.

An evolutionary approach best captures the considerable diversity and the voluntarist element in contemporary international relations. Although international structures constrain, statesmen and decision-makers at large possess a considerable freedom of action. What structuralist realists like Waltz fail to explain satisfactorily is the element of learning and innovation in international relations, as witnessed by the difficulty neo-realists have had explaining recent events such as Gorbachev's policy.[2] The dissolution of the USSR, the peaceful transformation of the international system in 1990 and the adoption by the Soviet leadership of Western ideas raise serious questions about the relevance of neo-realist theory. Indeed, the experience of 1989 is reflected in a new school in the debate on international relations theory, which stresses the role of ideas.[3] The onset of a new era of profound socio-economic change has added to the attraction of ideas-focused research.[4] Goldstein and Keohane emphasize that national interests are defined in the light of world views, principled ideas and causal beliefs shaped by

13

historical experience.[5] Ideas are argued to influence policy when '1) the principled or causal beliefs they embody provide road maps that increase actors' clarity about goals or ends-means relationships, 2) (when) they become focal points that define cooperative solutions or act as coalitional glue and 3) (when) they become embedded in political institutions'. Causal beliefs are of greatest relevance in this context. They 'are beliefs about cause-effect relationships which derive authority from the shared consensus of recognized elites'. And further 'Causal beliefs imply strategies for the attainment of goals, themselves valued because of shared principled beliefs and understandable only within the context of broader world views'.[6] Carlsnæs accords greater importance to the choices of statesmen, which he sees as being embedded in a dispositional structure and constrained by objective conditions.[7] Other theorists of a structurationalist disposition have suggested that international outcomes are often shaped by professional or 'epistemic' communities.[8] The latter proposition has a certain *prima facie* plausibility given the comparative advantages of knowledge-based groups in an information-scarce setting such as the international system. An even more radical attack on neo-realism has come from constructivists such as Alexander Wendt, who argues that 'anarchy is what states make of it'.[9] One thus detects a broad neo-idealist current in the debate among international relations theorists. A major challenge for realists seems to be to try to incorporate the role of ideas. Apart from stressing the element of learning and innovation in international relations, the ideas literature also draws the attention to the role of legitimacy as a political resource.[10]

Power and security are important motives in international relations. The security dilemma continues to haunt states, as does the obsession with relative gain. But technological globalization enhances transparency, which tends to reduce the security dilemma. It also improves the possibilities for diffusing ideas. Economic globalization creates new common problems prompting the formation of new pressure groups and the setting up of various types of joint governance structures. States remain the predominant, although not the only, actors. In low politics areas transnational actors abound and exert considerable influence, although their political impact is often difficult to trace. In high politics and constitutive areas the influence of transnational actors is likely to be much more limited. While the significance of domestic politics has increased in foreign policy formulation, its importance has probably been exaggerated. Recent contributions to international relations theory by Robert Putnam and others have argued that domestic political factors play a central role in the making of foreign policy. Decision-makers taking part in international negotiations are said to be involved in what Putnam calls 'a two-level game'.[11] They play a game with other state negotiators and a game with their domestic hinterland. Statesmen in two different states thus do not have the same freedom of action domestically at any given point in time. Significantly, domestic constraints may be an asset in international negotiations where there is a common wish to reach an agreement. Decision-makers in negotiations between democracies have to take into account the domestic political reality of their adversary. In his essay on bargaining Schelling similarly made the important point that 'if a binding public opinion can be *cultivated* (author's emphasis) and made evident to the other side, the initial position can thereby be made visibly final'. The point is that the domestic political factor may be and often is manipulated by statesmen. Much will then depend on how persuasively a negotiating position is communicated to the other party.[12] One suspects that many references to domestic pressures by foreign policy actors will be hard to back up with concrete evidence. Just as international commitments may be used as an alibi against domestic audiences, domestic constraints may be used as an alibi internationally.

Technological globalization enhances the knowledge of public opinion, but also risks creating an atomized citizenship that fails to influence foreign policy-makers. Only if married with organization does technological globalization seriously affect the distribution of power. The ability of the executive to manipulate public opinion thus needs to be taken into account. The executive does not simply passively respond to domestic demands but actively shapes opinion, making use of its superior resources in terms of information. International institutions may help state executives control domestic politics. A high degree of international institutionalization implies governance costs but also possibilities for executive information steering vis-à-vis domestic opinion, especially if one is dealing with governance systems with weak parliamentary controls. And political leaders are not helpless victims of a domestic setting. In some cases they may succeed in fundamentally shaping and re-shaping the values and principles of a state even in entrenched democracies, the Thatcher period in Britain being a case in point.

The domestic political argument is vulnerable in another sense too. It may be argued that domestic political pressures in foreign policy are much weaker than generally assumed. Notwithstanding a tendency towards democratization of foreign policy, even regional integration policy, which can be characterized as a special type of foreign policy with very considerable impact on national societies, continues to attract only limited attention among ordinary citizens. In Western Europe it remains the case that integration policy makers can count on a considerable 'permissive consensus' in the population favouring further integration, although in individual member states politicization of EU politics may be considerable.[13] However, knowledge of European politics is very limited at the level of the citizenship.

All in all, while realism is a useful approach to international relations it is clearly underspecified and in need of modification to account for the important role of ideas. Brooks has argued convincingly that it is necessary to differentiate within realism.[14] The existing international relations literature paints a simple two-dimensional picture, in which classical realism confronts structural realism, the English school generally being seen as a special position within the classical realist tradition with some affinities to pluralism.

Ideational realism is a tentative concept describing a third realist position. While accepting the primacy of state actors, it leaves some scope for state learning and innovation. It differs somewhat from classical realism in that it focuses on coherent sets of ideas shaped by historical learning and constrained by systemic factors. Goldstein and Keohane's notion of causal beliefs seems particularly helpful. At the same time, ideational realism accords strategy greater importance than does structural realism and is more optimistic as regards the possibility of cooperation in international relations. First of all, statesmen may learn from experience. Schroeder argues persuasively that the central weakness of neo-realism is that it simplifies the behaviour of states, thus making it difficult to make correct predictions. Neo-realist theory 'not only prevents scholars from seeing and explaining the various strategies alternative to balancing . . . but even blocks a genuine historical understanding of balancing conduct and the balance of power itself as a historical variable changing over time'.[15] He also points out with reference to extensive historical evidence that band-wagoning is more common than balancing and that states have devised new and imaginative ways of coping with anarchy, including 'niche behaviour' and 'transcending'. This brings us to our second point, that there is always more than one possible strategic response to any given structural challenge, and that state actors are capable of innovation. Thirdly, the

16

impact of systemic structure on state behaviour has probably been exaggerated by neo-realists. Systemic structures constrain, they do not determine as Waltz himself recognizes in *Man, the State and War*.[16] Systemic factors create incentives, they do not determine behaviour. Like a strong wind, systemic structure pushes the actor in a certain direction, but just as it is possible to walk against a strong wind, it is possible to ignore the logic of anarchy.[17] We would go further and argue that the (strategic) intentions of a state are more important than its (positional) role, which of course is a view with a long pedigree.[18] Some 'soft' neo-realists seem to recognize as much. Stephen Walt has argued convincingly that states do not balance against power but against fear.[19] This implies that given the right strategy a powerful state may limit the negative consequences of anarchy.

Strategy is a more important concept in international relations than are system, structure and discourse. During the 1980s the debate on international relations theory was dominated by Kenneth Waltz's structural realism, with writers like Barry Buzan and Robert Keohane adding modifications to neo-realism.[20] The 1990s have seen a shift in the debate with some of the assumptions of classical historical realism receiving new attention. At a fundamental level, the new interest in the role of ideas reflects a rediscovery of classical realism with its emphasis on agency and the historically generated particularities of states. The crucial point is that idealism in the epistemological sense is not incompatible with a realist behavioural logic.

In trying to incorporate the role of ideas into realist theory, one may pursue various lines of thought. At one extreme, one finds the constructivist argument that international politics is a permanent ideological building site with actors, among them academic communities, possessing great freedom to shape structures through the creation of new inter-subjective understandings. In a long historical perspective human agency is undoubtedly an important force. In any given historical situation, human beings are much more constrained. Analyses of contextual decision-making are therefore well advised to relate ideas to objective constraints. It would be equally unfortunate to substitute a neo-idealist structuralism for neo-realist structuralism. This is essentially what some discourse analysts do, when they argue that 'textual structures' constrain. This is an interesting idea, and useful to the extent that it helps us understand continuity in the choice of ideas. But as in the case of Waltzean neo-realism, it leaves us with the problem of explaining change. As Mearsheimer points out, it is far from clear 'what determines why some discourses become dominant and others lose out in the marketplace of ideas'.[21] Much discourse analysis comes close to static description and classification. What is more, there is a certain methodological arbitrariness to the way 'texts' and the individuals' 'constructing' discourses are selected. One looks in vain for criteria for selecting politically relevant texts. In the absence of general cross-national standards of measurement, discourse analysis also runs the risk of legitimizing the foreign policy of a given state. Discourse analysis may be helpful in explaining cases of ideological inertia, but generally it is difficult to see what it explains that cannot just as well be explained by a hermeneutic-evolutionary approach.

A more promising line of thought seems to be to resurrect the concept of grand strategy and to conceive of foreign policy as still primarily controlled by the executive.[22] Grand strategy could be argued to be the point where structural constraints and ideas intersect in a long-term plan of action. The choices on which grand strategies are based are influenced by causal beliefs shaped by a country's history. As Günther Hellmann points out in one of the few pleas for a rediscovery of grand strategy, 'grand strategies are not only the result of political conditions in the domestic and international environments but of broader cultural determinants as well'.[23] While recognizing the role of choice, the concept of grand strategy allows us to argue in terms of ideal-type choices relating to different types of objective constraints. In the existing literature the concept is defined rather narrowly as relating to security and military affairs, a reflection of the confrontational context in which much of this literature was conceived.[24] Posen characteristically defines grand strategy as 'a state's theory for creating security through military and diplomatic means'.[25] In a globalized world, where interdependence makes the use of military force more costly, the tools of grand strategy are likely to change. Economic, political, institutional and ideological sources of power gain in importance at the expense of military sources. Nordlinger points out that conceptions of strategy ought to be broadened to include a minimally activist strategy. Players in international politics have three, not two, options. They may cooperate, they may defect, but they may also choose not to play at all, to purposefully disengage.[26] In the post-Cold War era it thus seems helpful to define grand strategy broadly as *a state's theory about its international role and about how best to fulfil or defend that role*. Thinking in terms of grand strategy implies that foreign policy actors are rational and capable of long-term planning, an assumption that challenges a large part of the current institutionalist literature. There has also been a tendency to reserve the concept of grand strategy for big powers. But with technological globalization and a lower level of military conflict the formulation and implementation of grand strategies is no longer a no-go area for smaller states.

Grand strategy can be argued to be formulated within the constraining framework of 1) a strategic environment, which includes geopolitical realities, the degree of economic interdependence and the system's interaction capacity (in Barry Buzan's sense) and 2) a strategic culture, which may be subdivided into various strategic subcultures. For instance, one may also talk about an integration subculture.[27]

The fact that the formulation of grand strategy is assumed to be intimately related to certain international constraints allows the analyst to construct grand strategies, the relevance of which is contingent. At the same time, ideal-type grand strategies may be inferred from historical evidence, which may help enrich our debate about contemporary grand strategy.[28] In a recent article Alexander George asks the pertinent question, how lessons of history can be 'cumulated into policy-relevant theory'.[29] Thinking in terms of ideal-type grand strategies seems a useful way of bridging the gap between diplomatic history and international relations theory.

Notes

1. John Lewis Gaddis, 'International Relations Theory and the End of the Cold War', *International Security*. Vol. 17/3, Winter 1992/93.
2. The attempt by Taras and Zeringue to rationalize Gorbachev's policy in neorealist terms tracing the structural background to his grand strategy is not convincing. See Raymond Taras and Marshal Zeringue, 'Grand Strategy in a Post-Bipolar World: Interpreting the Final Soviet Response', *Review of International Studies*, Vol. 18, 1992.
3. An excellent survey is found in Marcus Jachtenfuchs, 'Ideen und Internationale Beziehungen', *Zeitschrift für Internationale Beziehungen*, 2. Jg., Heft 2, 1995.
4. See John Kurt Jacobsen, 'Much Ado about Ideas. The Cognitive Factor in Economic Policy', *World Politics*, no. 47, January 1995.
5. Judith Goldstein and Robert O. Keohane (eds), *Ideas and Foreign Policy: Beliefs, Institutions and Political Change*, Ithaca, N.Y.: Cornell University Press, 1993.
6. *Ibid.*, p. 10.
7. See Walter Carlsnæs, *Ideology and Foreign Policy: Problems of Comparative Conceptualization*. Oxford: Basil Blackwell, 1987.
8. See Peter M. Haas, 'Introduction: Epistemic Communities and International Policy Coordination', *International Organization*, Vol. 46, no. 1, Winter 1992.

9. Alexander Wendt, 'Anarchy Is What States Make of It: The Social Construction of Power Politics', *International Organization*, Vol. 46, no. 2, 1992, pp. 391–425.

10. John Kurt Jacobsen, *op. cit.*, p. 286.

11. Robert Putnam, 'Diplomacy and Domestic Politics. The Logic of Two-Level Games', *International Organization*, Vol. 42, Summer 1988. Peter B. Evans and Harold K. Jacobsen, *Double-Edged Diplomacy*, Berkeley and London: University Of California Press, 1993.

12. Thomas C. Schelling, *The Strategy of Conflict*, New York/Oxford: Galaxy Books, 1963, p. 28.

13. See Lindberg and Scheingold, *Europe's Would-Be Polity*, New Jersey: Prentice-Hall, 1971.

14. Stephen B. Brooks, 'Dueling Realisms', *International Organization*, Vol. 51, no. 3, Summer 1997.

15. Paul Schroeder, 'Historical Reality vs Neo-Realist Theory', *International Security*, Vol. 19/1, Summer 1994, p. 148.

16. Kenneth Waltz, *Man, the State and War*, New York: Columbia University Press, 1959 (1954).

17. See the discussion in Ole Wæver, *Introduktion til International Politik*, Copenhagen: Institut for Statskundskab, 1992.

18. Classical realists like Morgenthau stressed the intentional dimension of foreign policy.

19. See Stephen M. Walt, *The Origins of Alliances*, Ithaca, N.Y.: Cornell University Press, 1987.

20. Kenneth Waltz, *Theory of International Politics*, New York: Random House, 1979; B. Buzan, C.A. Jones and R. Little (eds), *The Logic of Anarchy*, New York: Columbia University Press, 1993.

21. John J. Mearsheimer, 'The False Promise of International Institutions', *International Security*, Vol. 19, no. 3, Winter 1994/95.

22. See also Stanley Hoffmann's related approach with its emphasis on the 'national consciousness' of a nation. See *inter alia* the inspiring analysis in Stanley Hoffmann, *The European Sisyphus. Essays on Europe 1964–1994*, Boulder: Westview, 1995. See also Robert O. Keohane, Joseph S. Nye and Stanley Hoffmann (eds), *After the Cold War: International Institutions and State Strategies in Europe 1989–1991*. Cambridge. Mass.: Harvard University Press, 1993.

23. Gunther Hellmann, 'Goodbye Bismarck? The Foreign Policy of Contemporary Germany', *Mershon International Studies Review*, Vol. 40, Supplement 1, April 1996, p. 28.

24. Here I agree totally with Hellmann, *op. cit.*, p. 29.

25. Barry R. Posen, *The Sources of Military Doctrine: France, Britain and Germany Between the World Wars*, Ithaca, N.Y.: Cornell University Press, 1984. For a recent analysis applying a slightly broader but still security-related definition of grand strategy see Christopher Layne, 'From Preponderance to Offshore Balancing: America's Future Grand Strategy', *International Security*, Vol. 22, no. 1, Summer 1997.

26. Eric A. Nordlinger, *Isolationism Reconfigured*, Princeton, N.J.: Princeton University Press, 1995, pp. 8ff.

27. The concept of strategic culture is discussed once again rather too narrowly in

Alistair Iain Johnston, 'Thinking about Strategic Culture', *International Security*, Vol. 19/4, Spring 1995.

28. For a fine example of the use of historical ideal-type strategies or models of statecraft see Josef Joffe, ' "Bismarck" or "Britain"?', *International Security*, Vol. 19/4, Spring 1995.

29. Alexander L. George, 'Knowledge for Statecraft: The Challenge for Political Science and History', *International Security*, Vol. 22/1, Summer 1997, p. 44.

3　The primacy of politics in European integration

The emphasis on grand strategy implies that political leaders at the highest level play a key role in regional integration. A large part of the theoretical literature on international cooperation challenges this claim. A recurring theme in much of the liberal and pluralist literature on the subject is that integration develops, as it were, behind the backs of political leaders and that supranational and societal actors play a key role in fostering closer integration. This approach is particularly influential within the German academic community, whereas American scholars have been less inclined to abandon realist assumptions.[1]

The pluralist interpretation of regionalism is a broad umbrella covering a range of different theoretical perspectives. One influential perspective essentially regards regionalism, including European unification, as determined by the economic forces of internationalization and its derivative europeanization, requiring the modern nation-state to adapt and engage in new forms of transnational and even supranational governance.[2] State actors are seen to be challenged by dynamic multilevel systems of governance as well as by new networks emerging as a response to functional differentiation and internationalization. Within this school, which builds upon some of the insights of functionalism and neo-functionalism, integration is mainly seen to be driven by material forces, although institutions are also accorded importance.[3] Modernization and its successor globalization are perceived as powerful structural forces forcing the hand of defensive politicians. Metaphorically speaking, integration is like a carnivorous plant which lures states down a deadly route.[4] Although economic internationalization is clearly a

22

phenomenon of growing importance, theories of internationalization focusing on responses to interdependence do not offer a convincing explanation of all aspects of regionalism, at least not in the European context.

The inclusion of political areas in European integration poses a major problem for these theories. European integration has not stopped at regulating economic life supranationally, but has proceeded to try to integrate high politics areas like foreign policy, security and citizenship. Some authors seek to rescue pluralism by arguing that even in the security area, nation-states are losing control. Thus Wallace and Wallace refer to the growth of security interdependencies and to changes in the definition of security.[5] They come close to explaining European integration after the Second World War as a response to an interdependence and transnational interaction 'of an unusual intensity'. Yet the extension of the security agenda has not led to the disappearance of traditional military security. Nor does the reference to security interdependence address the problem of foreign policy integration. A brief comparative analysis reveals that the European region is almost alone in trying to integrate high-politics sectors, which to my mind includes a common currency. Wallace and Wallace recognize the special political dimension in European regionalism, referring to 'a profound commitment to policies of stabilization' as a special feature of the European region.[6] Interestingly, their use of the term stabilization instead of say 'peace doctrine' seems to indicate a wish to reserve some space for realism in the overall interpretation of European regionalization. Yet this line of thought is not pursued. The interdependence perspective faces other disturbing anomalies in the European case. Historically, European integration was as much an attempt to re-establish interdependence as a response to economic interdependence, which in the 1950s was quite limited.

More importantly, theories of internationalization and european-ization fail to demonstrate convincingly why big states should want to integrate. Whereas they can explain the pro-integrative policies of small states, the economies of which are heavily dependent upon external markets, they have great difficulty explaining why large and quite self-contained economies, like that of France in the 1950s, should have wanted to create supranational bodies.[7]

Neo-functionalists also challenge the view that states can control processes of regional integration, pointing to unintended consequences which push the regional integration system towards higher levels of integration in a semi-automatic process.[8] But their theories are remarkably silent on the reasons why regional integration processes should be initiated in the first place. The key neo-functionalist concept is of course functional spillover, the idea that 'imbalances created by the functional interdependence or inherent linkages of tasks can be a force pressing political actors to redefine their common tasks'.[9] Neo-functionalists also posit a political version of spillover, arguing that various actors taking part in integration will gradually become socialized into transferring loyalty to the supranational level.[10] Bureaucrats taking part in transgovernmental networks tend to go native. Finally, Haas used the spillover concept in a third sense, arguing that supranational or national actors might manipulate the functional mechanisms of spillover.[11] Historical institutionalists have recently resurrected the basic neo-functionalist argument, supplementing it with new theories of undirected integration.[12] Pierson argues *inter alia* that regional integration processes once initiated tend to 'lock in' states for instance because of 'sunk costs'.[13]

Pollack tries to specify the domain within which neo-functionalist claims apply, arguing that the predictions of neo-functionalists hold for regulatory and to some extent distributive policy, but not for redistributive and constitutive policy.[14]

Although recent institutionalist approaches to the study of European integration have to some extent managed to combine intergovernmental and institutionalist theories, central propositions of neo-functionalists and historical institutionalists remain vulnerable. It is now generally accepted that regional integration is not an autonomous process. For spillover to occur, prior political decisions will have to be made.[15] This proposition can be seen as an elaboration upon second and third generation neo-functionalism. Lindberg and Scheingold thus introduced a concept of leadership in regional integration.[16] National and supranational leadership were seen as activators of the integration system's coalition-forming mechanisms. However, spillover and institutional dynamics are still regarded as factors creating unintended consequences. The possibility that the concepts of spillover and path-dependency may be subsumed under a realist-intergovernmentalist theory of integration focusing on grand strategy has not been considered. Yet strategic use of institutional strategies seems perfectly possible. Political leaders may anticipate and manipulate secondary effects of first decisions. Not only is this logically possible, it is also empirically likely given the often close connection between decision-makers and the academic communities giving birth to such integration theories.

This weakens the claim of neo-functionalism and historical institutionalism to a status as an alternative to intergovernmentalism and realism. It can be argued that of the three concepts of spillover commonly referred to, cultivated spillover is by far the most important concept, as the other types of spillover can be subsumed under cultivated spillover. Both functional and political spillover may form part of a political actor's strategy.

Even socialization may be part of a deliberate strategy. Indeed, in one of his self-critical works, Ernst Haas admitted that 'most neo-functionalists have not explicitly recognized, however, the crucial question of whether even this incremental style is not 'foreseen' and *manipulated* (author's emphasis) by certain heroic actors'.[17] The notion of politically 'cultivated' spillover is compatible with realist assumptions, provided we conceive of it as being applied by state actors. It seems perfectly possible for state actors to pursue a state strategy cognisant of and manipulative of functional linkages. Similarly, path-dependency may be amenable to strategic manipulation. An influential state with a strong commitment to integration may thus choose to apply institutional strategies as part of a long-term integration strategy. The pre-condition is that the rationality of the state in question is characterized by a long time-horizon. This presupposition is probably not valid for all states, but it could be valid for some. If we depart from the ideational realist assumption that states differ and may innovate, we may conceive of institutionalist strategies as part of the strategic repertoire of hegemonic states.

The institutionalist proposition that institutions are 'sticky' and resistant to change also *prima facie* seems difficult to reconcile with empirical evidence from European constitutive politics which shows a high frequency of quite wide-ranging institutional change.[18]

Moreover, neo-functionalists exaggerate the importance of welfare motives. As Haas recognizes in an article discussing the lessons of de Gaulle, 'pragmatic interest politics, concerned with economic welfare, has its own built-in limits'. And he continues 'integrative decisions based on high politics and basic commitments are undoubtedly more durable than decisions based on converging pragmatic expectations'.[19] Haas thus felt a need to introduce a new type of actor, the dramatic-political actor, but never developed a theory about the behaviour of such actors.

Pluralist interpreters of European integration may offer a serious counter-argument in response to the primacy-of-politics proposition.

They may accept the argument that regional integration structures are set up by political actors for essentially political reasons, but then go on to argue that over time the dynamics (and rationale) of regional integration change. A combination of a democratization of foreign policy and the emergence of new values begins over time to erode the old political agenda. At the same time, the integration process creates a range of vested interests and networks serving as stabilizers which keep the supranational vessel afloat even in stormy weather. The argument is essentially that a theory about the dynamics of regional integration needs to reflect the different characteristics of various phases in the process. Second-generation neo-functionalism did contain propositions about typical integration phases.[20] Yet these propositions in large part ran counter to the claim that in the later phases of integration politicians would lose control. Nye points out that, although the participating states will *inter alia* experience a reduction of alternatives as integration proceeds, one will also see a growing politicization as the integration process touches the more sensitive areas. This not only slows down the pace of integration, it also implies a greater role for elected leaders, who will be expected to respond to the concerns of the general public. What is probably true is that a process of regional integration tends to consolidate over time, as a result of the emergence of vested interests linked to the integration system.[21] This makes decisions on radical disintegration (or 'building-down') very costly. Gretschmann's comparison of regional integration to a game of chess in which earlier moves narrow down later choices is telling.[22] In other words, regional integration processes are hardly entirely under the control of political leaders, although politics take centre stage.

It seems *prima facie* plausible that the time-horizon of statesmen may have become shorter in the course of the last decades as a result of growing domestic involvement in foreign policy, although as pointed out above this involvement should not be exaggerated. Yet this does not necessarily imply that grand strategies are losing importance. It may simply imply that such strategies have over time become more difficult to implement. Moreover, if one distinguishes between normal and constitutive policy, one can argue that democratization has mainly touched normal integration politics essentially leaving constitutive politics as an executive *domaine réserveé* (see below).

A more voluntarist, liberal perspective regards integration as the product of a historical learning process.[23] Human beings are regarded as rational and inherently good. Cooperation is thus the natural state of affairs in international politics. Conflict is due to distorting factors such as ignorance, disinformation or misperception. Seen from this perspective, regional integration policy is a peace policy, and the process of regional integration is part of a neo-Kantian transformation of the international system. Regionalism is seen as the creation of 'peace in parts', a view held by many federalist theorists.[24]

Accepting the relevance of ideas, including the wish to avoid armed conflict, is not incompatible with a broad realist position. Morgenthau recognized that power was not always the final goal, although he thought it was always the immediate goal.[25] It is no coincidence that the subtitle of his book reads 'the struggle for power *and peace* (author's emphasis)'. The pursuit of peace is difficult to distinguish from the pursuit of stability. Stability can be expected to be an important goal for an enlightened realist actor. Regional stability is likely to be especially important for big states having a strong extra-territorial economic presence in a region. Moreover, the absence of armed conflict does not imply the absence of *Realpolitik*. Realism is not only a theory about conflict, but also and more fundamentally a theory about the pursuit of relative gain.[26] To make the absence of armed conflict the sole success criterion for liberalism is making life too easy for pluralists.

Neo-liberal institutionalists, most of whom straddle the divide between realism and pluralism, adopt a pragmatic view of the levels of cooperation achieved and achievable in a regional context. First of all, they find it unnecessary to formulate a specific theory about cooperation in a regional setting. This allows them to fit the European evidence into a larger picture of international collaboration. One of the advantages of a regime approach to regionalism is thus the possibility of making comparisons. While recognizing the continuing importance of states, regime analyses focus on the useful functions international regimes may fulfil for states, regimes being defined here in Krasner's sense as 'sets of implicit and explicit principles, rules and decision-making procedures around which actors' expectations converge in a given area of international relations'.[27] *Prima facie* the advantage of a regime approach to European integration is that it accounts for what must seem a paradox to more radical pluralist theories: the fact that nation-states have retained their strength as integration has proceeded. Realist applications of the regime concept can thus be expected to shed some light on Europe's state-centred integration system. Regime analyses of European integration typically argue that integration regimes have actually helped states perform domestic welfare-oriented tasks and thus helped them survive as viable political entities.[28] However, regime theory suffers from a serious drawback. Having been invented as a means of studying sectoral cooperation, the concept is not very helpful as a description of the overall integration structure. How does one aggregate the numerous sectoral analyses? Regime-oriented descriptions of the EU as a whole tend to become rather abstract. Jachtenfuchs characteristically talks about 'uneven Europeanization'.[29]

Although it offers some useful insights into the functions regional institutions may fulfil for states, as an overall approach to regional integration neo-liberal institutionalism suffers from two other and more fundamental flaws. First, apart from noting the special nature of regime building in the European region, it has little to say about the extra-ordinarily high level of institutionalization which is a characteristic feature of European regionalism. The functions normally accorded to regimes can be fulfilled at much lower levels of institutionalization than a supranational or semi-federal union. Why then should European political leaders have assumed the considerable governance costs relating to upholding and further developing the EU system? Nor does the strong political dimension in European institutionalization fit easily with liberal-institutionalist theory. Breckinridge tries to overrule this objection by arguing that 'its degree of centralization or institutionalization does not preclude the EU from having regime aspects'.[30] In other words, analyses of the EU should study both organizational and regime aspects. The idea is helpful in that it permits comparisons to be made between the EU and other instances of regionalism. A purely organizational analysis tends to exaggerate differences: In Breckinridge's words 'comparison of the EU with the ASEAN or the NAFTA centred on organizations could only stress the differences between them'.[31] Yet the problem of institutionalization is solved at the cost of leaving a very important feature of the EU unexplained.

Secondly, neo-liberal theory focuses on absolute gain and common regulative interests. Big-state bias in processes of regional integration thus runs counter to neo-liberal expectations. A preliminary comparative assessment nevertheless suggests the relevance of a hegemonic perspective on regional integration: in all major regionalist projects the largest state in the region has been the strongest protagonist of regionalization. That goes for Brazil in Mercosur, Indonesia in ASEAN, Kenya in the abortive East African Community and to a certain extent the US in NAFTA, although Mexico also played an important role in launching this initiative.[32] Now the mere fact of great power leadership in regionalist endeavours cannot be taken as an indication that regional integration is a zero-sum game. One version of the theory of hegemony claims that hegemons produce collective goods benefiting smaller states. Yet the prominent role of big powers in contemporary and past regionalist projects at least makes it pertinent to pose the question of big-power bias in such projects. Realism and its derivative, intergovernmentalism, thus seems the most appropriate point of departure when trying to understand the dynamics of regional integration. Given the weaknesses of structural explanations of modern international politics, our attention ought to concentrate on either intergovernmentalist theory or a new and more voluntarist theory of hegemonic leadership or a combination of the two.

Intergovernmentalism is essentially classical realism applied to the study of European integration. It is a rather loose label used to describe theories of regional integration which emphasize the predominant role of national governments and national interest. It should be added, though, that some recent institutionalist approaches to the study of the EU explicitly accept fundamental insights of intergovernmentalism.[33] The dividing line between intergovernmentalist and institutionalist approaches has thus become blurred of late. Notwithstanding important recent modifications of the theory by Andrew Moravcsik, intergovernmentalism remains a largely descriptive and somewhat vague theory. In his classical *The Limits of European Integration*, Paul Taylor hardly defines the concept at all, apart from stating that 'relations between European states are in their fundamentals much the same as those between states elsewhere'.[34] The concept of intergovernmentalism thus describes the nature of the relationship between states in Western Europe and normally appears alongside the concept of 'confederation', which is used to describe the end-state of a state-dominated integration process. Moravcsik's revised intergovernmentalism contains much more added analytical value, positing a number of typical intergovernmentalist bargaining modes including threats of exclusion. He outlines three likely determinants of interstate bargaining power: 1) unilateral policy alternatives ('threats of non-agreement') 2) alternative coalitions ('threats of exclusion') and 3) the potential for compromise and linkage.[35] Threats of exclusion are seen as deliberate attempts on the part of powerful member states to create negative policy externalities for other members. Although attentive to the special role of core states, Moravcsik stops short of developing a general approach to the study of big-power strategy and behaviour in regional integration. Moravcsik's rationalistic conception of state interests also, I shall argue, leads him to ignore some special ideational features of big-power leadership in the European region. While the attempt to explain European integration with reference to general theories of international relations is laudable, it runs the risk of producing rather anaemic accounts unless supplemented and enriched by ideational factors.

Given its emphasis upon the role of great powers, neo-realism has a certain *prima facie* attractiveness when it comes to explaining the special Franco–German role within the EU. Yet apart from its general weaknesses, which have already been discussed, structural realism has some particularly weak spots, the case of European integration being one. Its views on the possibilities of cooperation are generally too pessimistic to make it a useful basis for theorizing about European integration. Neo-realists dismiss the importance of agency in regional integration. The main point made by neo-realists is that the overall distribution of power in the international system is the primary determinant of state behaviour.[36] Neo-realists therefore expect the demise of bipolarity to have had major consequences for European politics. It is expected to have led to either a weakening of European integration, as the bipolar overlay disappears, or less likely to a European alliance with a view to balancing the American unipole.[37] Waltz's views on the likelihood of the emergence of a European pole are not entirely clear. However, we can infer that neo-realism does not expect states within a region to form cohesive and highly institutionalized structures, as the amount of mutual trust between states is expected to be limited. Since states are concerned about survival and relative gains, they inevitably tend to think in terms of worst cases. The crucial weakness of neo-realism thus seems to be its inability to provide an explanation of the high degree of institutionalization and notably its durability in the European region.

In a laudable endeavour to rescue neo-realism from the onslaught of real-life European cooperation, J. Grieco has raised the fundamental question whether realists are able to account for such radical transfers of sovereignty as those implied by the EMU project.[38] His answer is basically that a rational interest-based interpretation of the EMU decision can in fact be construed. Essentially, he argues, France and the smaller states in the EU are seeking to influence German monetary policy through a voice-opportunity strategy. Although Grieco's argument is interesting, it forces him to abandon stringent neo-realist premises in favour of a more voluntarist realism. Given the security dilemma, neo-realists expect neighbouring states to react to the strengthening of a major state not by moving closer to that state, but on the contrary by opting for distance and seeking to balance it. Moreover, the weakness of his voice-opportunity thesis is that it fails to explain the policy of the most powerful state (in this context Germany). Neo-realist theory expects rising powers to become more assertive, not more accommodating. Nor can the theory explain the deviating strategy of the UK in the European case. Grieco does, however, offer one possible explanation for the pro-integrationist policy of the most powerful state. He points out that it may regard transfers of sovereignty as necessary in order to counter international challengers. Yet this is an *ad hoc* hypothesis which is not developed theoretically. A hegemonic perspective *prima facie* fills both lacunae. It provides a rationale for German policy while casting the UK in the role of a counter-hegemonic force.

Notes

1. Although German theoretical contributions on the EU and international relations are often intellectually stimulating, it is probably fair to say that there is a tendency within at least part of the German academic community to substitute normative for explanatory arguments.
2. The literature on interdependence and globalization is extensive. Representative scholars are Kenichi Ohmae, *The Borderless World*, London: Fontana, 1991, and Michael Zürn, 'The Challenge of Globalization and Individualization. A View from Europe', in Hans-Henrik Holm and Georg Sørensen (eds), *Whose World Order? Uneven Globalization and the End of the Cold War*, Boulder: Westview, 1995.
3. Keohane and Nye's concept of 'issue-area' is clearly related to functionalist propositions concerning the technical logic of sectors. See their *Power and Interdependence: World Politics in Transition*, Boston: Little & Brown, 1977.
4. The wonderful metaphor is borrowed from Charles Pentland, *International Theory and the European Community*, London: Faber, 1973.
5. Helen Wallace and William Wallace, *Policy-Making in the European Union*, Oxford: Oxford University Press, 1996, p. 16.
6. *Ibid.*, p. 17.
7. See the argument in Alan S. Milward, *The European Rescue of the Nation-State*, London: Routledge, 1992, p. 20.
8. The neo-functionalist literature is of course huge. See e.g. Ernst B. Haas, *The Uniting of Europe*, London: Stevens and Sons Ltd, 1958; and Ernst B. Haas, *Beyond the Nation State*, Stanford: Stanford University Press, 1964.
9. See Joseph S. Nye, *Peace in Parts*, New York: University Press of America, 1987 (1971), p. 65.
10. In French this phenomenon is known as *engrenage*.
11. A good discussion of various types of spillover is found in Jeppe Tranholm-

Mikkelsen, 'Neo-Functionalism: Obstinate or Obsolete? A Reappraisal in the Light of the New Dynamism of the EC', *Millennium*, Vol. 20/1, 1991.

12. See in particular Mark Pollack, 'Creeping Competence: The Expanding Agenda of the European Community', *Journal of Public Policy*, No. 29, 1994, pp. 123–63, and notably Paul Pierson, 'The Path to European Integration: An Historical Institutionalist Analysis', *Comparative Political Studies*, No. 29, 1996, pp. 123–62.

13. Pierson, *op. cit.*

14. Pollack, *op. cit.*

15. See the discussion in Robert O. Keohane and Stanley Hoffmann, 'Conclusions', in William Wallace (ed.), *The Dynamics of European Integration*, London: Pinter, 1990.

16. Lindberg and Scheingold, *Europe's Would-Be Polity*. New Jersey: Prentice-Hall, 1971.

17. Ernst B. Haas, 'The Study of Regional Integration: Reflections on the Joy and Anguish of Pretheorizing', in Leon L. Lindberg and Stuart Scheingold (eds), *Regional Integration: Theory and Research*, Cambridge, Mass.: Cambridge University Press, 1971.

18. See the discussion of institutional inertia in Mark A. Pollack, 'The New Institutionalism and EC Governance: The Promise and Limits of Institutional Analysis', *Governance: An International Journal of Policy and Administration*, Vol. 9, no. 4, October 1996.

19. Ernst B. Haas, 'The Uniting of Europe and the Uniting of Latin America', *Journal of Common Market Studies*, Vol. 5/1967, pp. 327ff.

20. See Nye, *op. cit.*

21. See Thomas Pedersen, 'Political Change in the European Community: The Single European Act as a Case of System Transformation', *Cooperation & Conflict*, Vol. 1, 1992.

22. See Klaus Gretschmann, *European Monetary Integration: EMU Between the Common Good, National Interests and Regime Formation*, Esbjerg: The Torkild Kristensen Institute, Working Papers, 18/1997, p. 20.

23. Most of the federalist writings fall into this category, examples being Michael Burgess, *Federalism and European Union*, London: Routledge, 1989, and John Pinder, *European Community. The Building of a Union*, Oxford: Oxford University Press, 1991.

24. The expression 'Peace in parts' is taken from the title of Nye's important work, *Peace in Parts* (*op. cit.*), in which he discusses the five peace doctrines underlying much (neo-functionalist) thinking on regional integration.

25. Hans J. Morgenthau, *Politics among Nations. The Struggle for Power and Peace*. New York: Alfred A. Knopf, 1978 (1948), p. 29.

26. For a discussion of relative gain, see Duncan Snidal, 'Relative Gains and the Pattern of International Cooperation', *American Political Science Review*, Vol. 85, September 1991.

27. See Stephen Krasner, 'Structural Causes and Regime Consequences: Regimes as Intervening Variables', in S. Krasner (ed.), *International Regimes*, Ithaca, N.Y.: Cornell University Press, 1983, p. 2. See also Robert O. Keohane (ed.), *Inter-*

national Institutions and State Power: Essays in International Relations Theory, Boulder: Westview, 1989.

28. See the discussion in Robert E. Breckinridge, 'Reassessing Regimes: The International Regime Aspects of the European Union', *Journal of Common Market Studies*, Vol. 35, no. 2, June 1997.

29. Marcus Jachtenfuchs, 'Democracy and Governance in the European Union', *European Integration Online Papers*, Vol. 1, 1997.

30. Breckinridge, *op. cit.*, p. 181.

31. *Ibid.*, p. 185.

32. See the excellent surveys of the new regionalism in Louise Fawcett and Andrew Hurrell (eds), *Regionalism in World Politics*, Oxford: Oxford University Press, 1995, and in Andrew Gamble and Anthony Payne (eds), *Regionalism and World Order*. London: Macmillan, 1996.

33. For instance Mark Pollack, 'The New Institutionalism and EC Governance: The Promise and Limits of Institutional Analysis', *Governance*, Vol. 9, no. 4, 1996, p. 430.

34. Paul Taylor, *The Limits of European Integration*, London: Croom Helm, 1983, p. 60.

35. Andrew Moravcsik, 'Preferences and Power in the European Community: A Liberal Intergovernmentalist Approach'. *Journal of Common Market Studies*, Vol. 31, no. 4, December 1993, p. 499.

36. See Kenneth Waltz, *Theory of International Politics*, New York: Random House, 1979.

37. Buzan *et al.* thus argued in an early study of the post-Cold War era that the removal of overlay would lead to either fragmentation or integration. Their assessment was that integration was the most likely scenario. See Barry Buzan, Morten Kelstrup, Pierre Lemaître, Elzbieta Tromer and Ole Wæver, *The European Security Order Recast: Scenarios for the Post-Cold War Era*, London: Pinter, 1990.

38. Joseph M. Grieco, 'The Maastricht Treaty, Economic and Monetary Union and the Neo-Realist Research Programme', *Review of International Studies*, Vol. 21, 1995, pp. 21–40.

4 A theory of cooperative hegemony

The concept of hegemony

The concept of hegemony is slippery, having been the object of an extensive scholarly debate that cannot here be given the treatment it deserves.[1] The debate has concentrated upon the specific theory of hegemonic stability. The great advantage of this theory is that it constitutes a parsimonious theory which can be tested empirically. Concentration of power is expected to contribute to stability. Strong economic regimes are expected to depend on hegemonic power.[2] Within the resource-oriented current of hegemonic theory one can distinguish between a benevolent and a coercive strand.[3] The hegemonic stability theory associated with Charles Kindleberger casts the hegemon in a benevolent role. Its pursuit of selfish motives is claimed to indirectly benefit secondary states. It is argued that successful international (economic) cooperation is dependent upon the presence of a hegemonic leader. The hegemon produces collective goods that otherwise would not have been provided. Smaller states have an incentive to free-ride, but given its preponderance the hegemon can afford the free-riding. A more coercive interpretation of hegemony is found *inter alia* in Gilpin's work.[4] While retaining the notion of collective goods, Gilpin argues that the hegemon has the capacity to tax smaller states to pay for these goods. James and Lake identify three complementary and mutually reinforcing processes or faces of coercive hegemony.[5] The first face of hegemony is characterized by the use of positive and negative sanctions aimed directly at foreign governments in an attempt to influence

34

their choice of policies. The second face of hegemony involves the use of international market power. Here the hegemon seeks to alter the incentives and influence of societal actors in foreign countries, expecting these actors to exert pressure upon their governments. The third face of hegemony involves the use of ideological power to structure public opinion and the political agenda in foreign countries in order to influence what are seen to be legitimate and illegitimate policies.

The theory of hegemonic stability assumes that a materially predominant state in the international system will automatically be willing to project power. In *Power and Interdependence* Keohane and Nye modify this structuralist assumption, breaking the linkage between resources and behaviour. A materially powerful state will only act as a hegemon if it has the political will to do so.[6] The USA became materially preponderant as early as the 1920s but only became willing to assume a global hegemonic role in the 1940s. Once again this points to the importance of ideas and strategy.

Other writers, among these Gramscian neo-Marxists have undertaken helpful elaborations of the theory pointing out that apart from material resources hegemony may also be based on ideological or normative power.[7] Thus a state may possess a superior economic or political system which others emulate. This kind of ideological power has generally been seen to be structural, not a result of any deliberate strategy on the part of the hegemon. Thus Friis in her interesting study essentially interprets Germany's hegemonic power in Europe as based on ideological power, in the sense that it possesses an attractive societal model.[8] In his writings on regional integration Karl Deutsch could be said to have indirectly touched upon this aspect when referring to core areas serving as models for a wider region.[9] Yet, standard-setting is not sufficient to establish cooperation. A hegemonic leader also has to perform the function of 'broker', as Kaelberer points out.[10] Ikenberry and Kupchan stress that a hegemony based on coercive power cannot be in the interest of a big power. Having to use material capabilities to enforce the hegemonic order is simply too costly and cumbersome. Ideological hegemony on the other hand is cheap. The weakness of existing theories of ideological hegemony is that they neglect the political and strategic aspect of such a leadership. Ikenberry and Kupchan suggest that certain kinds of hegemons will deliberately try to encourage the emergence of a legitimate order by 'articulating principles and norms, and engage in negotiations and compromises that have very little to do with the exercise of power'.[11] Ideological hegemony may also be based upon socialization.[12] The main instrument of socialization for cooperative hegemons is economic power which tends to produce ideological adaptation (see also below).[13]

Going further down the voluntarist road, hegemony can also be conceptualized in terms of a grand bargain based on the existence of a specific pattern of interests. Ougaard's observations on the relationship between interests and hegemony may serve as a point of departure. In Ougaard's formulation:

> the concept of hegemony is relevant in situations with common basic interests and secondary but still significant contradictory interests. In such situations we can define the hegemon as the member of the system who, within the framework of the common interests, is able to provide for its own special interests in conflicts of a secondary nature.[14]

Clearly the chances of exercising legitimate informal leadership increase if a big power is able to satisfy interests common to all states in a region. It is, however, counterintuitive that hegemons should be satisfied with an arrangement in which they would only be able to defend their interests in conflicts of a secondary nature. In a modified version Ougaard's definition of hegemony may help us conceptualize a particular version of hegemony, that of cooperative hegemony, a form of hegemony involving concessions to secondary states. The notion of hegemony as based on a tacit contract according the hegemon a leading role and based on the defence of certain common interests seems a useful one.

Grieco has applied a version of the theory of hegemonic stability in a comparative study of what he calls regional institutionalization.[15] Examining the correlation between resource asymmetry and degree of institutionalization he finds that, whereas the USA/NAFTA and Brazil/Mercosur cases are in accordance with the hegemonic leadership thesis, the cases of Germany/EU and Japan/EAEC are anomalies. In the case of Europe there is a combination of the lowest concentration of regional economic resources among the groupings examined and the highest level of institutionalization. In the case of Asia there is a combination of very high concentration of economic resources but weak regional institutionalization. Grieco therefore concludes that hegemonic theory cannot explain regional institutionalization in a fully satisfactory way.

An ideational realism will want to move beyond a structural resource-based interpretation of big-power leadership in regional integration. Put differently: a theory of regional hegemony must be based on voluntarist premises. Some authors have made propositions which might be seen as elements in an ideational realist theory of regional, hegemonic leadership. Emphasizing the role of state actors, Crone has argued that although the degree of resource asymmetry in a region affects the chances of successful institutionalization, so do cognitive factors.[16] Crone can be said to apply Walt's theory of balance-of-fear to the problem of big powers and regional integration. Extreme resource asymmetry hardly leads to high levels of institutionalization, first of all because the hegemon feels that it can get what it wants by bilateral means and therefore does not have to invest in costly multilateral regimes. Secondly, the subordinate states in the region fearing domination have little incentive to join a regional structure set up by the predominant state. Crone's argument helps us understand the differences between European and Asian patterns of institutionalization. In Asia the USA had extreme preponderance until recently. The recent levelling of resource disparities in the region may, as Crone points out, have created new incentives for smaller Asian states to take part in APEC (Asia–Pacific Economic Cooperation). Inside the Asian region a certain levelling of resource disparities has taken place in recent years, although Japan remains predominant. This, too, may have facilitated regional institutionalization.

Conversely, in Europe US superiority was never quite as high as in Asia, and it has been declining in recent decades. Inside the European region, German material superiority is not overwhelming. This may give Germany's neighbours cause to believe that they can influence Germany within common institutions. This leaves us with one central puzzle. How can we explain the fact that the European level of institutionalization rose at the very time that Germany unified? A first possible answer is that even a unified Germany does not constitute a very powerful state within the European region. However, at the level of perceptions, the increase in territory resulting from unification was so large that it is natural to expect it to have caused anxiety. A second possible answer is that external balancing was seen to be more important than internal (regional) balancing. This is an argument compatible with Waltzian neo-realism. A third possible answer and the one that is accorded central importance in this study is that the rising hegemon may develop a strategy aimed at reducing anxiety amongst its neighbours.

The motives of cooperative hegemons

Traditionally, hegemony has been regarded as either benevolent or coercive. The concept of cooperative hegemony is based on the assumption that states primarily pursue relative gains, but emphasizes that powerful states may pursue relative gains by non-coercive or soft coercive means. The literature also tends to conceive hegemony as a unilateralist strategy. By contrast, cooperative hegemony describes a type of international leadership that is institutionally embedded. The third sense in which the concept of cooperative hegemony departs from conventional wisdom in the field is in thinking in terms of regional hegemony. To define hegemony in regional terms implies the existence of other hegemons. A theory of regional cooperative hegemony thus has an environmental dimension that is absent in the traditional theory of unilateral hegemony.

As pointed out earlier, why a big state should want to integrate with other states is not immediately clear. In relative terms, economic externalities are often limited in big states, although globalization is modifying even their autonomy. Moreover, a big state in a region will normally have alternative national options and therefore will have to incur considerable opportunity costs if it decides to integrate (as opposed to merely cooperate) with other states. However, systemic factors may cause the problem of scale in international politics to change over time. Regionalization is probably somehow related to modernization, although we assume that state actors will fit systemic changes into their political strategies. A big state lacking the resources to act as a global power on its own may find it attractive to merge with regional neighbours so as to increase its global influence.

The ideational realist will want to qualify the argument and ask what kind of big powers may want to opt for a strategy of regional institutionalization. First of all, cooperative hegemony is a grand strategy for comparatively weak big powers and for great powers in decline. A regional big power with limited military but superior economic capacity and extensive extra-territorial economic activities would pass the test. Such a power would have an interest in gaining secure access to markets in neighbouring states. To the extent that it had made large direct investments in the region it would be interested in harmonizing norms, standards and laws in the region so as to create an extended home market. A supranational order would be able to ensure a higher degree of stability and predictability than would an intergovernmental regime.

Secondly, we would expect a big power with a high population density to be interested in a high degree of regional institutionalization. For such a power regional institutionalization would imply access to a larger employment market and a larger space for leisure activities etc. Thirdly, and related to the foregoing, a big power with a significant diaspora in neighbouring states could be expected to promote regionalization, since the implication would be the removal of the physical borders between states. Regionalization would thus amount to an indirect unification.

Finally, a comparatively weak big power with an exposed geopolitical location and, related to this, a history of conflictive relations with its neighbours, might also qualify. Such a state would have a fundamental interest in reassuring its neighbours and enhancing its legitimacy, and if attempting to expand it might well want to do so behind the shield of a reassuring integration structure. Birthe Hansen similarly points out that 'a weak superpower will . . . be sensitive to the interests of other states'.[17] In a somewhat similar vein, Watson talks about diffused hegemony, a hegemony that none would agree to others exercising alone.[18] The question then arises of what type of regional state system would correspond to the needs of this type of big power.

The concept of asymmetrical federation

An ideational realist cannot be satisfied with Kenneth Waltz's and Robert Gilpin's abstract characterization of the organizing principle of international politics as a simple dichotomy between hierarchy and anarchy. History offers a rich menu of experiences on the basis of which one may construct ideal-type state systems. In recent years a number of more historically-oriented scholars within the discipline of international relations have thus tried to flesh out more specified typologies of international or regional orders. Adam Watson distinguishes between five types of state systems: multiple independencies; hegemony; suzerainty; dominion and empire.[19] For Watson, the degree of legitimacy is a central criterion for distinguishing between different systems. As we move towards the centralized end of the spectrum the importance of the consent of the ruled loses importance. The variety of international relations is also stressed by David A. Lake in his slightly different but overlapping discussion of a continuum of security relations, ranging from alliance (extreme anarchy) to empire (extreme hierarchy).[20] In a recent article, Daniel H. Deudney similarly points out that most realists have too simplistic a view of political order, arguing in terms of dyads and refusing to conceive of intermediate forms of order between federal states and interstate confederations. Deudney thus discusses what he calls the Philadelphian system which existed from 1787 to 1861 as just such an intermediate political order. It was a union of states with federal features, but the states retained very significant powers, for instance the right to policing, criminal law enforcement and a militia. Deudney also suggests a third structural principle of political order alongside hierarchy and anarchy, that of negarchy, which he defines as 'the arrangement of institutions necessary to prevent simultaneously the emergence of anarchy and hierarchy'.[21]

Asymmetrical federation is, one could argue, a further type of states system with security implications.[22] Cooperative hegemons may construct asymmetrical federations as part of their grand strategy (see below). The term federal asymmetry has been used by Ivo Duchacek.[23] According to Duchacek, federal asymmetry raises two problems. Firstly, a large and wealthy state in a federation may refuse to assume the economic burdens involved in assisting in the development of poorer areas in the federation. Secondly, a powerful state may provoke fear of domination in other states.[24] Here we are mainly interested in the second problem. However, our definition of asymmetry differs from that of Duchacek. As intimated by Duchacek himself, federal asymmetry in the objective sense is something of a platitude. Members of a federation always differ in size. The defining characteristic of asymmetrical federations, as used here, is that the organization of the federation is biased in favour of one or two major states, giving them a special role, and that these states deliberately seek such a special role. This special role of the more powerful state(s) may or may not be formally recognized. Asymmetrical federations may be established by a single decision or they may be the outcome of a series of asymmetrical constitutive bargains leading to the formation of an asymmetrical federation.

Symmetrical federations, on the other hand, are characterized by the fact that no major state seeks a special role in the federation. In such systems territorial politics and the realist behavioural logic will be weak. Such federations often have a senate or a functional equivalent granting all states equal representation.

We define *federation* broadly as 'a constitution with the following characteristics 1) there are two levels of government that rule the same land and people 2) each level has at least one area of action in which it is autonomous, and 3) there is some guarantee ... of the autonomy of each government in its own sphere'.[25] Riker thus distinguishes between peripheralized and centralized federations based on the number of areas of action transferred to the federal government. We assume that peripheralized federations and some centralized federations are compatible with a realist conception of state behaviour.

That regional institutionalization in a broad sense may be power-based is widely recognized. Krasner's concept of 'metapower' refers to 'the ability to change the rules of the game'.[26] Asymmetrical federalization is thus a classical case of a metapower strategy. Arnold Wolfers similarly has pointed out that states may pursue 'possessional' as well as 'milieu' goals.[27] The latter represent an indirect route to the satisfaction of the national interest. States seek to create an environment beneficial to the realization of certain national interests. Normally, states emphasizing milieu goals will thus have a longer time-horizon in their foreign policy than other states and will be willing to sacrifice short-term benefits. In a recent article Schroeder, in a criticism of Waltz, shows that historically state behaviour in many instances has not conformed to Waltz's expectations.[28] One of the anomalies mentioned by Schroeder is the use of what he calls the strategy of 'transcending', that is the attempt to solve a problem by reshaping it. Regional integration can be regarded as a way of solving traditional inter-state problems of balance by creating institutional structures that deflect inter-state tension and offer new ways of balancing.[29] In a recent study of Asian regionalization Kishore Mahbubani similarly emphasizes that 'the institutional perspective is compatible with both realism and idealism'.[30]

The claim that federal-style institutionalization may be compatible with a realist behavioural logic is slightly more controversial. Yet, as recognized by Buzan and Little, while federations are normally based on voluntary consent, they may also involve coercive elements.[31] Duchacek similarly talks about the 'extraconstitutional reality' in federations and in that connection refers to phenomena like 'federal asymmetry' and the possibility of 'intrafederal hegemony'.[32] Thus the formal distribution of powers in federations can give a quite misleading picture of the actual distribution of influence.

As regards the motives for federalization William Riker similarly stresses realist goals, concluding that historically federalization has most often been the result of a grand political bargain between major powers seeking peaceful aggrandizement and smaller powers seeking protection against external threats.[33] He thus talks about two necessary conditions of federalization: 1) the expansion condition and 2) the military condition. Although generally a neglected perspective in the literature on European integration the link between power-politics and federalization has been made in one brief examination of the European integration process.[34]

Two general points in Riker's theory are worth emphasizing. First of all, in Riker's understanding states integrate for essentially political reasons. Secondly, the initiative lies with the major powers, which opt for regional integration as an alternative to traditional military expansion. If we define realism broadly as a mode of international organization in which state behaviour is mainly concerned about relative gains, we can posit a typology of realist institutionalization.

Table 4.1 summarizes the relationship between realism and regional institutionalization.

Table 4.1 *Realism and regional institutionalization*

Degree of regional institutionalization

Strength of realist logic	High	Low
Strong	Empire	Unilateral hegemony
Medium	Asymmetrical federation	*Directoire*
Weak	Symmetrical federation	Pluralistic security community

To the extent that they are not global in reach, empires can be conceived as forms of regional institutionalization. They combine a high degree of institutionalization and a strong realist element. Unilateral hegemonies also contain a strong realist element, but are much less institutionalized. Unilateral hegemons normally possess overwhelming resource superiority, which gives them strong coercive power and enables them to offer collective goods even at the risk of major free-riding. Asymmetrical federations contain a less marked realist element. They are typically established by cooperative hegemons willing to share power and capable of exercising soft forms of power (see above). *Directoire* systems are state systems in which all big powers have special informal prerogatives, though without being able to impose their views in all areas. The main difference between asymmetrical federations and *directoires* is that the *directoire* is a much less formalized system of big-power rule. *Directoire* systems are more vulnerable than asymmetrical federations as they are not institutionally embedded and thus likely to enjoy a lower degree of legitimacy, but from the point of view of the big powers they also involve fewer risks. Symmetrical federations differ from asymmetrical federations in that they do not accord big powers a predominant role and contain significant minority guarantees for smaller states. In this type of political order, the sharp edges of territorial politics of states are lost. Finally, security communities are characterized by a combination of limited institutionalization and a weak realist logic. The most important cohesive factor in security communities is likely to be the existence of a shared political culture. In a sense, security communities reflect a latent cultural 'nation'.

German unification: a historical analogy

If, following Riker, we define the concept of federation broadly, history provides us with interesting parallels which illustrate the meaning of asymmetrical federation. The most striking analogies are the German Confederation of 1815 and the German Empire of 1871. Both political orders can be regarded as instances of asymmetrical federations. For purposes of illustration, such historical analogies may be quite useful as illustrated by Deudney's use of the American case.[35] A preliminary caveat is nevertheless in order. Clearly, historical analogies are full of methodological pitfalls. All things are never equal, which means that two different historical periods are never alike. Thus, for instance, at least two features distinguish the contemporary European scene from the German scene in the last century. First of all, the pattern of geographical asymmetry is somewhat different. The inequality in terms of resources is greater in the German than in the European case. Most of the German 'states' were small principalities. Still, there were also middle-sized and major actors in the German Confederation such as Bavaria and Württemberg. Besides, the two constellations are sufficiently similar to allow similar strategic consequences to be drawn. Secondly, the economic interdependence between the states is greater in Europe today than in the Germany of the last century. It should be noted though that to the extent that such interdependence is asymmetrical it can be manipulated by the most powerful state, interdependence being linked with geopolitical location. Asymmetrical interdependence is not a phenomenon that sets this century apart from the preceding one. In this connection one can refer to an interesting passage in one of Bismarck's writings. Bismarck points out that given their smallness, their location and their common borders with Prussia, the smaller states are anyway dependent on some arrangement with that country in areas like customs, transport, trade, mail or cartel conventions. Only Hanover, he continues, has alternative options (given its geopolitical location) and is capable of adopting an independent posture vis-à-vis Prussia. Therefore, Bismarck concludes:

> *Hannover ist deshalb der einzige unter den deutschen Mittelstaaten, in betreff dessen die deutsche Diplomatie Preussens ... unausgesetzt alle Anstrengung und Geschicklichkeit zur Anwendung bringen sollte, um seinen guten Willen für Preussen zu gewinnen und sein Misstrauen zu beruhigen.*[36]

The central institution of the German Confederation, which first assembled in 1816, was the Federal Diet (*Bundesversammlung*) in Frankfurt which was little more than a congress of ambassadors. Constitutional amendments required unanimity. Day-to-day business was dealt with on the basis of simple majority decisions in an inner committee (*Engerer Rat*) in which the eleven largest states had one vote each (*Virilstimme*) while the other states shared six votes between them (*Kuriatstimmen*).[37] In the case of a balanced vote, the president, Austria, cast the decisive vote.[38] In the plenary sessions the votes were weighed. The big states had four votes; the medium-sized states had three or two.[39] Although Austria and Prussia possessed only one vote each, in practice they were in most cases able to get their way in the inner committee by means of indirect pressure on the smaller states. Austria tended to boycott the sessions of the *Bund* if it did not get its way. Another tactic consisted of securing a majority in advance of the Diet's session in Frankfurt. Thus in August 1819 Austria convened a secret conference in Karlsbad, in which ten states, enough to secure a majority in the *Engerer Rat*, adopted a number of important measures which were subsequently pushed through the Diet.[40] During the early years of the *Bund*'s existence Austria was *primus inter pares* in the Confederation. This was illustrated by the fact that meetings of the Diet took place on the ground floor of the Von Thurn und Taxis Palace in Frankfurt, whereas an extravagant second floor was reserved for the Austrian presidency. Yet, during the first decades of the Confederation's existence, Austria ruled in tacit understanding with Prussia.

In his essay *Einige Bemerkungen über Preussens Stellung am Bunde* from 1858 Bismarck describes the period from 1815 to 1848 as a peaceful period, during which Austria adopted a relaxed attitude in the *Bund*, not interfering in Prussia's German policy as long as Prussia supported Austria in European matters. After 1851, Bismarck claims, Austria deliberately tried to use the *Bund* as a vehicle for Austrian hegemony. He also lists the means used by Austria to achieve this goal: personal ties, including various kinds of bribery; support for the Catholic parties in other principalities; the 'bought press'; and the linking of issues in the *Bund*. These tactics were used with a view to gaining control of a majority of the members of the *Bund*. Bismarck furthermore describes how Austria *seine Forderungen in bundesfreundlichen Worte kleidet* and how, whenever Prussia insisted on a minority view, Austria and its majority *ihm in der Diplomatie und der besoldeten Presse die Schuld der Uneinigkeit aufgebürdet, und diese Beschuldigungen nehmen die Färbung einer Anklage wegen Störung des Friedens im Bunde und Untergrabung seiner Institutionen an.*[41]

Bismarck's essay is silent about Prussia's own successful attempts in the 1830s and 1840s to build an economic power base by virtue of the *Zollverein* (the Customs Union), from which Austria was excluded. Friedrich Schlegel for one had warned of the political consequences of the *Verein*, referring to the new arrangement as 'a customs empire' (*ein Zollkaisertum*).[42] Nor was Austria enthusiastic about the enterprise. Austria's policy towards Prussia was based upon the premise that Prussia must never succeed in creating a situation in which Austria was treated as 'foreign' in Germany.[43] The fact of the matter was that from the 1840s onwards Prussia and Austria became engaged in a fierce and in many ways fascinating struggle for the leadership of the German Confederation. The story of the competing projects of German union cannot and need not be told in detail here. Suffice it to point out that Prussia's superiority in the economic and military sphere eventually won it the upper hand.

A decisive moment occurred in 1863, when Austria presented the last of a series of proposals for reform of the Confederation. The proposal envisaged a confederal structure led by a directorate of five with executive powers. Having aligned the majority of states behind it, Austria, at short notice, invited Prussia to take part. Bismarck tried to persuade the King of Prussia to decline to attend and only succeeded after lengthy conversations and a second invitation from Austria. The decision proved a wise one from the Prussian point of view. The middle states evidently did not want to bind themselves to Austria without a balancing Prussian presence.[44] Put differently: nothing could be done without Prussia.

The German Empire of 1871 constitutes a classical case of an asymmetrical federation, in that one member state was clearly dominant. Twenty-four rulers (four kings, six grand dukes, four dukes and eight princes along with the senates of three free cities) had created the Empire by a voluntary act of association.[45] Formally, all members were equal. In practice the King of Prussian was more equal than the remainder. The Prussian King thus wore two hats, being at the same time German Emperor and thus head of the imperial executive and chief of all armed forces in the Empire. Carr describes the German empire as 'an uneasy compromise between the forces of conservative federalism, the liberal unitary principle and the military might of Prussia'.[46]

The federal body of the Empire was the *Bundesrat*, an assembly of ambassadors from the various states. Its consent was needed for all legislation; it had a veto over constitutional changes and foreign policy was supervised by a special *Bundesrat* committee. Compared with the German Confederation, the institutional structure of the Empire was much more asymmetrical. In the *Bundesrat* Prussia had seventeen of the 58 seats, Bavaria six and the smaller states one each. In theory Prussia could be outvoted. In practice the smaller states never opposed Prussia on important issues. The *Reichstag* shared legislative power with the *Rat* but otherwise had limited powers. Thus the Chancellor and his ministers were not accountable to the *Reichstag*. The executive powers lay in the hands of the Chancellor, the office of which was usually combined with that of the Prime Minister of Prussia. The imperial government was responsible for defence, customs, currency, banking, communications and the civil and criminal codes. States had considerable residual powers in the fields of education, justice, agriculture, local government and religious matters. Only states could levy direct taxes whereas the empire was dependent for its revenue on indirect taxation. Some states enjoyed specific privileges. Originally, Bavaria, spokesman for the particularists, would only enter the Prussian-led North German Confederation, which had been set up by Prussia in 1867 following the military defeat of Austria, on the condition that it be granted an equal voice with Prussia. However, Bismarck managed to isolate and win over Bavaria, appeasing the particularists by agreeing to extend the powers of the *Bundesrat* and granting Bavaria some special privileges, including the right to a permanent seat on the military committee of the *Bundesrat*, separate representation at peace negotiations and the chairmanship of a committee on foreign affairs. In addition, along with Württemberg, Bavaria obtained so-called reserve rights, allowing the two states to retain control of their postal and telegraphic services and armed forces.

In summary, the experience of German unification in the last century provides an interesting illustration of the concept of asymmetrical federation. Asymmetries were deliberately being constructed by institutional and other means but within the confines of a legal order, the rules of which were time and again re-shaped to accord with territorial interests.

Types of asymmetry

As we have seen, asymmetrical federations have a considerable realist dimension. Asymmetry may assume various forms. All federations are geographically asymmetrical in the sense that not all states within the federations are equal. There will in most cases be at least one geographical core within the federation. California and New York are competing geographical cores within the American Union. To the extent that this core tries to exercise deliberate leadership we may talk about a hegemonic strategy aiming at federal asymmetry. Asymmetrical federations are thus consciously created. The primary state actors seeking to set up asymmetrical federations will be called cooperative hegemons.

One may furthermore distinguish between external and internal asymmetry. Under external asymmetry a set of institutions are erected in the region's geopolitical core but at the subsystemic level that is outside the regional institutions *per se*. External asymmetry typically involves strategic differentiation within the integration system (see below). External asymmetry may also be less formalized. Internal asymmetry can be defined as the shaping of the regional institutions in a way that favours the dominant state(s) disproportionately. Internal asymmetry can assume at least three different forms: 1) institutional asymmetry refers to a biased institutional system which grants the dominant state(s) a preponderant role. This role may be achieved for instance by trying to convert the core's population strength into political influence within the federation's institutions; 2) geopolitical asymmetry which refers to a federation which acquires a hegemonic centre as a consequence of strategic enlargement; and 3) structural asymmetry which refers to the creation of a supranational governing structure which in its basic features is congruent with the structure of the cooperative hegemonic state. This gives the latter state a comparative advantage in regional economics and politics, since regional politics will, as it were, become a continuation of national politics by the same means.

I have argued that asymmetrical federations are typically instituted by cooperative hegemons. The main sources of influence for cooperative hegemons are economic, political, institutional and ideological. But the emphasis in cooperative hegemony is on political and institutional sources of influence. Asymmetrical federations are less the product of structural factors than of a specific grand strategy. Asymmetrical federations are thus soft hegemonies, in which in a reformulation of Keohane 'a state is powerful enough to maintain the essential rules governing inter-state relations in a region, and willing to do so'.[47] Cooperative hegemons may or may not be legitimated, but will put a premium on legitimacy. Asymmetrical federations are typically decentralized unions with a weak formal political leadership. In such unions an informal core often compensates for the formal leadership deficit. This *ceteris paribus* adds to its legitimacy among secondary states.

The degree of acceptance is *ceteris paribus* higher in asymmetrical federations where hegemons enter into a contractual relationship with other states than in unilateral hegemonies in which order is established without prior negotiation. However, the possibility of defection is likely to be greater under unilateral hegemony than within an asymmetrical federation, since the process of federalization implies a very high degree of economic interdependence and societal interpenetration. Asymmetrical federations are closer to the hierarchy pole in the continuum of state systems than are unilateral hegemonies. On the other hand, cooperative hegemonies rarely possess the same military power vis-à-vis their subordinates as do unilateral hegemonies. In fact, this is one of the main reasons why the cooperative type of hegemonic strategy is chosen in the first place. In asymmetrical federations defection thus has to be prevented by non-military means.

Directional leadership

A strategy of cooperative hegemony implies the exercise of regional leadership. The concepts of leadership and hegemony are often conflated and do in some respects overlap. Ikenberry distinguishes between structural, institutional and situational leadership.[48] Malnes has suggested the useful distinction between problem-solving, positional and directional leadership.[49] Directional leadership involves structural leadership based on resource power but is a broader concept including leadership based on skills. Given the limited resource asymmetry in regions where processes of asymmetrical federalization will typically occur, we expect cooperative hegemons to place the emphasis on directional leadership. The concept of directional leadership may be further specified. It can be argued that directional leaders are mainly concerned with agenda-setting. Far from imposing their views in each and every re-distributive conflict, directional leaders place priority on setting the long-term goals of the organization.

Oran Young distinguishes between structural, entrepreneurial and intellectual leadership. The latter two forms of leadership seem more or less synonymous with situational leadership. This is the kind of leadership which depends on personal charisma, ideas and the ability to see and exploit opportunities. Since the cooperative hegemon has a preference for soft power, it will also have to rely to a considerable extent on intellectual and entrepreneurial leadership 'producing intellectual capital or generative systems of thought'.[50]

Lisa Martin has formulated the interesting concept of coercive cooperation which implies the exercise of leadership by a state not possessing overriding structural power capabilities.[51] Such a state is more interested in achieving cooperation than are the other members of a state system. While lacking the capability of a traditional hegemon, it is willing and able to pay to get cooperation. 'The tools of coercion are the "soft" ones of side-payments and/or threats to reduce or eliminate grants offered previously to recalcitrant states', as Grieco comments.[52] Coercive cooperation is, it could be argued, an aspect of the strategy of cooperative hegemony. The cooperative hegemon is more interested in regionalization than its partners and is willing to pay (in the broad sense of the word) to get the process of federalization moving. The power wielded by the hegemon is soft power in Nye's sense, especially cooptive power.[53]

From balance to overbalance

Cooperative hegemons emphasize cooptation. They seek to neutralize the balance of power mechanism. As Rosecrance writes in a different context 'the balance of power only works if non-committed powers can effectively balance those already aligned together'.[54] Rosecrance refers to the chances of the EU becoming the pivot of a new centralized world order. But his point is valid for intra-European affairs as well. If the EU 'contained a grouping that was too strong to be balanced against, the net effect would be cooptive of other states. Balancing yields to band-wagoning ... A strong central core would not produce balance and repulsion. It would produce overbalance and magnetic attraction'.[55]

Stephen Walt has pointed out that states do not balance power but fear.[56] The extent to which states appear threatening not only depends on capability, but also on other factors such as intentions. Whether or not a dominant state is balanced also depends on the behaviour of the dominant state.[57] Balance-of-fear realism thus abandons the purely structural approach in favour of a nuanced approach, combining structural and evolutionary explanations. This brings it close to classical realism and makes it a valuable point of departure for an ideational realism. Mastanduno uses Walt's theory to make inferences about the defensive grand strategies of consolidated unipoles. But there is no reason why it could not also be used to speculate about the grand strategy of aspiring hegemons with a relatively weak capability basis. An essential element in cooperative hegemony is precisely the reduction of fear with a view to preventing the formation of counter-hegemonic alliances.

Elaborating on this point we would argue that what Rosecrance is describing is an essential element in the strategy of cooperative hegemony, a defensive big-power strategy for big powers without overwhelming resource superiority and for declining hegemons. Such a big-power strategy is in any case probably only feasible under certain conditions. Under conditions of extreme asymmetry it is unlikely to succeed, because the smaller states in a region will refuse to commit themselves to a federalizing process, fearing the dominance of the big powers.[58] In this case the smaller states are more likely to opt for a policy of distance.

An ongoing federalizing process may also at some point come to face the problem of extreme asymmetry, either because of transformations enhancing the material power of the cooperative hegemon or because of changes in the policy of the cooperative hegemon or in the perception of the hegemon in the non-hegemonic states. However, the strategy of cooperative hegemony may also fail because the core is too weak. If the incentives to join the core in its federalizing project are too small, or if the threat of exclusion is not credible (e.g. because of weaknesses in the cohesion of a dual hegemony), the smaller states may defect. However, this will in part depend on the availability of alternatives. The challenge for cooperative hegemons consists of ensuring that the core is sufficiently strong and cohesive to foster band-wagoning behaviour but not so strong and coercive as to provoke balancing or a policy of distance on the part of the non-hegemonic states. Band-wagoning is often structurally determined, but it may also be the outcome of a deliberate strategy. Sum has shown how Japan seeks to stimulate a follower identity in the Asian NICs (newly industrialized countries) within the context of a 'flying geese pattern' which could be characterized as a variation on the theme of cooperative hegemony.[59]

Although economic capability is crucial in fostering band-wagoning, political tactics play a role as well. The cooperative hegemon may, for instance, threaten to set up a formalized substructure within the regional structure.[60] This we may call tactical differentiation. It confronts the non-hegemonic powers with the threat of losing influence, since by constituting a caucus the subsystem will often be able to preempt the decisions of the regional bodies. Moreover, the threat of forming a powerful subsystem at the core of a region confronts other states with an incalculable risk, since it is impossible to influence the future decisions of such a system, were it to be set up. Moravcsik, using the concept 'alternative coalitions', puts it succinctly 'exclusion can be expensive both because the non-member forfeits input into further decision-making and because it foregoes whatever benefits result... The coercive threat may bring about an agreement at a level of integration above the lowest common denominator'.[61]

Alternatively, the cooperative hegemon may choose the strategy of external asymmetry. External asymmetry typically takes the form of strategic differentiation that is the actual setting up of a core structure outside the regional institutions. The important point is that cooperative hegemons will seek to avoid defection and balancing and therefore will set up an open core structure. By leaving open the possibility of participation the core has a divisive effect on the periphery, making balancing difficult.[62] If the core commands a clear resource superiority within the region, non-membership will be, or will be regarded as, costly. One element in the strategy of cooperative hegemony may thus be tactical and strategic differentiation of the integration system.

One may point to several historical examples of differentiation in processes of unification. Once again German national unification is illustrative. Prussia set up the *Zollverein* in 1834 within the larger German Confederation.[63] Austria, at one and the same time rival and co-leader of the Confederation, was not a member of the *Zollverein*, the purpose of which was to strengthen Prussia vis-à-vis Austria. The *Zollverein* proved a perfect tool for Prussia. By strengthening the economic position of Prussia vis-à-vis Austria the *Zollverein* led to band-wagoning in the smaller German principalities. In 1867 following the Prussian defeat of Austria,

Prussia set up the North German Confederation and in 1871 Prussia assumed the primacy in the German *Kaiserreich* (empire). The Prussian King thus carried the additional title of German Emperor. The predominant role of Austria and Hungary within the Austro–Hungarian empire is another case in point.

From the point of view of integration theory these examples illustrate how deficiencies in the formal leadership structure of federations may be compensated for by informal leadership structures, a point also stressed by Ivo Duchacek.[64] From the point of view of hegemonic theory they illustrate the importance of economic and political sources of hegemonic power.

Exit, voice and loyalty in regional integration

Organization theory provides some useful insights into the strategic behaviour of cooperative hegemons in regional integration systems. First, as Hirschmann points out, the effectiveness of the voice mechanism is strengthened by the possibility of exit.[65] To the extent that a cooperative hegemon offers secondary states significant concessions, the latter gain an interest in the continuing existence of the integration system. This produces an asymmetrical pattern of exit options, giving the hegemon an exit option which the secondary state will not normally see itself as possessing. If the regional hegemon is economically very influential or if it is militarily indispensable to the defence of a region, it may obtain concessions by threatening to exit from the regional structure or parts of this structure.[66] One can draw a parallel between the oligopolistic behaviour of firms in the economic sphere and the behaviour of hegemons in the international political sphere. Oligopols will try to make exit impossible so as to allow them to raise prices. Similarly, it is logical to expect the cooperative hegemon to try to raise the price of exit for secondary states. It will try to reduce the alternatives available to secondary states, as the voice effectiveness of these states will in part depend on their alternative options. In order to wield major power, cooperative hegemons will first have to 'lock in' the smaller members of the regional system. Interestingly, neo-functionalists foresaw a gradual reduction of alternatives as integration proceeded.[67] It is perfectly possible to conceive of the reduction of the alternatives available to secondary states as an element in the strategy of cooperative hegemons. In the debate on European integration, reduction of alternatives has

52

normally been discussed in the context of a German policy of 'self-binding', but it is more helpful to interpret it as an element in the hegemon's strategy and behaviour towards the secondary members.

Hirschmann also points out that 'no-exit polities' stimulate compromising behaviour. He compares geographically and culturally isolated Japan to Argentina with its easy access to exit, arguing that the difficulty of exit in the Japanese case set rigid boundaries for the possibilities of political opposition.[68] Translated into the context of regional integration, this leads to the proposition that 1) as integration proceeds the price of exit rises and 2) this generates a more compromising behaviour vis-à-vis the hegemonic leader. One may object that the threat of exit on the part of the big state is pure bluff, since it risks damaging itself e.g. by losing important markets. The answer is that there are ways of reducing this boomerang effect and thus enhancing the credibility of an exit threat. Here strategic differentiation proves its worth. By combining the threat of exit with (preparations for) strategic differentiation the cooperative hegemon can make sure – and make visible – that unlike the secondary states, it does possess an exit option!

The credibility of the threat of exit varies with the degree of asymmetry in a region. Under conditions of extreme asymmetry the threat of exit is most credible. However, under such conditions it is also unlikely that the regional power will have managed to convince the other states in the region to take part in regionalization in the first place. For a cooperative hegemon with moderate superiority in terms of economic resources, the threat of exit is also unlikely to be credible, since the negative consequences of exit for the other members of the regional grouping will not be very salient. For the cooperative hegemon with clearly superior but not overwhelming resources, the threat of exit may on the other hand be both credible and damaging. This threat only becomes credible in the later stages of an integration process, however, once an asymmetrical economic interdependence has developed in the relationship between the hegemon and its regional periphery, making exit very costly for secondary states, and once the integration system has acquired a density that permits the hegemon to manipulate the nested games.

A final point concerns loyalty. As Hirschmann points out, high initiation costs may help repress exit and to some extent also voice. The member having paid a high price of entry will be prone to self-deception. In Hirschmann's own words 'recognition by members of any deterioration (in the organization, author) will therefore be delayed and so will be the onset of voice'.[69] This is a variation on the theme of cognitive dissonance which may help shed light on the EU's policy of requiring that new members accept *l'acquis.*

Hegemonic socialization

The cooperative hegemon is typically hesitant to use overt coercion vis-à-vis its neighbours since its powers of sanction are limited. This type of hegemonic leadership will therefore tend to concentrate on positive rather than negative ways of exerting influence. As mentioned above, the exercise of ideological power is a low-cost strategy for hegemons. Ideological consensus in the Gramscian sense will often emerge by force of example. A state may thus try to demonstrate its superiority in a region or globally by means of a kind of 'systemic competition'. Markovits and Reich put it succinctly 'assimilation is the sincerest form of flattery'.[70] But a state aspiring to leadership may also try deliberately to diffuse its values. It may try to socialize the smaller member states in a region into accepting its leadership. Ikenberry and Kupchan argue that secondary states will often adopt the values of the hegemon in order to reduce cognitive dissonance, i.e. a situation in which political leaders in the secondary state uphold norms of autonomy which are out of touch with the reality of economic dependence upon the hegemon. In the context of regional integration one could argue that a regional economic hegemon may succeed in indirectly obtaining support for its political objectives by expanding economically, thus establishing a structure of highly asymmetrical interdependence that spills over into the political–ideological sphere of dependent state behaviour.[71] In this sense, market power can be used strategically. Unfortunately this proposition is difficult to test empirically, since most individuals will be loath to admit that their views are not the outcome of a free decision. Yet, the timing of normative adaptation may be suggestive. For instance, foreign policy rhetoric in countries like Norway and Sweden changed quite abruptly in the late 1980s and early 1990s coinciding with the setting up of the EU's internal market and the threat of competitive losses that this posed to the EFTA countries.

The cooperative hegemon may also pursue a more direct and political strategy of hegemonic socialization, trying to formulate a set of values and symbols around which the region may rally. In that case the hegemon can be expected to devote extraordinary resources to 'region-building' efforts. At the same time, the hegemon can be expected to present its specific interests as the general interests of the region. Secondary members may discover needs they did not know they had. One way to legitimate a power-oriented regionalization process is for the hegemonic leader to link region building to regional stability, that is to the prevention of armed conflict in the region. The quest for non-violent aggrandizement thus almost inevitably becomes shrouded in peace rhetoric (see the case of German unification, p. 45). The weakness of this tactic is that it raises the question of when a region is sufficiently integrated to have made armed conflict impossible.

Side-payments and power-sharing

Economic influence is of fundamental importance for the cooperative hegemon seeking to stimulate band-wagoning behaviour. As Hoffmann writes 'the quest for control turns neighbours into adversaries and provokes balancing behaviour, whereas the drive for economic influence turns them into clients and breeds band-wagoning behaviour'.[72] A strategy of cooperative hegemony can therefore be expected to include the granting of side-payments, which is an effective way to obtain quick results in a negotiation.

Cooperative hegemony also implies a willingness on the part of the hegemon to share power, that is to offer an institutionalized voice-opportunity. A regional big power wanting to establish an asymmetrical federal structure in a region must be willing to share power on a permanent basis. Regional big powers with a tradition for power-sharing and federalism are therefore *ceteris paribus* best equipped to implement a strategy of cooperative hegemony. Cooperative hegemony implies inviting at least one other state to share in the leadership of the region, on the condition that it accepts the hegemon's leadership.

There are some methodological problems involved in measuring power-sharing. If the outcome of a given negotiation sequence between a hegemon and a secondary state is biased in favour of the secondary state, how can it be determined whether this is due to the hegemon's willingness to compromise or due to its weakness as a negotiator? In other words, can our theory of cooperative hegemony be falsified? In order to determine this we shall have to look for negotiating sequences in which the prospective hegemon consciously underperforms. Here a comparison with the same state's behaviour in bilateral bargaining sessions with countries outside the regional integration system could be useful. Intra-regional comparisons with the bargaining performance and bargaining style of other regional big powers not subscribing to the strategy of cooperative hegemony may also be helpful, although it will be difficult to separate voluntary concessions from structural imperfections deriving from internal characteristics of the states in question.

In what areas can the cooperative hegemon be expected to be most forthcoming vis-à-vis secondary states? In order to answer this question it may be useful to distinguish between different types of regional decisions. First of all, we may apply Hoffmann's useful distinction between high and low politics.[73] High politics are here defined as decisions in the areas of foreign and security policy, defence policy, monetary affairs and judicial and home affairs, as well as decisions on the overall institutional and procedural rules of the system.[74] Low politics are all other decisions. Secondly, I propose that we distinguish between constitutive and normal EU politics. Constitutive decisions refer to processes that establish or amend the basic rules of the game in a regional integration system.[75] This leaves us with the typology shown in Table 4.2.

Table 4.2   *Types of EU politics*

Types of EU Politics	High	Low
Constitutive	Hegemonic domain	
Normal		

One may object that constitutive decisions are also high politics in the sense that core values are affected. However, if high politics is defined narrowly as is the case here, it should be possible to avoid overlapping between the twin concepts.

We would argue that constitutive high politics constitutes the 'hegemonic domain' par excellence. The cooperative hegemon is expected to be most likely to offer voice-opportunity and share power in normal politics decisions, whether high or low politics, whereas it will be keen to maintain control in constitutive politics, especially in high politics decisions of a constitutive nature, the latter including decisions on the institutional and procedural rules of the regional system. The cooperative hegemon will seek to set the overall agenda of the regional system; it will seek to shape the basic rules and procedures of the regional institutional system with a view to exercising indirect rule, and in terms of substance it will concentrate on high politics sectors with international repercussions, notably security and defence matters but also external exchange rate policy. In theoretical terms, hegemonic leadership is *ceteris paribus* most likely to be accepted in areas in which hegemons produce collective goods. Defence (deterrence) is one such area, external exchange rate policy another. Other benefits of monetary integration, however, presuppose active participation by secondary states.

The purpose of power-sharing is to enable a big power in a region to exercise stable rule. One could also say that power-sharing is a way of winning legitimacy. Hegemonic power-sharing is not only about making choices between more and less important decisions, it is also about shaping the common institutions in ways likely to reassure less powerful actors. Certain systems of macro-political governance could be argued to be particularly effective in coopting weaker actors. Thus the system of consociation as defined by Lijphart and Taylor, apart from offering a model for conflict-prone societies, can also, we would argue, be used as a strategy for coopting smaller states in a process of asymmetrical federalization. Typical consociational mechanisms are broad coalitions, equal representation and the rotation of executive office.[76] Asymmetrical federations thus may include elements from other political orders.

Expansive gradualism

Since in any given negotiating sequence the cooperative hegemon is unlikely to accomplish all its goals, and since it is normally unable to act unilaterally to establish regional order, it must negotiate its way to regional primacy through a series of constitutive bargains. Here the strategy of cooperative hegemony differs from the unilateralism implied by traditional hegemony. This has several implications. The cooperative hegemon cannot impose its will at any given point in time and therefore can be expected to pursue a strategy of gradualism. Gradualism may thus be a reflection of weakness. But it may also reflect tactical acumen. Expansive gradualism capitalizes on the short time-horizon of human beings. As we have seen, a strategy of expansive gradualism can be deduced from neo-functionalist theory. Traditionally, the literature has conceived of spillover as essentially a process of self-reinforcing integration. It is more useful to conceive of spillover as a key element in a pro-integrationist strategy. The cultivation of spillover builds up pressure for further integration and mobilizes interest groups and other pressure groups against their own state. It devises integration plans which function like Russian dolls: inside each commitment, there is a further commitment.[77]

To the extent that a cooperative hegemon favours closer integration, it may well adopt a tactic of expansive gradualism. The concept of spillover can be conceived as a strategic device serving to fragment sensitive decisions on the transfer of sovereignty in order to secure the support of secondary states for an integration process led by a cooperative hegemon.

Regional identification

As pointed out above, the successful pursuit of a strategy of cooperative hegemony implies a tacit contract between the hegemon and secondary states. The hegemon articulates the common interests of the states in the region vis-à-vis outside powers and will also normally be expected to defend these interests. The global performance of the cooperative hegemon will be important in attracting the loyalty of other states in the region. But the functional logic can rarely stand alone. It will be supplemented by symbolic acts. Through acts and rhetoric the cooperative hegemon can try to build up an image as the defender and conscience of the region. We may call this regional identification. The cooperative hegemon can exploit advantages of scale. It is possible to talk about a group dividend, that is the fact that a number of states clustered in a region will find it easier to defend their interests vis-à-vis external powers if they act in unison. Significantly, however, the size of the group dividend will rise and fall depending on the power structure in the international system. This implies that the incentives for, and the feasibility of, regional identification fluctuate over time. Cooperative hegemons can be expected to fashion their concrete strategy with a view to the opportunity structure provided by the international constellation.[78]

In a unipolar system with a concentrated external challenge the group dividend will generally be very high, unless there is a very high degree of cultural–political similarity between the integrating region and the unipole. In a bipolar system the group dividend falls, but is still relatively high. In a multipolar system the group dividend will normally be moderate or low, since forming an alliance with the least threatening against the most threatening power(s) will constitute an attractive alternative to internal balancing through hegemonic region-building, with its attendant costs.

The size of the group dividend can also be expected to vary with the degree of conjunctural tension and détente in the regional and international system. Under conditions of international tension the group dividend rises, under conditions of détente it decreases. The hegemon's strategy of expansive gradualism can thus be expected to follow a stop–go pattern, in which the timing of new attempts to progress towards an asymmetrical federation will be dependent upon the international and regional constellation and climate.

Dual hegemonies

The strategy of cooperative hegemony may be pursued by one or two big states in a region. Dual hegemonies create special problems since there will normally be an imbalance of power between the two partners in the hegemonic core. Whereas asymmetry may have an integrative effect at the level of the region, provided it takes the form of unipolarity, institutionalized asymmetry within a subsystemic core is likely to produce tension. Constitutive politics at the level of the region will then come to revolve around a double asymmetry, i.e. the asymmetry between the hegemonic substructure and the wider regional system and the asymmetry within the dual hegemony. The two levels can be expected to interact with intra-hegemonic tension spilling over into the relationship between core and periphery and with peripheral states seeking to stabilize intra-hegemonic relations. The case of Prussia's and Austria's joint leadership within the German Confederation in the first half of the last century suggests that dual hegemonies are unstable. Whereas Austria and Prussia managed to exercise joint leadership in the German Confederation from 1815 to the middle of the century, the following years saw a fierce rivalry between the two powers, each trying to use the Confederation as a vehicle for its own expansionist aspirations (see above).

The case of German unification in the 19th century thus suggests that an important precondition for the durability of the dual hegemony is the introduction and maintenance of a system of parity even in the face of uneven development between the two hegemonic leaders at the level

59

of population and material resources. By way of analogy it could be argued that, apart from the nuclear stalemate, one of the important reasons for the relative stability in the international system during the bipolar period was that the USA was normally prepared to offer the USSR an at least nominal and in some respects also real political parity.

A summary

Let us briefly summarize our discussion. Stressing the role of positive inducements and institutional strategies we define cooperative hegemons as major powers which enter into a contractual and highly institutionalized relationship with other states with a view to expanding in a legitimate fashion. Cooperative hegemons seek to prevent balancing behaviour *inter alia* by granting secondary states concessions and seek to shape the rules and institutions of the regional integration system according to their interests.

From the concept of cooperative hegemony we may deduce a number of macro-institutional strategies. The key strategies relating to the way a biased regional order may be created are 1) strategic differentiation; 2) institutional asymmetry; 3) geopolitical asymmetry; and 4) structural asymmetry. The strategies vary in terms of both visibility and time-horizon. Table 4.3 summarizes these differences.

Table 4.3   *The strategy of cooperative hegemony: macro-institutional strategies*

Time-horizon	Visibility	
	High	Low
Short	Institutional asymmetry	
Long	Strategic differentiation	Geopolitical asymmetry Structural asymmetry

Strategic differentiation is characterized by a high visibility and a long time-horizon. This combination involves a certain amount of costs. It creates new divisions in the regional state system and unless combined with cooptive measures, it may provoke defection on the part of non-core members. Moreover, unlike tactical differentiation, strategic differentiation tests the core's cohesion. There may be costs in terms of loss of credibility if the core proves less cohesive than expected. Strategic differentiation is thus likely to be a transitional strategy. It may lead to institutional asymmetry, as the core seeks to legitimate its special position. Or it may, more dramatically, lead to fragmentation of the integration system, as the creation of a permanent core elicits hostile reactions or leads to unmanageable variable geometry. However, given the asymmetrical economic interdependence governing the relationship between core and periphery, fragmentation is not very likely.

Institutional asymmetry also normally has a high visibility. It encompasses issues such as institutional representation, which touch upon state influence and status. However, institutional asymmetry may be more or less visible. There is scope for imaginative design. The great advantage of institutional asymmetry is that it is an indirect way of redistributing resources. It multilateralizes a power struggle that would otherwise have been bilateral and thus even more visible.

Institutional asymmetry may operate within a short or a long time-horizon, but compared to strategic differentiation it has a more immediate effect on the distribution of power within the region. Structural asymmetry constitutes an attractive alternative in that its visibility is much lower. The effect on the distribution of power is much more indirect than in the case of institutional asymmetry. Enhancing the congruence between the domestic structures of the most powerful state and the structures of the regional system is also likely to be a long-term exercise. Geopolitical asymmetry too is a low-visibility strategy. It presupposes that the would-be hegemon has a very considerable influence in adjacent states wanting to adhere to the integration system. While unlikely to provoke strong opposition, this strategy is likely to be less effective than the other strategies of federal asymmetry as regionalization offers dependent states new coalition possibilities.

Table 4.4 (overleaf) provides an overview of the theory of cooperative hegemony.

The feasibility of a strategy of cooperative hegemony

The feasibility of a strategy of cooperative hegemony is likely to depend on several factors, some of which have already been touched upon. Four factors deserve to be highlighted. Firstly, as we have seen, the strategy of cooperative hegemony is most likely to succeed if the international system is unipolar. This implies an increase in the size and intensity of common interests for any given region which provides an opportunity

Table 4.4 *Cooperative hegemony and regional integration: an overview*

Paradigmatic assumptions	Ideational realism
Grand strategy	Cooperative hegemony
Regional political order	Asymmetrical federation
Macro-institutional strategies	Structural asymmetry Institutional asymmetry Geopolitical asymmetry
Dynamics of hegemonic integration	Expansive gradualism Cooptation Lock-in Regional identification Hegemonic socialization Side-payments and power-sharing Tactical differentiation

for cooperative hegemons to establish themselves as legitimate leaders of the region. Secondly, the degree of material asymmetry in a region is important. A high degree of regional institutionalization is unlikely in regions with extreme asymmetry, as this will stimulate a policy of detachment on the part of smaller states. Thirdly, the number of small and minor states in the integrating region is likely to be important. If the number of smaller states is high, the cooperative hegemon will find it increasingly difficult to carve out a privileged role for itself. As the number of smaller states increases, the cumulative cost of side-payments will increase. Besides, geographical enlargement may raise problems of decision-making efficiency leading to demands for federalization on a scale and of a nature not acceptable to the leading states. Theoretically, large-scale geographical enlargement may well pave the way for a symmetrical federation.[79] Enlargement on a major scale will tend to enhance institutional complexity to the point of unleashing a kind of institutional spillover effect. It should be added though that a large and rapidly expanding regional structure may also at least temporarily increase the power of the cooperative hegemon, since in a more complex setting there will be a greater demand for the informal leadership which only the hegemon can provide.

Fourthly, the hegemon's cultural–ideological assets are an important variable. Since asymmetrical federalization is a strategy for regional powers without a great superiority in terms of material resources, this kind of hegemonic rule relies heavily on soft power including ideological power and prestige. The attractiveness of the hegemon's 'way of life' therefore becomes a crucial parameter once a federalization process reaches the stage where national societies begin to merge. In the absence of great cultural assets, constructivist efforts to build a new and distinct regional value-system will become important.

Notes

1. A good discussion of the concept is found in David P. Rapkin, 'The Contested Concept of Hegemonic Leadership', in David P. Rapkin (ed.), *World Leadership and Hegemony*, Boulder and London: Lynne Rienner Publishers, 1990. See also J. Wiener, 'Hegemonic Leadership: Naked Emperor or the Worship of False Gods?', *European Journal of International Relations*, Vol. 1, no. 2, 1995, and David A. Lake, 'Leadership, Hegemony and the International Economy: Naked Emperor or Tattered Monarch with Potential?', *International Studies Quarterly*, Vol. 33, no. 4, 1993. For an attempt to deconstruct the theory of hegemonic stability see Isabelle Grunberg, 'Exploring the "Myth" of Hegemonic Stability', *International Organization*, Vol. 44, no. 4, Autumn 1990.
2. Robert O. Keohane, *International Institutions and State Power: Essays in International Relations Theory*, Boulder: Westview, 1989, p. 78.
3. See Duncan Snidal, 'The Limits of Hegemonic Stability Theory', *International Organization*, Vol. 39, no. 4, Autumn 1985.
4. See Robert Gilpin, *War and Change in World Politics*, Cambridge: Cambridge University Press, 1981.
5. See Scott C. James and David A. Lake, 'The Second Face of Hegemony: Britain's Repeal of the Corn Laws and the American Walker Tariff of 1846', *International Organization*, Vol. 43, no. 1, Winter 1989.
6. Robert O. Keohane and Joseph S. Nye, *Power and Interdependence*, Boston: Little & Brown 1977. See also Lykke Friis, *Den tyske magt*, Copenhagen: Politiske Studier, 1994, p. 49.
7. See e.g. Lears T.J. Jackson, 'The Concept of Cultural Hegemony: Problems and Possibilities', *American Historical Review*, Vol. 90, no. 3.
8. See Lykke Friis, *op. cit.* See also Lykke Friis, 'Germany as a Soft Great Power?', in Birthe Hansen (ed.), *European Security – 2000*, Copenhagen: Copenhagen Political Studies Press, 1995.
9. Karl Deutsch, *Political Community in the North Atlantic Area*, Princeton: Princeton University Press, 1957.
10. Matthias Kaelberer, 'Hegemony, Dominance or Leadership? Explaining Germany's Role in European Monetary Cooperation', *European Journal of International Relations*, Vol. 3, no. 1, March 1997, p. 51.
11. G. John Ikenberry, 'The Future of International Leadership', *Political Science Quarterly*, Fall 1996, pp. 396ff.
12. See John G. Ikenberry and Charles A. Kupchan, 'Socialization and Hegemonic Power', *International Organization*, Vol. 44, no. 3, Summer 1990.
13. *Ibid.*

14. Morten Ougaard, 'Dimension of Hegemony', *Cooperation & Conflict*, Vol. XXIII, 1988.

15. See Joseph M. Grieco, *Systemic Sources of Variation in Regional Institutionalization in Western Europe, East Asia, and the Americas.* Paper prepared for delivery at the Annual Meeting of the American Political Science Association, Chicago, 31 August–3 September, 1995.

16. See Donald Crone, 'Does Hegemony Matter? The Reorganization of the Pacific Political Economy', *World Politics*, No. 45, October 1992–July 1993.

17. Birthe Hansen, *Unipolarity – A Theoretical Model*, Copenhagen: Institut for Statskundskab, Working Paper no. 10, 1993.

18. Adam Watson, *International Society*, London: Routledge, 1992, p. 240.

19. *Ibid.*, pp. 13ff.

20. See David A. Lake, 'Anarchy, Hierarchy, and the Variety of International Relations', *International Organization*, Vol. 50, no. 1, Winter 1996, pp. 1–33.

21. Daniel H. Deudney, 'The Philadelphian System: Sovereignty, Arms Control, and Balance of Power in the American States-Union Circa 1787–1861', *International Organization*, Vol. 49, no. 2, Spring 1995.

22. My use of the concept of asymmetry is inspired by Duchacek's classical study, but the term is also used, albeit in a different fashion, in Peter M. Leslie, *Asymmetry and Integration: The Emergence of Regional Hegemonic Systems.* Paper prepared for presentation at the Annual General Meeting of the Canadian Political Science Association, University of Calgary, 12–14 June 1994. Interestingly, Leslie sets out to formulate a theory of regional hegemony. However, I am inclined to think that he places too much emphasis on purely economic hegemony, neglecting the institutional and political aspects.

23. Ivo Duchacek, *Comparative Federalism. The Territorial Dimension of Politics*, New York: Holt, Rinehart and Winston Inc., 1970.

24. *Ibid.*, pp. 282ff.

25. See William H. Riker, *Federalism. Origin. Operation. Significance*, Boston & Toronto: Little Brown & Company, 1964, p. 11. See also Alberta M. Sbragia, 'Thinking about the European Future: The Uses of Comparison', in Alberta M. Sbragia (ed.), *Euro-Politics. Institutions and Policy-making in the 'New' European Community*, Washington D.C.: The Brookings Institution, 1992.

26. Stephen Krasner, *Structural Conflict*, Berkeley: University of California Press, 1985, p. 14.

27. Arnold Wolfers, *Discord and Collaboration*, Baltimore: The Johns Hopkins Press, 1962.

28. Paul Schroeder, 'Historical Reality vs Neo-Realist Theory', *International Security*, Vol. 19/1, Summer 1994.

29. See Thomas Pedersen, 'Structure or Strategy: The Case of French European Policy after the Cold War', in Georg Sørensen and Hans-Henrik Holm (eds), *And Now What? International Politics after the Cold War*, Aarhus: Politica, 1998, pp. 103–24.

30. See Kishore Mahbubani, 'The Pacific Impulse', *Survival*, Vol. 37, no. 1, Spring 1995.

31. Barry Buzan and Richard Little, 'Reconceptualizing Anarchy. Structural Real-

ism Meets World History', *European Journal of International Relations*, Vol 2/4, 1996.

32. See Ivo Duchacek, *Comparative Federalism*, New York: Holt, Rinehart and Winston Inc., 1970, pp. 277ff.

33. William H. Riker, *op. cit.*

34. Friedrich Von Krosigk, 'A Reconsideration of Federalism in the Scope of the Present Discussion on European Integration', *Journal of Common Market Studies*, Vol. 9, no. 1, April 1968.

35. Despite its name the German Confederation could be regarded as an example of an extremely decentralized federal structure.

36. 'Hanover is therefore the only state among the German middle states, in relation to which Prussia's German diplomacy should constantly apply every effort and skill in order to obtain its support for Prussia and remove its anxiety', Otto Von Bismarck, *Werke in Auswahl. Zweiter Band. Das Werden des Staatsmannes 1815–1862. Zweiter Teil: 1854–1862*, Darmstadt: Wissenschaftliche Buchgesellschaft, 1963, p. 230.

37. William Carr, *A History of Germany, 1815–1945*, 2nd edition, London: Edward Arnold, 1979 (1969), pp. 4ff.

38. Heinrich Lutz, *Zwischen Habsburg und Preussen. Deutschland 1815–1866*, Berlin: Siedler Verlag, 1985, p. 38.

39. *Ibid.*

40. *Ibid.*, p. 48.

41. (Austria) 'dresses up its claims in pro-union rhetoric' … 'in the diplomacy and the bought press Austria and its majority puts the blame for every discord on Prussia, and these accusations take on the implication of a charge of disturbing the Union's peace and undermining its institutions', Otto Von Bismarck, *op. cit.*, pp. 204ff.

42. Wilhelm Treue, *Die Geschichte von Deutschland*, Stuttgart: Alfred Kröner Verlag, 1978, p. 529.

43. Lutz, *op. cit.*, p. 190. Lutz quotes a statement by Metternich.

44. Carr, *op. cit.*, pp. 91ff; Lutz, *op. cit.*, pp. 441ff.

45. Carr, *op. cit.*, p. 125. The following outline of the structure of the German Empire is based mainly on Carr.

46. *Ibid.*

47. See Robert O. Keohane and Joseph S. Nye, *op. cit.*, p. 44.

48. G. John Ikenberry, *op. cit.*

49. Raino Malnes, 'Leader and Entrepreneur in International Negotiations: A Conceptual Analysis', *European Journal of International Relations*, Vol. 1, no. 1, 1995.

50. Oran Young, 'Political Leadership and Regime Formation: On the Development of Institutions in International Society', *International Organization*, Vol. 45, no. 3, Summer 1991.

51. Lisa L. Martin, 'Institutions and Cooperation. Sanctions during the Falklands Islands Conflict', *International Security*, Vol. 16/4, Spring 1992.

52. Grieco, *op. cit.*, p. 4.

53. The effectiveness of cooptive power in contemporary world politics is stressed in Joseph S. Nye, *Bound to Lead*, New York: Basic Books, 1990.

54. Richard Rosecrance, 'Regionalism and the Post-Cold War Era', *International Journal*, Vol. XLVI, no. 3, Summer 1991, p. 385.
55. *Ibid.*
56. Stephen M. Walt, *The Origins of Alliances*, Ithaca: Cornell University Press, 1987.
57. Michael Mastanduno, 'Preserving the Unipolar Moment: Realist Theories and US Grand Strategy after the Cold War', International Security, Vol. 21/4, Spring 1997, p. 60.
58. See Crone, *op. cit.*
59. Ngai-Ling Sum, 'The NICs and Competing Strategies of East Asian Regionalism', in Andrew Gamble and Anthony Payne (eds), *Regionalism and World Order*, London: Macmillan, 1996, p. 214. See also Helen Wallace and William Wallace, *Flying Together in a Larger and More Diverse European Union*, The Hague: Netherlands Scientific Council for Government Policy, Working Documents 87, 1995.
60. The concept of threats of exclusion is discussed by *inter alia* Paul Taylor, 'The European Community and the State: Assumptions, Theories and Propositions', *Review of International Studies*, Vol. 17, 1991, and Andrew Moravcsik, 'Preferences and Power in the European Community: A Liberal Intergovernmentalist Approach', *Journal of Common Market Studies*, Vol. 31, no. 4, December 1993.
61. Andrew Moravcsik, 'Negotiating the Single European Act', *International Organization*, Vol. 45, no. 1, 1991.
62. For a discussion of subsystems in regional systems see Thomas Pedersen, 'Subsystems and Regional Integration – the Case of Nordic and Baltic Cooperation', in Susanna Perko (ed.), *Nordic-Baltic Region in Transition*, Tampere: Tampere Peace Research Institute, 1996.
63. William Carr, *op. cit.*
64. Ivo Duchacek, *op. cit.*
65. Albert Hirschmann, *Exit, Voice and Loyalty*, Cambridge, Mass.: Harvard University Press, 1970, p. 83.
66. Andrew Moravcsik, 1991, *op. cit.*
67. See Nye, *Peace in Parts*, New York: University Press of America, 1987 (1971).
68. Hirschmann, *op. cit.*, p. 61.
69. Hirschmann, *op. cit.*, p. 93.
70. See Andrei S. Markovits and Simon Reich, *The New Face of Germany: Gramsci Neo-Realism and Hegemony*, Graduate School of Public and International Affairs, University of Pittsburgh, Working Paper Series 28, p. 36.
71. See Ikenberry and Kupchan, *op. cit.*
72. Stanley Hoffmann, *The European Sisyphus. Essays on Europe 1964–1994*. Boulder: Westview, 1995, p. 261.
73. See the seminal article by Stanley Hoffmann, 'Obsolescent or Obsolete? The Fate of the Nation-State and the Case of Western Europe', *Daedalus*, Vol. 95, Summer 1966.
74. All of these sectors are commonly assumed to be closely related to statehood. Citizenship may also be said to be such an issue, but citizenship can be subsumed under the heading of judicial affairs.
75. Here I use the definition of 'constitutive politics' used by Anderson in his *A*

United Germany in Europe: Hard Interests and Soft Power, paper delivered at the 1995 Annual Meeting of the American Political Science Association, Chicago, 31 August–3 September 1995, p. 1.

76. See Arent Lijphart, 'Typologies of Democratic Systems', *Comparative Political Studies*, Vol. 1, no. 1, April 1968; Thomas Pedersen, *Three Faces of European Governance*, Institute of Political Science, Aarhus University, 1995, and Paul Taylor, *op. cit.*

77. The metaphor of Russian dolls is borrowed from George Ross, *Jacques Delors and European Integration*, Cambridge: Polity Press, 1995, p. 39.

78. The term 'opportunity structure' is also borrowed from George Ross, *op. cit.*, p. 5.

79. Of course, it may also lead to stagnation or more flexible forms of integration.

5 A new kind of nationalism

Large-scale wars are often followed by a period of foreign policy reappraisal in which new methods are applied with a view to making another war impossible.[1] In a sense then major wars have served as catalytic crises producing a measure of human learning that brings to mind Kant's idea of nature's hidden design.[2] Looking back upon the history of European relations one observes several conflicting patterns. First of all, the European experience lends some credence to Waltz's theory about the dominance of balance-of-power concerns. In the course of the last 500 years different states have risen to primacy and tried to establish an enduring military hegemony on the European continent. Rising hegemons have been confronted with balancing forces, whether it be single states or, more typically, alliances. For seven centuries Islam was seen as the main threat to Western Europe. The Turkish threat led to several attempts to unify Christians in the West and in the 17th century the Habsburgs led the decisive battles against Turkey, stopping the Turks at the gates of Vienna in 1683. The Netherlands and later France rose to primacy in Europe in the 17th century as a result of the Thirty-Years War which pitted the Catholic Habsburgs against a range of Protestant states and principalities, and showed religious motives interacting with power politics in a complex pattern. The 18th century thus became France's finest hour and French became the preferred language at every European court.

The revolutionary wars were to a large extent rooted in ideological contradictions, but Britain's involvement on the side of the anti-French coalition in the early 19th century was also and probably primarily motivated by balance-of-power considerations. The 19th century thus saw Britain rise to the status of global hegemon, the first such power in modern times. The revolutionary wars weakened France and simultaneously spurred on German national unification. German unification under Prussian leadership was thus to a considerable extent the product of military victory, and first and foremost victory over France. It is deeply symbolic that the new German Empire founded in 1871 chose as its national day the day of the battle of Sedan.[3]

The First World War could be interpreted as an abortive attempt on the part of expanding Germany and its allies to challenge Britain. British hegemony was widely regarded as relatively benign, in a sense an early instance of cooperative hegemony, although Gandhi, when once asked the question what he thought about British civilization is said to have retorted 'Oh, that would be a good idea'. It is much more difficult and problematic to analyse the Second World War in systemic terms. Here domestic and individual factors played a much more significant role, although external factors interacted with domestic forces of instability.[4] Russia climbed to the status of big power at a slower pace than Germany, starting its process of modernization in the 17th century under Peter the Great. The First and Second World Wars had the side-effect of mobilizing its enormous natural resources in the service of a missionary foreign policy, although for a brief period the new revolutionary state withdrew from international politics. Incidentally, like the rise of the USA, the rise of the USSR could be regarded as a classical case of what Toynbee would call the rise of the peripheral powers.[5] The Cold War emerged as an American attempt to balance Soviet expansion on the Eurasian continent and Chinese expansion in Asia.

Yet the history of European relations is also the history of human beings and their learning and innovation. The horrendous Thirty-Years' War prompted the first writings by Grotius on international law and the gradual recognition of state sovereignty as a basic principle in international relations. The following centuries saw a number of attempts to rectify the vicissitudes of anarchy. Kant's *Zum ewigen Frieden*, written in 1795 in the shadow of the Napoleonic wars, spawned a number of federalist plans for European peace.[6] It is true that the political impact of these plans in most cases remained limited. Yet ideas intervened to modify the effect of structural pressures. Thus there are periods in European history which fly in the face of neo-realist postulates. In particular, Waltz has great difficulty explaining why a multipolar power constellation in the first half of the 19th century coincided with stability, while the essentially bipolar constellation emerging at the beginning of this century produced war. One reason was that domestic politics intervened as a major determinant of conflict, causing the European elites to close ranks in the defence of the status quo in the first half of the century. But strategy also played an important role. Until the 1860s (some would say until 1890 and the departure of Bismarck) the Prussian government showed a certain amount of self-restraint in its pursuit of power.

It is possible to interpret the integration strategy of post-war Germany as to some extent the product of historical learning. More precisely, it can be seen as an attempt to break out of the logic of anarchy with its tendency to produce balancing behaviour, and as an attempt to draw the political consequences of the particularly damaging effects of the balance of power for a continental middle power like Germany. This lesson was in fact drawn much earlier than normally recognized. It is easy to overlook the very serious attempts made in the 1920s to stabilize European (and international) politics by integrative means.[7] Plans for a European Customs Union were discussed in 1929–30. In 1929 the League of Nations asked Aristide Briand to prepare a memorandum on a kind of European federation.[8] Briand worked in quite close understanding with Stresemann, the German foreign minister, and the UK government at the time seemed prepared to countenance the cession of sovereignty. A successful process of regional integration thus seemed underway when Stresemann suddenly died in 1929 and the world economic crisis broke out, throwing the European economies into disarray. A Franco–German committee set up in 1929 continued to function until 1932, but to little avail.

The new emphasis in the second half of the 1920s on a binding form of international cooperation was not revolutionary in the sense of abandoning national thinking. Both the French and the German politicians seemed to conceive the integration plans as essentially new tools which could be used to build the grand nations that both dreamt of. Yet integration would regulate inter-state competition in new ways and channel it in non-violent directions. It was no coincidence that Briand launched his 'federal plan' at a time when Germany seemed as a result of Stresemann's dogged policy of reassurance to be recovering much of its international freedom of action. Seeing that a bilateral collaboration with Germany would benefit Germany more than France, Briand tried to create a wider framework within which to embed Franco–German collaboration. As far as the Germans were concerned, Krüger points out

70

that the European conceptions of the leading group in the German foreign ministry were far from endorsing federal plans, whether for a 'Pan-Europa' or for a unified *Mitteleuropa* (Central Europe). Interestingly, German decision-makers in the 1920s regarded European integration as an element in their revisionist policy. In Krüger's words:

> *Selbstverständlich lag eine Diskrepanz darin, dass man im Auswärtigen Amt an einen wie auch immer gearteten europäischen Zusammenschluss nur dachte auf der* Basis eines Generalausgleichs mit Frankreich und ohne Versicht auf Revisionsforderungen (author's emphasis), *während Briand eher umgekehrt eine Stabilisierung Europas auf der Grundlage des Status Quo im Sinne hatte.*[9]

The thinking in both France and Germany was quite pragmatic in terms of methods, with the Germans stressing economic integration and France political issues, not least security.[10] At the end of the 1920s the German foreign ministry seemed to be envisaging an economically integrated Europe based on a Customs Union, but with variations according to sectoral needs. It was felt that such a union would in itself be so powerful that a protectionist policy vis-à-vis the USA could be avoided.[11] Stresemann did however speak of the long-term need for the European economies to erect a common defence against the USA.[12]

In the end the combination of a deteriorating economic climate, the re-emergence of traditional nationalism in Germany and the death of Stresemann brought these endeavours to a halt. A new grouping assumed the leadership in German foreign policy. It had little patience with plans for European unity, concentrating instead on short-term demands such as Germany's right to equal treatment and national independence. In March 1931 the idea of union re-emerged in an altogether different guise, when Germany and Austria launched an ambitious plan for a separate German–Austrian Customs Union.

Thus the policy of inter-national unification also served at times as a cover for much more traditional power politics. The two countries did however take care to describe their initiative as part of a process of European union. After pressure from the Western powers which regarded the move as an indirect *Anschluss* and could refer to clauses in the Treaty of St Germain forbidding such initiatives, the agreement was cancelled.[13]

The new debate on European integration which emerged after the Second World War thus could and indeed did build upon the experience of the 1920s. Some of the most prominent political actors of the 1950s like Adenauer had even taken an active part in the debate on European integration in the 1920s. It is not difficult to recognize

Stresemann's policy of building up trust in Adenauer's reliable *West-bindung* (Western integration). But in other respects, too, the Federal Republic's European policy bore ressemblance to the policy of the 1920s. The emphasis on economic forms of integration recurred in the 1950s and continued to be a hallmark of German policy.

Even more than the First World War, the Second functioned as a catalytic crisis for the Germans. In the defeated countries the nation-state had lost legitimacy more so in Germany than in any other European country. This meant that there was now a much more fertile ground for sowing the ideas of close integration than there had been 20 years earlier. It was not surprizing that Germany (with Italy) should have been in the forefront of the ensuing debate about new forms of political authority in Europe. The two countries found it difficult to enter the international scene on their own and had little to lose.

A central feature of the new German Grand Strategy was its emphasis on stability. Fundamentally, the Federal Republic had to build up *Vertrauenskapital,* a capital of trust. A consistent demonstration of will-ingness to share power within a binding integration structure was an essential element in this endeavour. But given the constraints on the Federal Republic's freedom of action, the transfer of sovereignty to supranational bodies would intrinsically be more beneficial to the FRG than to other West European states. Integration thus meant rehabilita-tion for the Germans – first legally, then politically. Moreover, in the context of the immediate post-war period it seemed quite impossible for Germany ever to become unified, unless this were to occur within some sort of reassuring framework. In other words, legitimate power meant institutionally embedded power. In addition, integration was a peaceful and indirect way of removing borders and thus creating new opportun-ities for German industry and society. Wæver talks about Germany's preference for 'invisible' expansion at the societal level.[14]

Finally and not least, regional integration fulfilled some very basic security needs. Adenauer regarded Western (both US and West Euro-pean) backing as essential to countering the Soviet threat and in particular to defend West Berlin. A fear of encirclement also continued to haunt German politicians. The spectre of a Franco–Russian alliance was the primary fear. It is telling that Adenauer had made a timetable listing the situations when Russia had formed an alliance with France against Germany.[15]

As Garton Ash points out, the foreign policy of the Federal Republic was a complex mixture of nationalism and idealism. Its European policy

72

had a certain affinity with that of Stresemann. In Ash's apt formulation 'as with Stresemann, there was the mixture, so difficult to analyse, of genuine Europeanism and genuine nationalism, of more or less affected Europeanism for foreign audiences but also of more or less affected nationalism for domestic audiences'.[16] West German politicians in fact set out to redefine the very language of foreign policy. *Realpolitik* disappeared from German public discourse, German academics propagating the new paradigm of interdependence. As Ash puts it: 'in this rhetorical world, there were no conflicts ... national interests were always to be discreetly covered like Victorian piano-legs by curtains marked "Europe", "peace", "cooperation", "stability", "normality" or even "humanity" '.[17]

In his study of Bonn's *Ostpolitik* (Eastern policy), Ash points out that the reality of West German policy was much more hard-nosed and old-fashioned than its public appearances would lead to believe. It is not unnatural to expect much the same to have applied to German EC policy. In fact, one may draw some interesting parallels between German *Ostpolitik* and *Westpolitik* (Western policy). Characteristically, interdependence was not only regarded as a reality which required adaptation but also as a deliberate goal in German foreign policy. Hans-Dietrich Genscher spoke repeatedly of the virtues of *Verflechtung* (interdependence). Ash quotes him as saying that 'a web had to be created which no longer allows any country to get out of this association without severely damaging their most vital interests'.[18] Other West German politicians spoke of 'system-opening cooperation' (Von Weizäcker) or *Wandel durch Annäherung* (change through rapprochement) (Bahr). The purpose of this strategy towards the East was hardly convergence but rather a kind of 'subversion by example'. In other words, the effects of interdependence were intended to be asymmetrical. The Soviets and East Europeans were to be exposed to Western (German) habits and would emulate these habits since they were assumed to be superior.[19] Adenauer talked about *eine Sogwirkung* (a magnetic effect) in the East.

The important conclusion to be drawn from this is that the West German foreign policy elite regarded the fostering of ties of interdependence as a way of exercising political influence. It is tempting to draw a parallel with Germany's regional integration policy in the West. Whilst bringing back stability, integration would tie Western Europe to Germany and, it was hoped, transform Germany's neighbours in the process.

This kind of thinking did not emerge out of the blue. German thinking on integration and unification had always had a power-oriented strand. Here it seems legitimate to establish a link between German thinking on national (German) unification and on European unification, since European integration can be seen and is being seen by many analysts as in some respects a process of nation-building. German national unification was based on a process of economic integration epitomized by the Customs Union (*Zollverein*) founded by Prussia in 1834. As we have seen, the middle of the 19th century was in Germany a period rich in conceptual debate with the so-called *grossdeutsche* (greater German) current envisioning the unification of all German peoples on the continent pitted against the *kleindeutsche* (lesser German) current, which made a plea for a small but efficient German entity centring around Prussia.[20] Reacting to the successful Prussian attempt to create a 'lesser Germany', the Austrians represented by Freiherr von Bruck launched an alternative plan for a central European customs union which was to include both Prussia and Austria. The Austrian plan which was rejected by the Prussians was not without ulterior motives. It essentially aimed at weakening Prussian power by dissolving it in a larger framework.[21] Friedrich List, the famous German economist, advocated a customs union including Germany, Belgium, Holland, Denmark, and Switzerland.[22]

In the late 19th century German thinkers such as Gustav Cohn launched plans for *Gross-staatenbildung* (formation of a large state); the so-called Brentano plan of 1884 spoke of a central European customs union, and a current of thinking which could be called continental pan-Germanicism emerged. The most important work within this tradition is undoubtedly Friedrich Naumann's *Mitteleuropa* published in 1915, which advocated the formation of an economic union in Central Europe.[23] In the European debate in the 1920s this economic regionalism, whose stronghold was Germany, merged with a current which had a more cultural focus and struck a distinctly pessimistic note emphasizing Europe's cultural decline and the need for Europe to unify. French writers and thinkers like Valéry, Gide and Gaston Riou are representative of this current, but the German Spengler and the Dutch–Austrian Coudenhove-Kalergi, the latter at one stage based at the Hofburg in Vienna, were also convinced of Europe's cultural superiority and saw regionalism as the way to assert it.[24] The symbol of Coudenhove's Pan-Europa founded in 1923 was the red cross and the golden sun, the cross being the symbol of the medieval crusaders but used by Coudenhove as a symbol of international humanitarianism, and the sun being used as a

74

symbol of the European spirit which should enlighten the world.[25] Among German Catholic politicians West European integration was widely regarded as the continuation of the Holy Roman Empire of the German Nation.

In a similar vein, the efforts to integrate Western Europe after the Second World War were essentially motivated by the national interests of Germany, a defeated power who, in the light of the disatrous consequences of traditional nationalism and influenced by American thinking, set out to re-define the concept of national interest. Its strategy of cooperative (or institutionalized) hegemony placed great emphasis on long-term interests, gradualism, the virtues of stability, and not least the need to merge and share power regionally in order to enhance power internationally.

In *Europe in the Making* Walter Hallstein, one of the leading ideologues of the ECSC (European Coal and Steel Community), and of German descent, reflects upon the importance of 'time' in 'the European problem'.[26] Not only is time the most important factor in getting people used to change:

> Time also justifies the method of seeking unity not in every sphere but, to begin with, in those spheres which stir up fewer emotions and where the practical reasons for fusion are compelling and obvious; in pursuing matters of common advantage, in fighting common dangers, in working together jointly in the political field, ideas and habits of thought and action become integrated in 'time'.

The quotation is a fine illustration of the strategic use of neofunctionalist theory on the part of German EC politicians.

On the whole, France also formed part of the revolutionary current in the post-war debate on European cooperation. And it was not surprising that the UK was among the more hesitant countries when it came to ceding national sovereignty and moving closer to its European neighbours. After all, the British nation-state had led Britain to victory in alliance with America and other non-European countries.[27] Although Churchill, recognizing the geostrategic benefits of European integration, played a major role in putting the goal of unification on the agenda, he and other British leaders did not envisage Britain as forming part of an integrated Europe.[28]

Notwithstanding the efforts of many personalities from small European states during the debates in the late 1940s and the successful concrete steps taken by the Benelux sub-group, the initiative for the first supranational body in Europe, the ECSC came from Germany and

France. The Schuman declaration of 9 May 1950 is normally seen as the founding document of the European communities. It is customary to describe the ECSC initiative as a French initiative. This is at best a half truth. In fact, the declaration had been preceded by a German initiative. In March 1950 the German Chancellor, Konrad Adenauer, gave two interviews to the American journalist, Kingsbury-Smith, in which he proposed a union between France and Germany. In his first interview, on 7 March, Adenauer briefly described the reasons for his proposal.[29] He described the union as a way of solving the Saar problem and other problems. Adenauer said that he was deeply worried about the recent steps taken by France on the Saar issue, which came close to a *de facto* annexation, and he wanted to forestall a nationalist German reaction. However, there was a wider dimension to the proposal. The Franco–German union was to be the foundation of a United States of Europe. It would set free enormous forces and *Europa retten* (save Europe). In his second interview on 21 March, Adenauer furthermore drew attention to the growing tension in relation to the USSR, describing this as 'one of the most important reasons' why he had made the proposal. As regards the strategy to be followed, Adenauer explicitly referred to the German *Zollverein* of 1834, which had paved the way for German political unification. Taking the so-called Customs Parliament of the *Zollverein* as a model, he proposed the creation of an economic parliament involving France and Germany.[30]

In his memoirs Adenauer goes on to describe de Gaulle's positive reaction to the proposal. De Gaulle is quoted as having said that 'thanks to the common efforts of Gauls, Germans and Romans, Attila had been defeated on the Catalan plains'.[31] De Gaulle thus stressed the opportunity which regional integration provided for balancing hostile third powers.

When Schuman launched the Schuman plan in May 1950, Adenauer immediately threw his weight behind it. In his memoirs he describes the plan as the best way to eradicate the old nationalism. But he also talks at length about the advantages of a European economic space: *ein einheitlicher Wirtschaftsraum für mehr als 150 Millionen Menschen, den wir anstreben, würde dem Wirtschaftsraum der Vereinigten Staaten gleichen, deren staunenswerte Entfaltung von Wohlstand und Kraft dadurch möglich wurde, dass keine staatliche Hindernisse dem freien Güteraustausch entgegenstanden.*[32] Commenting upon the signing of the Treaty of Rome, Adenauer adds more bluntly that 'nur die Zusammenfassung zu einem gemeinsamen europäischen Wirtschaftsraum konnte auf die Dauer die Länder Europas gegenüber anderen Wirtschaftsgebieten auf der Erde konkurrenzfähig machen und erhalten'. And further: *dafür einzutreten, dass Europa ein kraftvolles, geeintes Europa würde, war die dringende Aufgabe der jetzt lebenden Europäer.*[33]

During the negotiations on the ECSC the French and Germans were playing a leading role assisted by the highly influential Monnet. In his memoirs Monnet describes the essence of the negotiations as a Franco–German attempt to persuade and reassure Italy and the Benelux countries. Monnet supported by Hallstein emphasized the importance of the supranational bodies, with Monnet most concerned about the high authority and Hallstein focusing on the court and the assembly. The Benelux countries on the other hand were sceptical about the high authority and wanted a council of ministers. Luxembourg's representative was keen to insert an escape clause in the treaty, introducing the notion of a vital interest which was later to reappear in the Luxembourg compromise.[34] Hallstein urged the Benelux countries and Italy to subordinate their economic interests to the grand political goal. Trying to reassure the smaller countries, he referred to the general principles inscribed in the preamble and the treaty, notably the principle of equality. These principles would be upheld by the court and the assembly.[35] The Benelux countries kept on opposing the supranational design for several months, the Dutch representative demanding a right for the council to give political directives to the high authority and the Belgian objecting to the expression 'fusion of sovereignty'.[36]

Monnet writes in his memoirs that in his press statement after the first conference between the six he took care to insert a specification to the effect that a unilateral withdrawal of a member state would not be possible. A withdrawal – and its conditions – would have to be negotiated.[37] During the formative period of European integration, the big West European states and notably Germany thus appear to have been the most fervent advocates of a federal-style structure, whereas the small member states adopted a mainly intergovernmental stance.[38]

Notes

1. One of the best recent interpretations of European history is Norman Davies, *Europe. A History*, Oxford: Oxford University Press, 1996.
2. Incidentally, this idea is reminiscent of Adam Smith's notion of the beneficial effects of the market's 'hidden hand'.

3. William Carr, *A History of Germany, 1815–1945*, 2nd edition, London: Edward Arnold, 1979 (1969), p. 125.

4. Incidentally, the case of the Second World War confronts Waltzian neo-realism with serious normative problems. A strict Waltzian reading of the Second World War would lead to the conclusion that Nazi Germany simply tried to balance British or Anglo-Saxon hegemony. Taken to its extreme, neo-realism thus absolves individuals of their responsibility for political decisions (or non-decisions).

5. Arnold J. Toynbee, *A Study of History*, London: D. C. Somerville, 1960 (1934). One of Toynbee's central points is that the (geopolitical) centre powers tend to exhaust themselves, leaving the scene to the peripheral powers.

6. Kant's publication was itself inspired by the writings of Abbé St Pierre who in 1713 under the influence of the Spanish War of Succession had drafted a plan for perpetual union between the European states.

7. See the excellent survey in Elisabeth du Réau, *L'Idée D'Europe au XXe Siècle*, Paris: Edition Complexe, 1996.

8. Notwithstanding the ambitious terminology, Briand appears to have been thinking in terms of a confederal structure.

9. 'Obviously there was a difference in that in the German foreign office one only conceived of a European unification, however fashioned, based on a general compromise (*Ausgleich*) with France and without giving up revisionary demands, while Briand, on the other hand, had in mind a stabilization of Europe on the basis of the status quo.' Peter Krüger, *Die Aussenpolitik der Republik von Weimar*, Darmstadt: Wissenschaftliche Buchgesellschaft, 1985, p. 490.

10. *Ibid.*, pp. 490ff.

11. *Ibid.*, p. 492.

12. *Ibid.*, p. 489.

13. Elisabeth du Réau, *op. cit.*

14. See Ole Wæver, 'Hvordan det hele alligevel kan gå galt', in Gottlieb and Jensen (eds), *Tyskland i Europa*, Copenhagen: SNU, 1995, p. 301.

15. Thomas Pedersen, 'Europa – Tysklands anden nation', in Henning Gottlieb and Frede P. Jensen (eds), *Tyskland i Europa*, Copenhagen: SNU, 1995, p. 71.

16. Timothy Garton Ash, *In Europe's Name*, London: Vintage, 1994, p. 358.

17. *Ibid.*, p. 359.

18. *Ibid.*, p. 268.

19. *Ibid.*, p. 273.

20. See Heinrich Lutz, *Zwischen Habsburg und Preussen. Deutschland 1815–1866*, Berlin: Siedler Verlag, 1985, pp. 271ff.

21. See Peter M.R. Stirk, 'The Idea of Mitteleuropa', in Peter M.R. Stirk, *Mitteleuropa. History and Prospects*, Edinburgh: Edinburgh University Press, 1994.

22. *Ibid.*, p. 6.

23. Friedrich Naumann, *Mitteleuropa*, Berlin: Georg Reimer, 1915.

24. See Réau, *op. cit.*, p. 72ff.

25. See Gaston Riou, *S'Unir ou Mourir*, Paris: Valois, 1929, and Count Coudenhove-Kalergi, *An Idea Conquers the World*, London: Hutchinson, 1953.

26. Walter Hallstein, *Europe in the Making*, New York: Norton & Company, 1972, pp. 328ff.

27. Michael Charlton, *The Price of Victory*, London: BBC, 1983.
28. Sean Greenwood, *Britain and European Integration since the Second World War*, Manchester and New York: Manchester University Press, 1996, pp. 46ff, quotes Churchill as saying *inter alia* 'we help, we dedicate, we play a part, but we are not merged'.
29. Konrad Adenauer, *Erinnerungen 1945–1953, Bd. I.*, Frankfurt am Main and Hamburg: Fischer Bücherei, 1967 (1965), pp. 300ff.
30. *Ibid.*, p. 302.
31. *Ibid.*, p. 304.
32. 'a unified economic area for more than 150 million people, which is what we aim at, would be on a par with the economic area of the United States, whose astounding display of welfare and power was made possible by the fact that no state barriers stood in the way of the free exchange of goods'; *ibid.*, p. 413.
33. 'only the merger of Europe in a common European economic area could ensure that Europe's nations were and remained competitive with other economic areas of the world in the long term'. (And further) 'working to make Europe a powerful, unified Europe was the urgent task for the contemporary European', Adenauer, *Erinnerungen 1955–59. Bd. III*, Frankfurt am Main and Hamburg: Fischer Bücherei, 1969 (1967), p. 267.
34. Jean Monnet, *Mémoires*, Paris: Fayard, 1976, pp. 380ff.
35. *Ibid.*, p. 384.
36. *Ibid.*, p. 390.
37. *Ibid.*, p. 382.
38. The memoirs may be biased in the sense that Monnet tries to cast his own (and the German) government in the role of idealists, but first of all, Monnet must have been aware of the fact that false claims might be challenged by 'eyewitnesses' (and I am not aware of any such challenges). Secondly, Monnet's account is quite detailed, which adds to its credibility.

6 The Gaullist interlude

It is no coincidence that, except for the European Defence Community which was killed by the French national assembly in 1954, the 1950s were both a period of progress in European integration and a period of Franco–German intimacy. The small member states did at times provide intellectual leadership as in the case of the common market, but overall France and Germany dominated the process of integration. Even the Dutch initiative on the common market should be seen in the context of a Franco–German meeting in April 1955, which was meant to give new impetus to 'European cooperation' but did not specify within which framework this was to occur. This provoked anxiety in the Benelux countries (as well as in Italy) and made it seem all the more urgent to relaunch the cooperation between the six.[1] The content of the Treaty of Rome very much reflected French and German priorities. The EEC was thus essentially a compromise between the German interest in market liberalization and the French interest in support for agriculture. In addition France obtained a treaty on cooperation in nuclear energy, a topic that attracted a lot of attention in France at the time. The position of the two biggest members in the Council of Ministers was quite comfortable. A blocking minority consisted of two larger member states or one larger member state plus Belgium or the Netherlands.[2]

The advent of de Gaulle in 1958 changed this state of harmony. De Gaulle had been among the leading opponents of the ECSC and the Defence Community. The premise of the German-inspired integration strategy was that all member states, including the major ones, should be willing to share power, albeit asymmetrically, forego short-term benefits in the interest of long-term stability and engage in nested negotiating games. De Gaulle broke with all of these principles and instead opted for a strategy of autonomy and *directoire*. Of treaties he said that 'they are like roses and young girls. They last as long as they last'.

Under his turbulent reign, France turned away from supranationalism and tried to transform the Community into a confederal entity with France as *primus inter pares*. A new 'Gaullist method' centring on confrontations on high politics issues and a more rigid national supervision of supranational bodies began to make its presence felt, in sharp competition with the traditional 'Monnet method'.[3] At the same time de Gaulle adopted a confrontational line vis-à-vis the USA. The theoretical rationale behind de Gaulle's moves was the strategy of *directoire* with its preference for big-power leadership within a looser institutional framework. As his confederal Fouchet plan failed in 1962 de Gaulle tried to set up a bilateral Franco–German leadership structure outside the Community institutions.

It would, however, be superficial to contrast French nationalism with German post-nationalism. Although for historical reasons and because of its internal federal structure the Federal Republic was generally more disposed to share power regionally than France, Germany and France both wanted to use the Community as a platform for exercising leadership. But under de Gaulle France abandoned Hallstein's, Schuman's and Monnet's community method, developing a preference for *directoire* or external asymmetry within the context of membership of the Community. Germany had a preference for the less visible and more institutionally embedded internal asymmetry.

Significantly, de Gaulle did not challenge EC membership. He soon saw the political as well as the economic benefits that France could reap from membership of the EEC in particular. However, he made a point of the fact that France had other ways of exercising influence than through the EC. In 1958 de Gaulle proposed the formation of a global *directoire* of three countries – the US, the UK and France – ignoring the FRG.[4] It is a testimony to the Federal Republic's role of a *demandeur* in international relations at the time that Adenauer nevertheless accepted to enter into a close bilateral collaboration with France a few years later. However, de Gaulle had managed to regain some of the lost sympathy in the FRG during the Berlin crisis in 1961 when he showed himself to be a stauncher supporter of Germans than the USA. The Elysée treaty of 1963 introduced regular meetings between the two countries in the areas of defence, education and youth. The treaty stipulated that the defence and armed forces ministers of the two countries should meet at least once every three months. In the field of education, meetings would be held at similar intervals. The chiefs of staff should meet at least once every two months as would the ministers for family and youth affairs.[5] In the field of foreign policy the two governments agreed to consult each other on all important questions of foreign policy 'with a view to reaching as far as possible an analogous position'. In the field of defence it was agreed that the two countries should endeavour to mutually approximate their doctrines with a view to reaching common concepts. The treaty also foresaw exchanges of military personnel. The nuclear area was, however, a no-go area for de Gaulle. The joint declaration which served as a preamble to the treaty referred to the solidarity between the two countries and described the increased cooperation as an indispensable stage on the way towards a united Europe. The two countries thus found it necessary to legitimate their privileged partnership by shrouding it in Europeanist rhetoric. The final provisions echoed concern about the cohesion of the Community and consequently contained an undertaking that the two governments would keep the other member states of the EC informed of the developments of Franco–German cooperation. One notes, however, that the other members would only be informed of the development of the cooperation – not of the activities.

Before the new treaty could even be implemented it ran into severe difficulties. The German *Bundestag* insisted on attaching a preamble to the treaty in which the FRG's loyalty to the Atlantic alliance was stressed. This undercut Adenauer's credibility and provoked some disillusionment in France. The subsequent replacement of Adenauer by the Atlanticist Erhardt opened up a gulf between Paris and Bonn which even the best of diplomats could not bridge. As president of the Commission, Hallstein meanwhile played the game of spillover very skilfully. As early as 1961 he launched a plan for closer monetary cooperation.[6] In 1965 France and Germany clashed over a package of reforms put together by Hallstein, which linked the implementation of the Common Agricultural Policy to a strengthening of the powers of the Commission and the Parliament.[7] The upshot was de Gaulle's empty-chair policy which led to the Luxembourg compromise on the national veto. The confrontation was not only due to French intransigence. Hallstein had engaged in a risky political gamble. Moreover, de Gaulle's policy was rational given its premises. If de Gaulle were to stop supranationalism, now was the time. On 1 January 1966, the principle of majority decisions in council was to take effect. At a deeper level, what de Gaulle did was to challenge the materialist incrementalism underlying Hallstein's doctrine. He sacrificed benefits accruing to French farmers on the altar of political principles.[8]

The period from the mid 1960s until the early 1980s thus became a rather fallow period short on progress in the direction of European union. As seen from the FRG, the problem was that under de Gaulle and his right-wing successor France was unwilling to share power and could neither be made to accept log-rolling or side-payments nor offer the smaller members the voice-opportunity necessary to ensure their support for Franco–German leadership. This French abstinence had a crippling effect on German EC policy. Without French support and the legitimation of German intentions that this support implied, Germany could not take the ambitious initiatives that it wanted to take. The absence of progress in the supranational 'state-building' meant that influence had once again to be measured and exercised at the inter-state level, where the FRG continued to lag behind.

Pompidou did soften the Gaullist stance, allowing the entry of the UK into the EC, and showing a certain interest in the idea of a European Monetary Union (EMU), but on institutional matters his thinking was as confederal as that of de Gaulle. The matter-of-fact Pompidou also found it difficult to collaborate with the more lofty Brandt. What is more, Pompidou seems to have been somewhat jealous of Brandt's international standing.[9] The German government actively pursued the goal of EMU, placing the emphasis on coordination of economic and monetary policies. Such coordination 'would benefit German trading interests by guaranteeing free trade among the six, while eliminating embarrassing pressures for evaluation'.[10]

Under Giscard d'Estaing the Franco–German duo was revitalized. Yet the freedom of Giscard was severely constrained by his Gaullist partners in his centre–right coalition and he was compelled to adopt a quite conservative stance on institutional issues such as the role of the Commission. It is telling that one of France's few institutional initiatives during this period was the creation of the European Council in 1974. Giscard did however accommodate Germany on the issue of direct elections to the European Parliament after some hesitancy.

In the 1970s France also defended its privileged position within the EC institutional system with great energy. In 1978 the impending enlargement with Greece and the Iberian countries inspired Giscard d'Estaing to write a letter to the other heads of state and government suggesting that 'three wise men' look at the future of the EC's institutions. According to Jenkins, Commission President at the time, who had several conversations with Giscard on the subject, the French President wanted to cut down the power of the Commission, reduce its political role and 'half to amalgamate it with the Council secretariat and with COREPER'. The other thought at the back of Giscard's mind was apparently to revert to the *directoire* idea and to reform the Council of Ministers 'so as, after enlargement, to give greater power to the major countries'.[11] Giscard was also apparently concerned about the institution of the presidency. At one point he told Jenkins that the presidency 'ought to be done on a semi-permanent basis by someone who had been a major figure in the national government of a big country'.[12] Could it be that he was making plans for his own future? Although nothing came of the letter, it provoked a debate which delayed consideration of the Spanish application.[13]

The Gaullist straightjacket did not prevent Giscard from forging closer ties with Germany. The leadership deficit from which the EC had suffered from the mid 1960s to the mid 1970s was largely removed under Giscard and his counterpart Helmut Schmidt. But whether due to their common technocratic outlook or as a result of the continuing pressure from the Gaullists, new initiatives such as the European Monetary System assumed a more informal and less supranational form. The story of the birth of the EMS need only be dealt with briefly in this context. It is not quite clear who first came up with the idea. Simonean quotes Giscard as having replied to a similar question quoting Napoleon that *en matière de paternité, il n'y a que des hypothèses* (when it comes to paternity, there are only hypotheses)'.[14] Simonean's own view is that the scheme was 'principally German in origin'. This is confirmed by Roy Jenkins, who in his diary describes how Schmidt first broached the issue on the first day of the Copenhagen European Council on 7 April 1978. Schmidt's proposals had however been discussed with Giscard at a meeting in Rambouillet a week earlier and the two leaders were in full accord.[15] In his memoirs Schmidt does not take the credit for having invented the EMS, simply referring to the initiative as having emerged out of discussions between the two.[16] This seems to be a typical case of Germany providing the conceptual raw material for closer integration and France acting as the Union's entrepreneur. Schmidt puts it this way: *angesichts der Prestigeempfindlichkeit anderer – nicht nur der Franzosen – durfte (und darf) Bonn keineswegs als Führungsmacht der EG erscheinen, sondern musste (und muss noch für lange Zeit) (author's emphasis) immer wieder*

Paris den Vortritt lassen.[17] The qualification is important; Schmidt seems to envisage Germany assuming a more prominent role some time in the future. In the context of his discussion of the EMS initiative, Schmidt stresses the secretiveness of the preparations for the scheme. Neither the national burocrats nor the Brussels administration (apart from Jenkins) were informed, writes Schmidt adding sarcastically that *die Bürokraten als erstes alle Gründe zusammentragen würden, die gegen das Unternehmen sprachen, um sie dann in den Medien zu lancieren.*[18]

Although the plan itself was thus essentially conceived by Schmidt and his advisors in the chancellery, the general impetus for closer monetary cooperation seems to have come from Giscard, who had called for a revival of the EMU idea the year before. The Bremen summit in July 1978 endorsed almost every aspect of the Franco–German plan. There was some dissatisfaction with the secret discussions, notably those including the British too, but these complaints apparently subsided as the importance of the plan became clear.[19]

Schmidt's initiative appears to have been inspired by two motives in particular. First of all Schmidt, whose initiative was very much his own and elicited hostile reactions from the *Bundesbank*, wanted to create a new global monetary actor capable of challenging US dominance. Schmidt was extremely upset about the way the Carter administration was conducting monetary policy in the 1970s and about the fall of the dollar in particular. At one point he went as far as saying that 'no American President could lead the alliance while presiding over such degradation of the dollar as he had witnessed during his period as Federal Chancellor'.[20] At the same time an EMS might provide the FRG with a useful cover against American pressure on the Germans to reflate.[21] This 'alibi' function had of course been an important motive behind Germany's wish to set up the EPC (European Political Cooperation) in 1970. Secondly, an EMS would give German industrialists a lead in price competitiveness on world markets, as the Deutschmark would be tied to weaker currencies and thus less prone to re-evaluation.[22] While sharing Schmidt's global analysis Giscard d'Estaing also felt that by linking the franc to a stronger currency French inflation could be kept in check. Skjalm speculates that Giscard may also have been motivated by a wish to bind his Gaullist coalition partner in the economic policy.[23]

During the second half of the 1970s Germany and France thus helped the EC edge its way out of the crisis which had dominated it in the first half of the 1970s. The Community had to all intents and purposes overcome its leadership deficit, although it might have benefited from a clearer British presence in that leadership. Simonean relates how Schmidt and Giscard held bilateral meetings prior to almost every European Council and how in most cases the two dominated the Councils. The duo not only took initiatives, but also unblocked disagreements. The effectiveness of the collaboration was aided by the fact that both leaders spoke fluent English and had a common background as finance ministers. Why then, one may ask, did the constitutional reforms of the EC not commence in the late 1970s? Part of the answer is undoubtedly that Giscard was still feeling too constrained by his Gaullist coalition partners. In addition, the duo apparently did not wish to sideline the British. Despite the closeness of Franco–German collaboration, no systematic attempt were made to exclude the British from European constitutive initiatives. Schmidt in particular appears to have been unwilling to marginalize the British. This attitude may be explained at two levels. At the level of ideology, one may point to the solidarity between two socialist leaders. Ideology does not, however, appear to have played a major role in Schmidt's foreign policy, as witnessed by his partnership with Giscard. To the extent that ideology played a role in securing the UK access to the EC core, this was probably due to his anticipation of a negative reaction from his party to any attempt to marginalize the UK. The most important part of the explanation should probably be found at the level of national interest. Wanting for economic reasons to keep the British inside the Community, the FRG did not want to put too much pressure on the UK government at a time when exit was still an option for the UK.

Unlike his successor, Helmut Schmidt did not take a great interest in grand institutional plans for European integration. His attention concentrated on economics, not least international economics. Nevertheless, under his leadership the FRG managed to set up the EMS, the importance of which tends to be underestimated. The EMS must be regarded as an important, and somewhat neglected, case of institutional asymmetry. It constituted a regional set of rules biased in favour of the biggest member state in the EC, protecting it against pressure for re-evaluation of its currency and granting its export industry a major competitive edge. The political drawback of the EMS was first of all that the asymmetry was not balanced by political voice-opportunities and secondly that it was a weak institution, in which exit remained an option.

Notes

1. Pierre Gerbet, 'Le Rôle du Couple France–Allemagne dans la Création et le Développement des Communautés Européennes', in Robert Picht and Wolfgang Wessels (eds), *Motor für Europa?*, Bonn: Europa Union Verlag, 1990, p. 79.
2. See Martin Westlake, *The Council of the European Union*, London: Cartermill, 1995, p. 91.
3. Helen Wallace and William Wallace, *Policy-Making in the European Union*, Oxford: Oxford University Press, 1996.
4. See Jonathan Story and Guy de Carmoy, 'France and Europe', in Jonathan Story (ed.), *The New Europe*, Oxford: Blackwell, 1993, p. 187.
5. Franco–German treaty signed in Paris on 22 January 1963. Printed in Roger Morgan and Caroline Bray (eds), *Partners and Rivals in Western Europe: Britain, France and Germany*, London: Gower, 1986.
6. See the overview of monetary integration in the *Frankfurter Allgemeine Zeitung*, 10 March 1989, p. 3, 'Eine Vorstufe zur Eurozentralbank?'
7. Story and de Carmoy, *op. cit.*, p. 188.
8. See the theoretical interpretation of the empty-chair incident in Ernst B. Haas, 'The Uniting of Europe and the Uniting of Latin America', *Journal of Common Market Studies*, Vol. 5/1967, p. 326.
9. Haig Simonean, *The Privileged Partnership*, Oxford: Clarendon Press, 1985, p. 96.
10. *Ibid.*, p. 82.
11. Roy Jenkins, *European Diary*, London: Collins, 1989, p. 311.
12. *Ibid.*, p. 279.
13. Simonean, *op. cit.*, p. 289.
14. Simonean, *op. cit.*, p. 281.
15. Jenkins, *op. cit.*, pp. 244ff.
16. Helmut Schmidt, *Die Deutschen und ihre Nachbarn*, Berlin: Siedler Verlag, 1990, p. 221.
17. 'in view of the sensitivity about status of other states – and not only France – Bonn could never and may never look like the EC's leading power, but had to (and still has to *for a long time*) (author's emphasis) let Paris lead', *ibid.*, p. 173.
18. 'the burocrats would first of all gather all the arguments for opposing the scheme and subsequently launch them in the media', *ibid.*, p. 221.
19. Simonean, *op. cit.*, p. 282.
20. Jenkins, *op. cit.*, p. 247.
21. Karsten Skjalm, *Det Europæiske Valutasamarbejdes Politiske Økonomi*, Aarhus: Institut for Statskundskab, Aarhus Universitet, 1995, p. 100.
22. Jonathan Story and Marcello de Cecco, 'The Politics and Diplomacy of Monetary Union: 1985–1991', in Jonathan Story (ed.), *The New Europe. Politics. Government and Economy Since 1945*, Oxford: Blackwell, 1993, p. 329.
23. Skjalm, *op. cit.*, p. 103.

7 Tactical differentiation: the Single European Act

The revival of European integration

The year of 1984 saw a reactivation of Franco–German consultations and a call for a relaunching of Europe. The seeds of this new impetus in Franco–German cooperation, which was to lead to the reactivation of the EC, were sown in the early 1980s. For Germany the new interest in Franco–German cooperation was partly motivated by security concerns, the Soviet invasion of Afghanistan in 1979 being a seminal event.[1] But more important was the wish to find ways of balancing the USA, a wish that had grown ever stronger since the early 1970s. The new Kohl–Genscher government continued Schmidt's overall European policy but introduced important changes. First of all, it placed a new emphasis on tactical differentiation as a way of pushing integration forward. Secondly, while continuing to promote economic integration, the Kohl–Genscher goverment also took broader initiatives aimed at polit-ical unification.

The idea of a revival of European integration was first mooted publicly in a speech by the German foreign minister, Hans-Dietrich Genscher, to his party, the FRP. Speaking at the so-called *Dreikönigstreffen* in Stuttgart on 6 January 1981, Genscher called for the conclusion of a treaty on European Union.[2] In his speech Genscher, who on this occasion seemed to be acting in a personal capacity, stressed political rather than economic needs. He was first and foremost concerned about the deteriorating climate between the superpowers. According to Genscher, the fundamental objectives of European union were to be

88

development of a common foreign and security policy, extension of the scope of economic integration, closer cooperation in the cultural sector and legal harmonization. The initiative was partly motivated by domestic politics. Genscher wanted to assert his leadership over the party and more importantly felt a need to distance himself from what he regarded as Chancellor Schmidt's declining interest in Europe.[3] Genscher subsequently sought the support of the Italian government. There were some disagreements between the two sides. Whereas Genscher wanted a treaty, the Italians preferred a more flexible arrangement that would not call for national ratification. Moreover, the Italian pressure for an increase in the EC budget met with stiff German resistance. The disagreements did not, however, prove insurmountable.[4]

The French socialist government showed very little interest in the German–Italian initiative. Instead it published its own memorandum on a 'relaunching of Europe' on 8 October 1981. The document proposed closer cooperation in a number of economic and social areas. The approach of the document was pragmatic as far as institutional matters were concerned. It argued that no institutional reform was needed. Instead it recommended a return to the provisions of the Treaty of Rome including the provisions on majority voting.[5]

The German–Italian talks led to a joint German–Italian proposal published on 4 November 1981. The aim of the proposal was to gradually transform the Community into a Union, but it was cautious as regards the concrete steps to be undertaken, proposing *inter alia* a return to the decision-making procedures of the Treaty of Rome, a strengthening of the European Parliament, the creation of a new specialized Council, including a defence council, an expansion of the scope of the Community, including a completion of the internal market, a closer monetary cooperation and a closer foreign and security policy cooperation with a small secretariat for political cooperation and cooperation regarding international aspects of public order and cultural affairs. It also proposed to sign a 'European Act' to be reviewed five years later.[6] An important element in the draft treaty was the attempt to create bridges between what the ten did in the Community framework and what they did or might do in other frameworks such as EPC, culture etc. The proposal also envisaged according the European Council a 'strategic' role.[7] Perhaps as 'bait' to the French, the proposal suggested that this more coherent structure be headed by the European Council.[8]

In the ensuing discussions with their EC partners the Germans and Italians failed to make progress. The episode illustrates how difficult it is for the integration process to advance without Franco–German agreement. The reason why Germany had turned to Italy was probably uncertainty as to the direction French European policy would take under the socialists, but the German government may also have wished to jolt France into action. In any case, France clearly resented losing the initiative in European constitutive policy. The French also failed to show much interest when the German government presented a series of proposals during its presidency in the first half of 1983. France's European policy seemed more or less in limbo, the economy smarting from the series of devaluations undertaken from 1981 to 1983, and the socialist government seemed uncertain as to what conclusions to draw in its European policy. Only in March 1983 did Mitterrand come down on the side of Delors and the pro-integrationists.[9]

Despite the cool reception, the Genscher–Colombo plan could not be ignored. Following a period of fruitless discussions in an *ad hoc* study group, the member states agreed on 'a solemn declaration on European Union' at the Stuttgart summit in June 1983. The declaration was a major disappointment for the Germans. It was little more than a declaration of intent. The idea of a binding treaty was dropped, there was no clear endorsement of the principle of majority voting and the European Parliament was only strengthened at the margins.[10]

The atmosphere was thus one of gloom in Germany and the rest of the Community, when in the first half of 1984 Mitterrand surprised everybody by announcing France's willingness to contemplate changes in the Treaty of Rome. Several factors explain this initiative for a European revival. First of all, the failure of the socialists' national growth strategy had caused a shift of emphasis from the national to the European level in French economic policy. At the same time, Mitterrand was becoming deeply unpopular at home. New European initiatives seemed helpful as a way of improving Mitterrand's image. There is a sense in which Europe became a safe haven for a president fleeing a domestic economic crisis. At the same time, the European issue was a useful means of sowing division within the right-wing opposition.

Secondly, and more importantly, France's traditional anxiety about a possible German drift towards neutrality was reawakened in the early 1980s, as large sections of the German population went into the streets protesting against the INF double-track decision. Mitterrand felt that there was a need to solidify the anchor that tied Germany to the West. At the same time, Mitterrand's speech in the *Bundestag* in January 1983 in support of the controversial double-track decision on the deployment of intermediate range nuclear missiles was partly intended to create good-will in Bonn which might help Mitterrand in his new European offensive. In his speech to the *Bundestag* Mitterrand went far, quoting Victor Hugo's expression *consanguinitè* (consanguinity) from a speech in 1842 about Franco–German relations.[11]

Thirdly, the second enlargement of the EC led to the admission of Greece, whose maverick president, Papandreo, almost brought the Community to a standstill at the European Council in Athens in December 1983. In Athens, for the first time in its history, the EC was unable to agree on a joint communiqué. Spain and Portugal were waiting in the wings. To a certain extent Mitterrand was exercising crisis management. At the same time, Mitterrand and his advisers were leaning towards the view that enlargement required institutional reform of the EC, an assessment shared by the Germans and, more importantly, the British. The Greeks soon became the scapegoats for a much wider crisis touching on core issues like the CAP and the budget. The tough stance of Margaret Thatcher on the budgetary issue raised acute problems, as did Franco–German disagreement on monetary compensatory amounts for agricultural exports. The fact that the crisis was now touching the very foundation of the Community, the CAP, set the alarm bells ringing in Paris as well as in Bonn.

Yet it would be wrong to interpret the French initiative as merely a rescue operation. It also had strategic dimensions. The age-old French rivalry with the USA continued, sharpened by the ideological clashes between French socialism and Reagan's fierce neo-conservatism. Although Mitterrand himself does not appear to have been particularly anti-American, his experiences in the first years of the socialist reign had reinforced his belief that a European alternative to American supremacy in the West was needed. The clash with the US came to a head when in March 1983 the USA launched its Strategic Defense Initiative project, which posed a direct threat to French nuclear policy. Thus France's European offensive focused upon the technological field, but it also emphasized the need for European monetary unity. In France's balancing strategy, which had the support of most of France's political class, the Deutschmark played a key role.[12] Initially, Mitterrand adopted a pragmatic approach but, spurred on by Germany, gradually began to take on board some of the ideas of the institutional-ists, to the point of agreeing to break some Gaullist taboos in European policy.

Consolidating the core

Despite Mitterrand's gesture in the *Bundestag* 1983 was not an entirely happy year for Franco–German cooperation. The Germans could hardly be blamed for suspecting that France was unwilling to allow Germany a breakthrough if the reform of the Community could be turned into a French success by postponing the discussion for six months. The atmosphere between Bonn and Paris was not the best at the end of 1983. In November 1983 in connection with the 42nd Franco–German summit in Bonn, Kohl gave a dinner speech in which he indirectly criticized France for a lack of willingness to compromise, referring amongst others things to the decisions made at the Stuttgart summit in June. Mitterrand responded by giving a speech in which he attacked German acquiescence vis-à-vis the USA and hinted at the difference in status between the two countries, saying *inter alia* '*Nennen wir die Dinge beim Namen. Die Hauptschwierigkeit besteht darin, dass die politische Wille, zu dessen wichtigsten Vertretern Sie, Herrn Bundeskanzler, gehören, nicht leicht mit militärischer Macht und Realität einhergehen kann*'.[13]

In early January 1984 a Franco–German meeting was ominously postponed to February. But the Germans seemed determined to get European integration moving. Putting pressure on the new French presidency to take bold European initiatives, Kohl spoke on German radio about the need for a relaunch of European cooperation: '*Der Geist der Römischen Vertrage, der Geist von Messina . . . ist offensichtlich gegenwärtig in Europa nicht zu erkennen*', Kohl said with a dig at the French.[14]

The Kohl–Genscher government evidently placed greater priority on EC matters than its predecessor. Under Kohl the chancellery assumed a higher profile in EC policy, which provoked some friction between Kohl and Genscher. Moreover, Kohl began placing greater emphasis on a bilateral link with France, signalling his willingness to embark upon a two-speed process if necessary.[15]

Notwithstanding the acrimony of some Franco–German exchanges, the French government seemed to be gradually moving closer to the German–Italian view as regards the need for institutional reform. This change had been on its way for some time. In 1982 the French had taken a step of great symbolic importance when in May during the Belgian presidency they had failed to defend the Luxembourg compromise and joined a majority in overruling a British veto on agricultural prices.[16]

On 2 February 1984 Mitterrand and Kohl held a long and probably crucial confidential talk at Schloss Edenkoben in Germany.[17] They agreed not only to make a determined joint effort to solve the concrete problems facing the EC, but also, on the basis of the Treaty of Rome, to take new initiatives to further political cooperation in the EC and in bilateral relations. The security area was to be included in bilateral talks.[18] Kohl and Mitterrand were reported to have discussed a bilateral union involving a joint government and a common parliament at the meeting.[19]

The bilateral meeting elicited an immediate reaction from Italy. Prime Minister Craxi told Kohl that he only regarded Franco–German cooperation as useful '*wenn sie nicht neue Ungleichgewichte innerhalb der EG hervorriefen*'.[20] Craxi appears to have been worried by the fact that Kohl had mentioned the possibility of 'a two-gear' Europe without specifying what he meant by that.[21] On 7 February 1984 Mitterrand gave an important speech in The Hague in which he called for a new departure in European integration, comparing Europe to 'an abandoned building site'. Without being very specific Mitterrand asked the rhetorical question of how one could envisage a European military power, which most people seemed to regard as necessary, without a unified political power. He added vaguely that '*le moment est venu d'accorder à nos institutions une cohérence qui leur manque*'.[22] Whereas the Germans would use economic integration as an argument for political integration, Mitterrand was trying to use security as a catalyst for political integration.

In mid-February in a speech to military officers from the *Bundeswehr* in Travemünde, Kohl added to the new momentum in the European debate by announcing that he intended to take a new initiative aimed at European unification after the European elections in June. He would seek to formulate a policy which ensured that the slowest ship did not determine the pace of integration. He added that he would pursue the creation of a common European security policy, the core of which would be the close Franco–German cooperation.[23] The speech added to the pressure on Mitterrand to act – and act decisively – while at the same time sending a signal to the UK that it risked being excluded from a core of more closely integrating member states.

These signs of a new German (and Franco–German) policy of differentiation within the EC were not lost on the UK government. Nor were their implications. The UK responded by signalling a serious concern about the state of affairs in the EC. The British foreign minister, Sir Geoffrey Howe, thus gave a speech to the Royal Institute of International Relations in Brussels on 20 February 1984 in which he expressed support for the pragmatic programme of action agreed to at the Stuttgart summit, a highly watered-down version of the Genscher–Colombo plan. Ignoring the debate about institutional reform, he focused on a number of concrete problems, highlighting the need for a thorough market liberalization in Western Europe. Despite the strict intergovernmentalism of the speech it was obvious that the British government wanted to be seen to share the concern of the French and Germans about Europe's competitiveness. In Howe's words: *Europas ganze Zukunft als grosse internationale Industriemacht steht auf dem Spiel* ('Europe's whole future as a big industrial power is at stake').[24]

France and Germany had now evidently mended fences and this enabled the duo to exercise leadership within the EC. Following another Franco–German meeting in preparation for the European Council in Brussels in March 1984 Kohl told German TV that 'experience has shown that this idea (the Franco–German axis) awakens discontent. For this reason it is neither Mitterrand's policy nor my own. However, the FRG and France form the centrepiece of the future Europe, and we must therefore try to make this work between ourselves, and we are following the right lines'. Willy Brandt, the former German Chancellor, supported Kohl saying that 'nothing is possible in Europe if impossible between the FRG and France'.[25]

The March European Council in Brussels failed to solve the EC's crisis. Mitterrand reacted by raizing the stakes. Mitterrand's calculation was that not less Europe but 'more Europe' was what was needed to help the EC overcome its crisis. He thus called upon those who wanted to build Europe to meet again at a conference which was to take place within a few weeks. Mitterrand emphasized that '*personne n'en est exclu*' (nobody is excluded). At the same time he said that the content of the deliberations was more important than the number of participants.[26]

In late April the two foreign ministers, Genscher and Dumas, met to discuss the British budgetary issue as well as the admission of Spain and Portugal and the future financing of the EC. In connection with this meeting Genscher was quoted by the *Frankfurter Allgemeine Zeitung* as having told a newspaper that in his view France and Germany were the *Kernzelle* (nucleus) of the EC. He also emphasized the security dimension of the bilateral cooperation, adding that Europe had to define its security interests and play a more influential role within NATO. Genscher pointed out that it was not the USA but the various European governments which relegated Europe to second place.[27] The statement highlights the two key elements in the reactivation of European integration in the mid-1980s: the importance of security in re-invigorating

Franco–German cooperation and the two countries' decision to apply the tactic of differentiated integration.

On 20 May Kohl and Mitterrand met in Saarbrücken, once again trying to find a solution to the British budgetary problem. Taking the high ground, Kohl told journalists *inter alia* that 'solidarity ensures that the economically strong help the weakest. We consider that every Deutschmark invested in the Community's future is an advance payment for the future of liberty'.[28] By referring to its role as *Zahlmeister* (paymaster) Kohl was casting Germany in the role of leader of the Community, the country defending the principles and the long-term interests of the Community.

Mitterrand's opening

On 24 May 1984 Mitterrand gave a crucial speech in the European Parliament in Strasbourg. The speech signalled a new departure in France's European policy, but also evoked memories of the pro-integrative policy of the Fourth Republic. For 25 years France's European policy had essentially been dictated by the Gaullists. Now a socialist president broke that mould. While his thoughts on the need for reinforced industrial and technological cooperation were at this stage already well known, Mitterrand had new and surprising things to say about the institutional framework of European cooperation. Without directly mentioning the name of Spinelli, he essentially endorsed Spinelli's approach, which implied a revising of the founding treaties.[29]

Breaking the Gaullist taboo of majority voting, Mitterrand asked the rhetorical question '*comment l'ensemble complexe et diversifiée qu'est devenue la Communauté peut-il se gouverner selon les règles de la Diète de cet ancien Royaume de Pologne dont chaque membre pouvait bloquer les décisions?*'[30]

Recalling the numerous new institutions and practices created by the member states to address new problems, he said '*à situation nouvelle doit correspondre un traité nouveau*' (a new situation requires a new treaty).[31] Apart from reforms of the decison-making procedures, new areas ought to be included in the treaty, notably *l'Europe politique* (the political Europe). Mitterrand was, however, far from being dogmatic on institutional matters. He expressed openness towards more flexible methods such as a multi-speed Europe or variable geometry, provided such new methods were complementary in relation to the central structure.

Mitterrand's speech to the European Parliament was greeted with satisfaction in Germany. The spokesman for the German government said that Mitterrand had addressed problems which Bonn also would like to highlight. The German government particularly welcomed Mitterrand's reference to the need for a revision of the decision-making procedure in the Council. Germany would, he indicated, do everything to support moves aimed at the creation of a European Union.[32]

On 28 May 1984 a Franco–German summit was held in Rambouillet. Kohl, Mitterrand and several ministers participated. On this occasion Kohl gave his full support for the proposals made by Mitterrand in his speech to the European Parliament. The two countries' foreign and defence ministers held a separate meeting, in which they discussed a revival of the Western European Union and closer foreign policy and defence cooperation between the two countries. They also discussed the joint construction of an attack helicopter.[33]

In the run-up to the Fontainebleau summit on 25–26 June which would crown the French presidency, the French foreign minister Dumas told the French daily Le Matin that France would indicate the direction which the EC ought to take but that it obviously could not impose a specific method upon the rest. In a veiled threat to the UK Dumas said that he considered it likely that intensified cooperation could take place in a circle of 'fewer than ten'.[34]

The spirit of the 1950s

The Fontainebleau summit became the turning point in the debate on a reform of the EC. Not only did the heads of state and government find a solution to the British budgetary problem thus unblocking other important dossiers, they also made a number of other important decisions pointing towards the future: 30 September would be the deadline for the finalization of negotiations on adhesion with Spain and Portugal and more importantly, a working group presided over by the Irish senator, James Dooge, was asked to prepare suggestions for an improvement of the functioning of European cooperation in several areas, including the Community area and the area of political cooperation. In the conclusions from the summit there was an explicit reference to the 'Spaak committee' which had prepared the Rome Treaty. This immediately raised the level of ambition. But apart from that the mandate stepped carefully, avoiding references to the concept of European Union or to the draft treaty of the EP.[35]

Another working group presided over by the Italian Adonnino was asked to prepare proposals under the heading 'Europe of the citizen'. Among the areas referred to were education, youth, reduction of frontier controls, public health and research. Moreover, Kohl and Mitterrand agreed on the appointment of Jacques Delors as new President of the European Commission from 1 January 1985. One month after Fontainebleau, Kohl and Mitterrand signed an agreement on free movement, which prefigured the Schengen accord.[36]

In his diary, Attali gives a more detailed account of this crucial summit. '*En cas d'échec tout est prêt pour fonctionner à neuf* (in case of failure everything is prepared for functioning in a group of nine') Attali writes, adding '*Guigou a bien travaillé. Londre le sait*' ('Guigou has worked well. London knows'), confirming the new importance of the strategy of differentiation in French EC policy. According to Attali, Kohl and Mitterrand decided over breakfast on the second day of the summit to hand over the Commission presidency to Delors.[37] Although he was in principle in favour of a German as president, Kohl made a point of not pressing his claim. He told Mitterrand he had nothing against a Frenchman provided the new president did not oppose the political initiatives which Kohl and Mitterrand were planning.[38] Thatcher told Mitterrand that she could accept Delors, whom she respected for having reined in the Mitterrand government's initial left-wing policies, but not the left-wing Claude Cheysson.[39] On 18 July the EC governments named Delors to the presidency of the Commission.

On the delicate question of the budget, Thatcher had the day before demanded first a 90 per cent rebate then 'much more than 70 per cent'. During their breakfast Kohl and Mitterrand decided on 65 per cent as the maximum. This position was subsequently presented to Thatcher by Kohl in session as the 'position of the nine'. Thatcher reacted by demanding 66 per cent and the deal was struck.[40] Thatcher's diary confirms Attali's account on the essential points, which adds to its credibility.[41]

From the perspective of this study, the important point is that Thatcher recognizes Franco–German leadership as being important in EC constitutive politics. In her own words 'President Mitterrand's and Chancellor Kohl's breakfast the following morning probably cleared the way for a settlement'.[42]

The decisions at Fontainebleau inspire Hubert Vedrine to make some cutting remarks about the dynamics of European integration. '*L'Europe des années 1980 est le pur produit d'une forme moderne de despotisme éclairé*' . . .

'la construction européenne a été une démarche volontariste et élitiste par excellence'.[43] The crucial decisions on the relaunching of Europe, he goes on, were basically taken by three persons: Kohl, Mitterrand and Thatcher, and twenty persons on the suggestions of three or four of them set in motion the process of creating a political Europe and a Europe of the citizens, the latter being accorded merely a symbolic function. Not that he laments this state of affairs. In Vedrine's view the EU's elitism is motivated by a justified fear of re-awakening the sleeping nationalist demons in the European peoples.

The Dooge committee

In July 1984 Ireland took over the presidency. But France evidently sought to retain a guiding role. In August Mitterrand sent a letter to the Irish Prime Minister recalling amongst other things the goal of progressively creating a European Union. He also drew attention to his own proposals *que mon représentant dans le Comité pourra développer* ('which my representative in the Committee will be able to develop').[44]

Mitterrand and Kohl had envisaged a committee composed of high-ranking and politically independent persons. Yet some of the other member states were quick to appoint civil servants to the committee. In early September just before the start of the talks, the German Chancellor expressed his dissatisfaction with some of the nominations. As German representative and chairman of the committee, Kohl wanted to appoint Karl Carstens, former President of the FRG, but Kohl was unable to control the procedural discussion. He apparently overplayed his hand in demanding the chairmanship without first having consulted the French and did not press the point. Besides, Kohl made a *faux pas* in suggesting Carstens, whose wartime record was not uncontroversial. In addition, there appears to have been some division within the German government, the foreign ministry putting pressure on Kohl to appoint one of its officials.[45] Eventually, the foreign ministry won this fight, the German chair being filled by Jürgen Ruhfus, a high-ranking official from the foreign ministry. The composition of the committee thus became a quite heterogeneous mixture of high-ranking civil servants and political figures. The representatives also differed in terms of their relationship to their heads of state or government.

The dominant figure soon became the Frenchman, Maurice Faure, who was a former minister and a signatory of the Treaty of Rome. Faure had the confidence of Mitterrand, which gave him a considerable freedom of action. The French President's clear prerogatives in the foreign affairs area gave Mitterrand a head start in his competition with the German Chancellor, who had to harmonize his views with a foreign ministry held by a coalition partner. It is a testimony to his influence that Faure was asked to prepare an overall report for the second meeting of the committee. His report in many ways prefigured the committee's final report.[46] France's key role enabled the Germans to wield indirect influence in the committee via their close relationship to France. The Germans appear to have been more ambitious than their partners in all areas except the monetary. Even here, however, the Germans were flexible in part because it was difficult to express a strong commitment to European union while at the same time resisting monetary union, an essential element in any union.[47] The German side did however register a reservation on the promotion of the ecu.[48] Although the German level of ambition was very high, Germany adopted what at first glance looked like a pragmatic approach, taking care not to be isolated in the negotiations. Yet the expression 'pragmatic' is hardly an accurate description of the German position. It would be more correct to describe it as reflecting a gradualist strategy. As they stated explicitly, the Germans always considered the results achieved as *Etappenziele* (intermediate goals), although without specifying the goal towards which they were aiming.[49]

During the autumn Mitterrand and Kohl met on several occasions. On 22 September at the initiative of the Chancellor the two met in Verdun. It was on this occasion that Mitterrand took the hand of Kohl, a symbol of the reconciliation achieved.[50]

Characteristically, the summit at the end of October 1984 in Bad Kreuznach was devoted mainly to military cooperation. Attali quotes Mitterrand as saying '*il faut faire ensemble tout ce qui ne vous est pas interdit, c'est à dire l'espace, les armes chimiques, le laser*' ('we must do everything together which you are not prevented from doing, that is to say space, chemical weapons, lasers'). Kohl agreed, saying that France and Germany must start out together. He was very sceptical as regards the possibility of achieving anything in a circle of twelve or even six.[51] The meeting led to a resumption of cooperation on a European satellite, a French plan meant to counter the American SDI project, as well as on military cooperation.

As had become customary, the two leaders met for breakfast on the second day of the Dublin summit in December 1984. The summit itself does not appear to have taken up much of their time. Instead they discussed how to celebrate the 40th anniversary of the ending of the Second World War. Kohl expressed the hope that there would be no allied military parades in Berlin and received Mitterrand's backing. Mitterrand said he had an idea: he wanted the two Europes to meet without the Americans to celebrate the anniversary: '*c'est l'Europe que se construit*' ('it is Europe that is being built'). Attali quotes Kohl as having answered '*Oui. Les Etats-Unis ne seraient pas très utiles*' ('Yes. The United States would not be very useful').[52]

At the summit Senator Dooge presented the preliminary report of the institutional committee. The report put forward a majority position with the minority positions represented in the form of footnotes. The recommendations of the report were quite radical. Most importantly, the report called for an intergovernmental conference to negotiate a draft treaty on European union.[53] The French were entirely satisfied with the result. Attali refers to the report as *préparé pour l'essentiel par la France et le Quai D'Orsay, sous l'égide de Maurice Faure* (an old hand from the debates in the 1950s).[54]

The Milan summit

In February 1985 Mitterrand met with Bettino Craxi, whose government had just taken over the presidency of the EC. During a discussion of the institutional reforms, Mitterrand summarized his assessment of the situation in the EC, pointing out that six countries were ready to go ahead, while four were putting the brakes on: the UK, Denmark, Ireland and Greece. Mitterrand's analysis was clear: '*sur ces quatre, il y a deux irréductibles, le Danemark et la Grèce. Le Royaume-Uni n'aime pas rester isolé des trois autres grands pays. Quant à l'Irlande, la Communauté est son salut, car sans elle, elle redevient une colonie anglaise*'.[55] Mitterrand went on to make a plea for a joint effort by France, Germany and Italy.

During the first half of 1985 global issues intervened to disturb the Franco–German rapprochement. Kohl found it difficult to refuse German participation in the American SDI project and he agreed with the American administration that a new GATT round ought to open soon. France was opposed to both initiatives, deciding to launch its alternative Eureka project, the purpose of which would be civilian. Nevertheless, the two leaders on the whole managed to maintain the momentum in the discussion on EC institutional reform.

Meeting on 25 March to prepare the upcoming European summit in Brussels, Mitterrand and Kohl decided to let their advisers work out a draft treaty on European union based on the Dooge report. Kohl wanted this preparatory work to be followed by an intergovernmental conference to be decided upon at the Milan summit in June.[56] The advisors did not commence their work until the end of April, probably because of the Bonn G7 summit.[57]

The summit at the end of March 1985 failed to produce any clear decisions as regards how to reform the Community. The final Dooge report was discussed. It recommended the creation of a European Union with an integrated market, the reinforcement of the powers of the Commission and the European Parliament, the introduction of majority voting in the Council and a common foreign policy with a permanent secretariat for political cooperation separate from the Council and the Commission. The latter idea, which had originated in Paris, was of course anathema to the Commission which feared that its role in EC external relations would be undercut.

In her diary, Margaret Thatcher takes the credit for having put the internal market at the top of the reform agenda at the March summit. Thatcher calculated that the UK was unable to resist the pressure for a reform of the EC. But she was determined to play a major role on issues of substance.[58] She relates how at the summit she 'launched an initiative on deregulation'. And yet, as a general goal, the objective of a single market was already on the agenda, as seen by the inclusion of this objective in the Genscher–Colombo plan.

On the Franco–German side a group of advisors led by Attali and Teltschik met in May to work on the details of a draft treaty. Apparently the German level of ambition was very high. According to Attali, Teltschik was willing to examine all aspects of European cooperation in detail, announcing his government's willingness to endorse all or almost all of the Dooge report. Kohl was also willing to move in the field of technology and monetary policy, including free movement of capital.[59] Teltschik even wanted to discuss a 'military Eureka'. He enquired about the possibilities of Matra and Messerschmidt joining forces with a view to developing a truly autonomous European nuclear shield.[60]

As the Milan summit approached Mitterrand began to have second thoughts about the preparatory work of the advisors. In a critical note to Attali Mitterrand wrote: *vous formalisez ici à l'excès la conversation que je dois avoir avec le chancelier . . . j'ignorais cette rencontre préparatoire qui ne me paraît pas nécessaire.*[61]

Compared to the previous year Mitterrand seemed much less enthusiastic about accelerating European integration. He may have been influenced by the Franco–German wrangle on relations with the USA, which did not bode well for a future European foreign policy. He may also have had second thoughts about forcing the pace, perhaps fearing that he would lose the British.[62] A week before meeting Kohl he told his advisors that before the meeting it was better to keep a low profile and not raise false hopes as to the results which could be achieved.[63] Mitterrand was probably also slightly miffed by the fact that on 12 June the German agricultural minister had on a direct order from Chancellor Kohl laid down a veto in the council.[64]

If Fontainebleau was an important event in the revival of the EC, Milan was decisive. At the end of May 1985, Kohl and Mitterrand met to prepare the summit. Attali accords this preparatory meeting, in which the two leaders became reconciliated after the G7 summit, extraordinary importance, quoting the two at length. The mood was not the best. According to Attali a large part of the meeting was devoted to the SDI question and a possible European response. Kohl reassured Mitterrand that Germany was in favour of a European initiative in the field of high technology. What he had in mind was a division of labour between the USA and Europe with the Europeans concentrating on the civilian sector, perhaps involving Japan. According to Kohl, Nakasone was willing to collaborate with the French and Germans. Kohl explained the low German profile quoting Adenauer as once having said that '*quand la France ou la RFA font la même chose, les conséquences en sont différentes*'.[65]

As regards the reform of the EC, France and Germany were under some pressure to show leadership by means of a bold gesture. A fierce competition between the UK and France and Germany had developed. Reacting to the rumours of intensive Franco–German preparations, the UK had moved quickly, submitting a pragmatic but substantive proposal to the Stresa meeting of foreign ministers in early June 1985. The British were essentially arguing that improvements in the EC's functioning could be introduced by means of gentlemen's agreements and a return to the practice of the treaties without there being any need for a new treaty. They were thus trying to lure the other two big member states into accepting a more pragmatic and less time-consuming reform procedure. In concrete terms, the UK had amongst other things proposed a strengthening of foreign policy and security cooperation through the creation of a small permanent secretariat.[66] It suggested that the use of majority voting should be increased by mutual agreement, that use of the veto should be justified at the level of foreign ministers and that areas where the veto could no longer be invoked should be agreed at meetings of the European Council. George points out that the British softening on the issue of majority voting was due to concern lest the Greek socialist government block the freeing of the internal market.[67]

During the Franco–German meeting it became clear that the French were less keen on holding an IGC than the Germans. Kohl said to Mitterrand that it might be necessary to hide behind an IGC if the results of the Milan summit were unsatisfactory, whereas Mitterrand warned '*la conférence intergouvernementale est un échappatoire*' ('the intergovernmental conference is an evasion').[68] He also expressed reservation regarding a strengthening of the European Parliament, refusing to give the Parliament the right to levy taxes, a point raised by Kohl.[69] As regards decision-making, Mitterrand was in favour of returning to the Treaty of Rome and giving up the right of veto. Considering it unlikely that he would obtain this, he told Kohl that one must make the veto exceptional. Kohl seemed mainly concerned about the issue of a common security policy and enquired about the possibility of signing a bilateral treaty on security policy.[70]

The UK paper had been discussed with Kohl but not, it seems, with Mitterrand – an attempt by the British to split the Franco–German axis by emphasizing the concrete areas in which London and Bonn had common interests. Thatcher relates how she got the impression from her meeting with Kohl that he was sympathetic towards the British paper. Nevertheless, just before going to Milan she learnt that France and Germany had tabled their own proposal, which, it soon appeared, was almost identical to the British one.

In the run-up to the summit a remarkable episode appears to have occurred on the Franco–German side. During the month of June 1985 the top advisors of Kohl and Mitterrand had coopted the Italians. The three delegations had made very considerable progress in the direction of a joint proposal for a new treaty. According to Attali, Kohl's view was that the French and Germans should together work out a draft treaty to be handed over to the Italians on 20 June, that is a week before the summit. Italy would then present the draft to the summit as its own proposal. In fact, Attali and Teltschik had already involved the Italians in early June, probably at Mitterrand's initiative. Attali writes sarcastically: *Teltschik et moi faisons semblant de nous voir pour la première fois sur le projet. Ruggiero fait semblant d'être dupe.*[71]

A number of important issues were discussed including the possible integration of the WEU into the European Union, the creation of a general secretariat for political cooperation and whether or not the FRG ought to have a permanent seat in the UN security council. Attali quotes Teltschik as having said that '*il s'agit de créer un vrai pouvoir politique à côté de la Commission et, indépendamment d'elle, un véritable ministère des affaires étrangères européen, ayant droit de contrôle sur les votes de la France et la Grande Bretagne à l'ONU*'.[72]

On 26 June the group met again and by then a draft treaty was apparently more or less ready. Germany and Italy proposed some last-minute changes in the preamble, which Attali supported because they strengthened the idea of European union. The Germans accepted that the draft could use the term 'union' referring to foreign and security cooperation alone, leaving out the issue of democratization. They also accepted that the proposed secretary general would be called 'Secretary General of the Union'. This was the old French idea of creating a political leadership separate from the supranational Commission. The Italians and Germans insisted on moving further on the Parliament, but agreed to defer the subject to the summit negotiations. The eventual joint Franco–German proposal was rather meagre, focusing on political cooperation, which seemed to indicate a loss of interest in the main substance of the Dooge report. It was left to the Italian presidency to decide whether or not it wanted to present the draft treaty as its own proposal. If not it was decided to publish it as a Franco–German proposal prior to the summit.

The next day however, Kohl, whether in order to demonstrate German leadership or in an attempt to appease the opposition, announced the existence of a Franco–German draft treaty on European union in a speech to the *Bundestag*, without having consulted the French or the Italians.[73] The Italians reacted angrily, feeling that they had been manipulated, perhaps also afraid that Germany's high level of ambition might throw the summit into disarray.[74]

Confirming Attali's version of these events, Vedrine argues that a new treaty could have been endorsed at Milan, had not the Chancellor disclosed the Franco–German agreement.[75] Realizing that the project had caused alarm, France and Germany hastened to downplay its importance, calling it a working paper.[76]

Despite this stumbling start the summit produced a breakthrough on constitutive reform. The first day's discussions ended in deadlock, three countries (the UK, Denmark and Greece) opposing the idea of an intergovernmental conference. Early on the second day the German foreign minister, H.-D. Genscher, pressed for a decision tabling a text which stated a clear goal: *Die Europäischen Union beginnt; die Mitgliedstaaten werden über die Ausgestaltung einer Union abschliessen. Es wird eine Regierungskonferenz eingesetzt, die den Entwurf des Vertrages bis zum 31 October erarbeitet. Er wird auf dem Europäischen Rat in Luxembourg beraten und beschlossen.*[77]

This 'bathroom paper', which Genscher himself calls it, appears to have been dictated by Genscher to his secretary through his bathroom door on the morning of the second day.[78] As several countries continued to veto treaty changes, the Italian chairman, Bettino Craxi, pulled off a great surprise by drawing attention to the fact that a majority of member states were in favour of convening an intergovernmental conference.[79] The presidency appears to have been under some pressure to go down this road. According to Genscher, whose account is quite detailed, which adds to its credibility, he himself gave the decisive push, whereas Mitterrand warned that a vote might split the Community.[80] Gerbet confirms this account, claiming that on this occasion the locomotive was Italy supported by Germany.[81] It seems almost a general rule in EU politics that whenever the Franco–German duo is malfunctioning Germany and Italy get together to fill the leadership vacuum.

Article 236 in the Treaty of Rome permitted a decision on the calling of an IGC to be taken by simple majority but so far no one had dared to make use of this provision and few people expected it to be used in Milan. France still appeared to be hesitant as regards the merit of holding a conference. After all, France had submitted a paper to the conference which proposed the use of majority decisions without any change in the treaty.[82] However, Mitterrand eventually joined Kohl in supporting a conference.[83] A majority was in favour of calling an IGC, with the UK, Denmark and Greece opposed. Thatcher was surprised and angry. Schlüter, the Danish Prime Minister, spoke of 'rape'. The Greek Prime Minister used the expression 'coup d'état' disputing the legality of the decision.[84] The Greek Prime Minister further angered Margaret Thatcher by insisting that, if there was also to be an IGC, he could not agree to the implementation of the agreement that had already been reached on the abandonment of the veto on matters relating to the creation of the internal market.[85]

In a move which may have been decisive, Thatcher agreed to take part in the IGC. George describes the decision as resulting from advice from her foreign minister and her personal advisor on EC matters, David

Williamson, who both argued that the other countries were less committed to institutional reform in practice than they were in theory and that the outcome of the negotiations would therefore be modest. They furthermore argued that by participating constructively in the intergovernmental conference Britain would make it difficult for France and Germany to hide behind the British, which would force them to reveal their real commitment.[86] In Thatcher's own words she 'saw no merit in an empty-chair policy'.[87] Such a stance could in her view only be justified if a major principle was at stake. Somewhat surprisingly, she later thought this had not been the case, referring to the basic agreement with the other member states on issues of substance. Even Thatcher wanted an enhanced political cooperation and a single market.

Yet the 'method' could surely be argued to be an issue of principle. Why, one must ask, did she not hold that view? Apart from the fear of being isolated from a continental bloc, one suspects that, perhaps slightly overestimating her power, Thatcher regarded the IGC as a tempting opportunity for a free-market crusade on the continent. A treaty centring on the internal market might be used to 'lock in' some of the liberal principles she cherished.

Looking back, Thatcher has second thoughts about the decision at Fontainebleau to set up the working group on closer European cooperation. It was the Dooge committee which came up with the idea of holding an intergovernmental conference. The idea having been put on the table, it came to appear the perfect vehicle for almost everyone's ideas about European development, as Thatcher rightly points out.[88] Yet the implications of accepting the idea of treaty changes were to prove far-reaching, as this enabled Germany and France to negotiate asymmetrical bargains with their partners.

The intergovernmental conference and the Single European Act

Between September and December 1985 the IGC held six rounds of negotiations. It was decided to deal with economic and political matters in a single conference at the level of foreign ministers. Yet each aspect was prepared by a specific working group. The Commission appears to have played an important role in these negotiations. It tabled proposals in areas like environment, research and cohesion and Delors devised the new 'co-operation procedure' between Council and Parliament, arguing that national parliaments lost influence as a result of the introduction of majority voting and that a compensating democratic guarantee had to be created. Grant goes so far as estimating that Delors and his officials wrote 60 to 70 per cent of the Single European Act.[89] This is undoubtedly an exaggeration, but from a theoretical perspective it is certainly interesting that an actor with no formal powers at IGCs should have assumed such an important role as did the Delors Commission.

It is not quite clear to what extent Delors had the blessing of the French government. Grant's analysis suggests that overall Delors was pragmatic, taking great care not to antagonize the big member states, notably Germany, whose support he needed in his daily work. Delors appears to have been particularly sensitive to German attitudes and on constitutive issues he was often closer to the German than to the French view.[90] The Commission of course benefited from the fact that the presidency was held by a small country, Luxembourg, which for purely practical reasons welcomed assistance. Moreover, the Commission was able to act quickly, tabling often very detailed papers which sought to incorporate member state views. Germany, on the other hand, had difficulty operating under the considerable time pressure, especially since a lot of difficult internal compromises had to be worked out. However, Germany was occasionally able to channel German positions to the negotiating table via the Commission.[91]

Germany and France were not alone in putting pressure on the hesitant states, although the core strategy had been devised by the two countries. Italian and Dutch politicians thus spoke of the possibility of some of the ten moving ahead without the others.[92]

On 2 and 3 December 1985 the heads of state and government met in Luxembourg for the final negotiations on a reform of the Community. In a typical French gesture Mitterrand had invited the Polish General Jaruzelski to Paris on the day after the summit, thus making sure that most of the media attention would be focused on him at the press conference following the summit.

The negotiations proved difficult (in part perhaps due to German annoyance at this last-minute French move). The summit lasted 28 hours, ending at 10 o'clock after some acrimonious exchanges.[93] Two years after the summit Mitterrand told Vedrine that three minutes before the end of the negotiations it seemed certain that the summit would end up a failure because of British and Danish resistance. At that point, however, Delors, Mitterrand and Kohl intervened with a plea for an accord to be reached. France and Germany also made it clear that in case the twelve could not move ahead together, a smaller grouping would go it alone. This had an effect on Thatcher, who, after having demanded a suspension of the session, returned to give her approval.[94] Not only did the decision to convene the IGC represent a breach of a convention, the conclusion of the final text of the *acte unique* also required the use of threats of exclusion.[95]

One of the most difficult dossiers was monetary affairs. France with Delors were aiming for a clear commitment to monetary integration. On this point Germany's position was unclear. At the early stage of the negotiations, Germany made the inclusion of a monetary chapter dependent upon approval by national parliaments, a provision which in a sense would have constituted a step backwards compared to the existing state of affairs. However, the German delegation soon realized that without some result on monetary integration the negotiations might break down. Wanting at almost any cost to reach a result, Germany decided to make concessions.[96] The softening of the German position had been facilitated by the fact that on the eve of the summit France and Italy had accommodated German demands, promising some liberalization in the laws governing transfer of capital. This made it easier for Kohl to compromise.[97]

In her diary Thatcher records her amazement at the sudden change of heart by the Germans on this issue during the summit. According to her, only a few days before the summit Kohl had assured her that Germany was 'totally opposed' to changes in the Rome Treaty on monetary affairs.[98] Now Kohl said he was willing to include monetary affairs in the treaty. Thatcher managed, however, in bilateral talks with the Chancellor to reduce the commitment to monetary integration by adding the phrase 'cooperation on economic and monetary policy'. Eventually, the summit endorsed a German proposal making further steps in the direction of monetary integration dependent upon the calling of a new IGC in accordance with Article 236. This was an important victory for Germany, since it allowed Germany to link changes in the monetary sphere to other constitutive changes. At the insistence of the Commission the term ecu was mentioned in the text.[99]

Another area of disagreement was the definition of the internal market. Here Germany and Delors wanted a very broad definition, whereas the UK was more restrictive. Although the broad definition largely prevailed, the UK obtained a number of explicit exceptions as regards the removal of physical borders. Majority voting was introduced in a number of areas, first and foremost areas relating to the internal market. The British obtained an exception for fiscal matters. The Commission and the presidency had demanded that the deadline of 1 January 1993 for completion of the internal market be made legally binding, but had to accept that it would merely be a political commitment. Nevertheless, the fact that a deadline was agreed upon proved important, especially because of the Commission's skilful use of the deadline in its campaign for the internal market.

The powers of the European Parliament also posed problems. Here the majority managed to push through a compromise solution – the cooperation procedure – which was regarded as not sufficiently integrative by Italy, the champion of the EP, and as too ambitious by Denmark, which subsequently held a referendum on the treaty. The FRG obtained most of its demands in this area except for a wide-ranging proposal regarding the involvement of the EP in constitutional affairs.

In a proposal of 24 September 1985, the German government had proposed a pragmatic two-level approach. In a number of areas relating to low politics, the EP would be granted a cooperation procedure. According to this procedure the EP and the Council were in principle to be placed on an equal footing. Thus in case of disagreement, a conciliation committee composed of six members from each body would be convened. Yet the Council would have the final word. In several other areas of greater importance the German government proposed a new procedure called 'common legislation' granting the EP a *de facto* right of veto, as its approval would be needed for a Council decision to take effect. This procedure would be introduced in three important areas: 1) constitutional matters (Article 236). Changes in the treaties would need the approval of a majority in Parliament 2) the admission of new members (Article 237). Such admissions would again require the approval of a majority in Parliament and 3) association agreements with third countries (Article 238). Such agreements would likewise need the approval of the EP. Of these two sets of proposals the former was adopted in a modified form as the new cooperation procedure did give Parliament enhanced powers though without instituting the conciliation committee, while two of the three proposals in the latter category were adopted. The proposal regarding Article 236 was not adopted.

A treaty on political cooperation was agreed upon in the final stages of the summit. It was a long-standing goal of the French to establish a general secretariat for foreign and security affairs. In the run-up to the Milan summit, France and Germany had submitted a joint proposal to that end. The idea was that the EC would appoint a General Secretary for the European Union, who would have responsibility for political cooperation. He or she would be appointed by the European Council for a four-year period. The General Secretary would be assisted by a general secretariat (see above).[100] Yet the idea was vehemently opposed by the member states supporting the Commission, as well as by the UK. The question of the link to economic cooperation still had to be addressed. It was referred to the foreign ministers' meeting of 19 December. It was the Commission which had insisted on the unity of the modifications to the Treaty of Rome and the treaty on political cooperation. France also wanted to 'cap' the two sections of the new treaty, but for different reasons. Whereas the Commission feared that the EPC structure might undermine the single institutional framework and by implication the Commission's powers, the French government wanted to strengthen the European Council. This must have placed Delors in a slightly precarious situation. Two weeks before the summit France had tabled a proposal on *l'acte d'union européenne* which included the idea of creating a general secretariat for European union, an idea that, as we have seen, had been endorsed by the FRG. The presidency, hardly keen on the French idea of a general secretariat, had refrained from putting this proposal on the agenda before the summit. Instead it had asked the member states to submit their reactions to the proposal in writing. There was broad agreement on the unity act idea (with only Denmark opposed), whereas there was considerable scepticism towards the idea of a general secretariat.[101] Two days after the summit the presidency submitted a text based upon the French draft, but without the most controversial formulations on the secretariat. The presidency probably calculated that the French proposal had fewer chances of being adopted if dealt with as an isolated issue at a meeting of foreign ministers than at the final IGC summit, where Mitterrand would have been able to link it to other issues. Delors argued, with some effect it appears, that a separate intergovernmental text would have weakened the Community's institutional system.[102] The presidency text was adopted by the foreign ministers on 19 December 1985.[103]

The art of packaging

Constitutive decisions in the EU can be divided into primary decisions which change the treaties and secondary decisions implementing the often very general commitments contained in the treaties. The signing of the Single European Act was followed by ambitious attempts on the part of the Delors Commission to wring further powers out of member states through an expansive interpretation of the Act. The Delors tactic was to tie proposals together in packages making them look inseparable. To this end the rhetoric of spillover was effective.[104] At the same time, Delors took great care not to antagonize the major national players. After very tough negotiations with the UK government in particular, the Commission managed to secure support for a package of budgetary measures known as the 'Delors package' in February 1988. At first it had seemed that Delors would fail. Margaret Thatcher refused to sign the plan in June 1987 and the Copenhagen summit in December the same year ended in failure. Only with the energetic support of Helmut Kohl did Delors manage to push through the package.[105] The Luxembourg summit had merely agreed on a significant increase in real terms 'within the limits of financial possibilities'.[106] Now the overall ceiling on EC spending rose from 1.05 per cent of Community GDP in 1988 to 1.2 per cent of GDP in 1992, which amounted to 70 billion ecus in 1992 prices. The structural funds which were meant to assist the less developed economies and to compensate them for the market pressures of the internal market were doubled over six years. Member states thus transferred powers to Brussels in two ways, through constitutive changes and new laws and through the transfer of money to the Community budget.[107] By 1988 Jacques Delors had acquired a remarkable status. The EC-sceptical press referred to him as the 'czar of Brussels'. A more fitting comparison would perhaps have been with the Pope and the German Emperor who together ruled Europe in the Middle Ages, just as Delors and Kohl seemed now to be on the verge of ruling Western Europe.

Cooperative hegemony and the case of the Single European Act

Among analysts of European integration a key question has been whether political or economic actors were paramount in relaunching European integration in the early 1980s. Although European multinationals undoubtedly exercised a considerable amount of intellectual leadership, the political leaders in Germany and France, assisted by Jacques Delors, deserve the main credit for the initiative. Cowles has shown convincingly that the European Round Table of Industrialists was influential in raising the debate about Europe's industrial decline.[108] A close interaction between the Round Table and the Commission developed in the early 1980s, although it would be going too far to argue that the Round Table dominated these talks. A comparison between statements made by members of the Round Table and the internal market plan demonstrates this clearly. The famous speech held by the President of Philips, Wisse Dekker, in January 1985 calling for a European revival carried the title 'Europe 1990'. Indeed, in his speech Dekker referred several times to the fact that Philips had drawn up a five year plan covering the years from 1985 to 1990.[109] Whatever inspiration the Commission may have drawn from the plan, Mr Dekker did not succeed in selling his timetable. The deadline became 1992 and not 1990.[110]

The Franco–German duo played a key role in the chain of events leading to the adoption of the SEA. Their role was especially important at the early stage of the process. President Mitterrand gave the green light for a new approach to reforms of the EC. And had not Italy known that it could count on German and French support, it would hardly have called the controversial vote on the convening of an IGC in Milan. Delors exercised a certain amount of intellectual and even entrepreneurial leadership, but as we have seen, he was France's and Germany's choice and Chancellor Kohl had made it clear to Mitterrand that the precondition for his support of Delors was that Delors did not trespass upon German (or French) national interests. The much vaunted Delors package thus had the blessing of Kohl.

The SEA negotiations constitute a hard case for the cooperative hegemony proposition since the largest state among the less integrationist countries was led by a strong leader with a solid domestic base who was determined to put a spoke in the wheel of the Franco–German wagon. And yet, France and Germany managed to make headway, introducing a wholly new approach to Community reform – that of treaty changes. The French representative in the Dooge committee, assisted by his German colleague, played a decisive role in rallying support for the idea of an intergovernmental conference. The main cause of the breakthrough was France and Germany's use of the tactic of differentiation. Both during the early procedural stage and at the final stage of negotiations in Luxembourg the two countries made effective use of the threat of exclusion. This constituted a new departure especially for Germany, which under Schmidt had made considerable efforts to keep the British on board. France on the other hand had a long-standing sympathy for differentiated integration. Nevertheless, the pressure for tactical differentiation seemed to come mainly from Germany, which was determined to push integration forward.

Leadership was also exercised by other actors. Italy often worked in close collaboration with Germany. Just as Italy had backed Genscher's early plan for reactivating integration, it was the Italian presidency which made the legal but somewhat controversial decision to call a vote on the convening of an IGC in Milan – apparently after consultations with the Germans. The UK, while overrun on procedural matters, proved an effective negotiator on substantive issues. The Delors Commission managed to exercise a quite impressive leadership at the IGC, despite the fact that according to the treaties it had nothing to do there. The Commission performance at IGCs is thus a valuable test of neo-functionalist and institutionalist propositions. Yet the fact that the Commission President at the time was French complicates our analysis. We know very little about the relationship and the degree of coordination between Delors and the Elysée. We do know, however, that in his actions Delors to a significant extent anticipated the views of the German government. Teltschik is quoted by Grant as having described Delors as a mediator between Mitterrand and Kohl and as having often tried to make Mitterrand understand the German point of view.[111] It should also be recalled that, France and Germany having been instrumental in electing Delors for the Commission presidency, and Delors being keen to be re-elected, his autonomy was bounded. This does not imply that the Delors Commission as a whole was a mere instrument, but it does commend caution in assessing Delors' role.[112]

The fact that during the decisive negotiations on the SEA the presidency was occupied by the smallest member state, Luxembourg, adds to the difficulties in making general inferences about the Commission's role. The second half of 1985 was not a typical period in European politics in terms of formal leadership resources. At the same time, this raises the interesting question of the extent to which the timing of constitutive changes is manipulated by France and Germany with a view to bypassing the formal leadership. From a realist point of view, it would be logical to expect France and Germany to try to time new constitutive initiatives with the aim of ensuring that the presidency was in the hands of either a small and uninfluential country, a friendly member country, or France and Germany themselves. Unfortunately, we have no access to sources which may enlighten us on this point.

The main factors motivating France and Germany to exercise leadership during the SEA negotiations largely confirm our expectations.

External balancing was one of the motives behind the reactivation of the duo and by implication of European integration. Germany was keen to protect European détente from the assertive security policy of the Reagan administration. France was more concerned about the implications of the SDI project, about technological competitiveness and about monetary issues. The external factor stressed by Sandholz and Zysman in their classical analysis of the SEA should not, however, be overemphasized. A participant in the negotiations suggests that the external factor was more a negotiating tactic than a serious concern, arguing that Jacques Delors used the spectre of an external threat to 'sell' the deal on an internal market and institutional reform.[113] The rhetoric of external balancing was an effective tactical weapon against the left-wing socialists in the peace movement, as a major part of the movement had anti-American attitudes. The reactivation of the WEU in 1984 should also in part be seen in that light.[114]

As we have seen, intra-hegemonic rivalry on the European scene played a part in reactivating integration. French concern about a possible German drift towards the East did play a considerable role in making Mitterrand lift some of the historical vetos on French participation in the construction of a European Union. At the same time, our account challenges some of the existing analyses of the SEA in that it highlights the very active and effective German efforts to relaunch European integration. The new French opening towards Europe was welcomed in Bonn, because it provided the FRG with the cover necessary to relaunch its initiatives for a European Union. Moreover, the new French willingness to share power opened up new opportunities for the Germans, allowing them to enmesh the French in an institutional structure that might help neutralize France's advantages in terms of national freedom of action.

The British mainly exercised negative influence at Luxembourg. Yet the internal market and the strengthening of EPC were positive British achievements. In a sense, the British scepticism was only natural, as the British government had from the start been sceptical about the very idea of treaty changes. The acceptance of treaty changes was the biggest single concession made by the British during the SEA process. The very notion of an IGC proved the thin end of a wedge. Smaller members obtained side-payments in areas like environmental protection (Denmark) and regional policy (Ireland, Greece).

Whereas France failed in its attempt to set up a general secretariat for foreign and security policy, one cannot help noticing the German imprint on the SEA. The internal market was a long-standing German goal, although the British thought that the internal market programme might be used to open up the protected service sector in the German economy. The new powers of the Parliament were inspired by German proposals. At a general level there is a striking resemblance between the Single European Act and the German–Italian plan published in 1980. Let us recall that the Genscher–Colombo plan had proposed a return to the decision-making procedures of the Treaty of Rome, that is an introduction of qualified majority voting, a strengthening of the European Parliament, an extension of Community competences, efforts at completing the internal market, a closer monetary cooperation, a closer foreign and security cooperation and cooperation regarding international aspects of public order as well as cultural affairs. It had moreover been proposed to sign a 'European Act' to be reviewed five years later. A key element in the proposal had been the wish to create a greater coherence between the economic and political aspects of EC cooperation. Of these ideas only the wish for closer judicial and cultural collaboration and the proposal for a defence council failed to find its way to the SEA.

The crucial point from the German point of view was that a dynamic process of constitutive change in the Community had been initiated. The strategy of expansive gradualism had been stressed in the Genscher–Colombo plan. Europe had to merge if Germany were to prosper economically and politically, but not at the cost of political instability. A European Union that provoked anxiety would be defeating its purposes.

Notes

1. Hartmut Bühl, 'Deutsch–Französische Sicherheitspartnerschaft', *Dokumente*, Heft 5, 46. Jahrgang, October 1990, p. 372.
2. See Eckart Gaddum, *Die Deutsche Europapolitik in den 80er Jahren*, Munich and Vienna: Ferdinand Schöningh, 1994, p. 205.
3. Gianni Bonvicini, 'The Genscher–Colombo Plan and "The Solemn Declaration on European Union" (1981–1983)', in Roy Pryce (ed.), *The Dynamics of European Union*, London: Croom Helm, 1987, p. 176.
4. *Ibid.*, p. 177.
5. The French memorandum is printed in *Europa-Archiv*. Folge 2, 1982, pp. D 41ff.
6. Gemeinsamer Deutsch–italienischer Vorschlag für die Fortentwicklung der Europäischen Gemeinschaft zur Europäischen Union. Entwurf vom 4

November 1981 für eine Europäische Akte und eine Erklärung zu Fragen der Wirtschaftlichen Integration', *Europa-Archiv*, Folge 2, 1982, pp. 50ff.

7. Bonvicini, *op. cit.*, p. 183.

8. Jean de Ruyt, *L'Acte Unique Européen*, Brussels: Editions de l'Université de Bruxelles, 1989, p. 32.

9. Charles Grant, *Delors. Inside the House that Jacques Built*, London: Nicholas Brealey Publishing, 1994, pp. 50ff.

10. Gaddum, *op. cit.*, pp. 234ff.

11. Hubert Vedrine, *Les Mondes de François Mitterrand*, Paris: Fayard, 1996, p. 291.

12. See Thomas Pedersen, 'Structure or Strategy: The Case of French European Policy after the Cold War', in Georg Sørensen and Hans-Henrik Holm (eds), *And Now What? International Politics after the Cold War*, Aarhus: Politica, 1988, pp. 103–24.

13. 'Let us call things by their name. The main problem is that the political will, one of whose most important representatives is you, Herr Chancellor, cannot easily deal with military power and military reality.' The dinner speech is quoted in *Europa-Archiv*, Folge 2, 1984, pp. D 46ff.

14. 'The spirit of the Treaty of Rome, the spirit of Messina . . . is evidently not to be found in Europe today', *Frankfurter Allgemeine Zeitung*, 8 January 1984, p. 2.

15. This is the assessment of Gaddum, *op. cit.*, pp. 241ff., who has interviewed Joachim Bitterlich, the most important advisor to the chancellor on European affairs.

16. Jean de Ruyt, *op. cit.*, p. 33.

17. *Agence Europe*, 3 February 1984.

18. *Frankfurter Allgemeine Zeitung*, 4 February 1984.

19. Gaddum, *op. cit.*, p. 242.

20. 'provided it does not create new imbalances inside the EC', *Frankfurter Allgemeine Zeitung*, 15 February 1984, p. 2.

21. *Agence Europe*, 25 February 1984.

22. 'the moment has come to give our institutions the coherence that they lack': the speech is printed in *François Mitterrand, Réflexions sur la Politique Etrangère de la France*, Paris: Fayard, pp. 267ff.

23. *Frankfurter Allgemeine Zeitung*, 16 February 1984, p. 1.

24. Howe's speech is printed in *Europa-Archiv*, Folge 7, 1984, pp. D 200ff.

25. Quoted in *Agence Europe*, 27 February 1984.

26. *Le Monde*, 22 March 1984 and *Frankfurter Allgemeine Zeitung*, 22 March 1984, which informs that it is now no longer a taboo to talk about a 'Europe of nine' (i.e. without the UK).

27. *Frankfurter Allgemeine Zeitung*, 30 April 1984.

28. *Agence Europe*, 21 May 1984, p. 3.

29. The speech is printed in *François Mitterrand, Réflexions sur la Politique Extérieure de la France*, Paris: Fayard, pp. 280ff. Spinelli had prepared a draft treaty on European Union approved by the European Parliament on 14 February 1984. See *Europa-Archiv*, Folge 8, 1984, pp. D 209ff.

30. 'how can the complex and diversified entity that the EC has become be governed according to the rules of the Diet of that old Polish Kingdom, in which each member could block the decisions?', *ibid.*, p. 284.

31. *Ibid.*
32. *Frankfurter Allgemeine Zeitung*, 26 May 1984.
33. *Frankfurter Allgemeine Zeitung*, 26 May 1984.
34. *Frankfurter Allgemeine Zeitung*, 29 May 1984.
35. De Ruyt, *op. cit.*, p. 51. Patrick Keatinge and Anna Murphy, 'The European Council's Ad Hoc Committee on Institutional Affairs (1984–85)', in Roy Pryce (ed.), *The Dynamics of European Union*, London: Croom Helm, 1987, p. 219.
36. Vedrine, *op. cit.*, p. 297.
37. Jacques Attali, *Verbatim I, 1983–1986*, Paris: Fayard, 1993, pp. 999ff.
38. *Ibid.*, p. 1000.
39. Grant, *op. cit.*, p. 58.
40. Attali, *op. cit.*, p. 1002. Given the anti-British sentiment in the French foreign policy elite, Attali is probably less credible on the question of the negotiations with the UK than on the description of the Franco–German influence at the summit. It should be added though that his account is broadly confirmed by that of Vedrine.
41. A minor difference between the two accounts is that whereas, according to Attali, Kohl and Mitterrand agree on 65 per cent as the maximum concession, Thatcher says that in a bilateral meeting with her Mitterrand mentions 60 per cent as the maximum.
42. Margaret Thatcher, *The Downing Street Years*, London: HarperCollins, 1993, p. 543.
43. 'The Europe of the 1980s is the pure product of a modern form of enlightened despotism' ... 'European construction has been a voluntarist and elitist procedure par excellence', Vedrine, *op. cit.*, pp. 297ff.
44. Attali, *op. cit.*, p. 1042.
45. Keatinge and Murphy, *op. cit.*, p. 221.
46. Gaddum, *op. cit.*, p. 243 and p. 248.
47. Gaddum, *op. cit.*, p. 249.
48. Keatinge and Murphy, *op. cit.*, p. 226.
49. Gaddum, *op. cit.*, p. 277.
50. Attali, *op. cit.*, p. 1062.
51. Attali, *op. cit.*, p. 1084.
52. Attali, *op. cit.*, p. 1118.
53. Keatinge and Murphy, *op. cit.*, p. 228.
54. 'essentially prepared by France and the French foreign ministry under the aegis of Maurice Faure', *ibid.*
55. 'of the four, there are two incorrigibles, Denmark and Greece. The UK does not like to be isolated from the three other big countries. As for Ireland, the Community is her salvation, for without it she becomes once again a British colony', Attali, *op. cit.*, p. 1173.
56. Attali, *op. cit.*, p. 1197.
57. Attali, *op. cit.*, p. 1218.
58. Thatcher, *op. cit.*, pp. 546 ff.
59. Attali, *op. cit.*, p. 1230.
60. Attali, *op. cit.*, p. 1234.
61. 'here you go too far in formalizing the conversation that I have to have with the

chancellor ... I did not know about this preparatory meeting which does not seem to me to be necessary', Attali, *op. cit.*, p. 1230.

62. Keatinge and Murphy, *op. cit.*, p. 231.
63. Attali, *op. cit.*, p. 1234.
64. Gaddum, *op. cit.*, p. 253.
65. 'when France or the Federal Republic do the same thing, the consequences are different (for the two countries, author)', Attali, *op. cit.*, p. 1238.
66. De Ruyt, *op. cit.*, p. 57.
67. Stephen George, *An Awkward Partner. Britain in the European Community*, Oxford: Oxford University Press, 1994, p. 179.
68. Attali, *op. cit.*, p. 1240.
69. Assuming that Attali is credible we can infer from this that the idea had been suggested by the German side during the preparatory talks.
70. Attali, *op. cit.*, p. 1240.
71. 'Teltschik and I pretended to be meeting for the first time on the project. Ruggiero pretended to be fooled', Attali, *op. cit.*, p. 1245.
72. 'it is a question of creating a genuine political power alongside the Commission and, independently of it, a genuine European foreign affairs ministry with a right to control the votes of the UK and France in the UN', Attali, *op. cit.*
73. *Le Monde*, 29 May 1985, p. 1 and p. 3. Kohl's eagerness to show his European credentials should be seen in connection with the heavy criticism from Helmut Schmidt, the former Chancellor.
74. Attali, *op. cit.*, p. 1257.
75. Vedrine, *op. cit.*, p. 396.
76. De Ruyt, *op. cit.*, p. 61.
77. 'the European Union begins; the member states will decide on the construction of a Union. An Intergovernmental conference will be convened, which will work out the draft treaty until 31 October. The treaty will be discussed and decided upon at the European Council in Luxembourg', Gaddum, *op. cit.*, p. 257.
78. Hans-Dietrich Genscher, *Erinnerungen*, Berlin: Siedler Verlag, 1995, p. 373.
79. Grant, *op. cit.*, p. 72.
80. Genscher, *op. cit.*, p. 373.
81. Pierre Gerbet, 'Le Rôle du Couple France–Allemagne dans la Création et le Développement des Communautés Européennes', in Robert Picht and Wolfgang Wessels (eds), *Motor für Europa?*, Bonn: Europa Union Verlag, 1990, p. 115.
82. According to Gaddum, *op. cit.*, p. 256.
83. Attali even suggests that it was on French insistence that Craxi called a vote, but this seems less credible. Attali, *op. cit.*, p. 1259.
84. See de Ruyt, *op. cit.*, p. 62.
85. George, *op. cit.*, p. 182.
86. George, *op. cit.*, p. 183.
87. Thatcher, *op. cit.*, p. 551.
88. Thatcher, *op. cit.*, p. 550.
89. Grant, *op. cit.*, p. 75. Delors' own claim is 85 per cent.
90. Grant, *op. cit.*, *passim*.

91. Gaddum. *op. cit.*, p. 265.
92. Richard Corbett, 'The 1985 Intergovernmental Conference and the Single European Act', in Roy Pryce (ed.), *The Dynamics of European Union*, London: Croom Helm, 1987, p. 242.
93. De Ruyt, *op. cit.*, p. 79. De Ruyt quotes Tindemans.
94. Vedrine, *op. cit.*, p. 396.
95. Interestingly, Vedrine calls his chapter on the SEA *Le Forcing Européen.*
96. De Ruyt, *op. cit.*, p. 79.
97. Corbett, *op. cit.*, p. 247.
98. Thatcher, *op. cit.*, p. 554f.
99. Gaddum, *op. cit.*, p. 267.
100. See *Franco–German Draft Treaty on European Union*, presented at the European Council in Milan on 28–29 June 1985, Copenhagen: Danish Ministry of Foreign Affairs.
101. De Ruyt, *op. cit.*, p. 87.
102. Grant, *op. cit.*, p. 74.
103. Grant, *op. cit.*
104. See George Ross, *Jacques Delors and European Integration*, Cambridge: Polity Press, 1995, p. 41.
105. *Ibid.*, p. 42.
106. Corbett, *op. cit.*, p. 249.
107. Grant, *op. cit.*, p. 79.
108. See Maria Green Cowles, 'Setting the Agenda for a New Europe: The ERT and EC 1992', *Journal of Common Market Studies*, Vol. 33/4, December 1995.
109. See *Europe 1990*, speech given by Dr W. Dekker at the Centre for European Policy Studies in Brussels, on the occasion of the presentation of the programme *Europe 1990 – An Agenda For Action*.
110. There is some uncertainty as to who actually thought up the idea of 1992 but according to Grant it originated in the Commission. See Grant, *op. cit.*, p. 67.
111. Grant, *op. cit.*, p. 141.
112. While Grant offers what appears to be a sober description of Delors' role, Ross's portrait is too panegyrical.
113. Obviously this assessment may reflect the observer's own subjective views.
114. See Thomas Pedersen, '*EF – en supermagt i svøb? Vesteuropæisk sikkerhedspolitisk samarbejde udenfor NATO*', unpublished dissertation, Copenhagen, 1989.

8 Structural asymmetry: the Maastricht Treaty

Although the press treated it rather disparagingly at the time the Single European Act contained the seeds of further integration.[1] The domestic market had been defined sufficiently broadly to permit linkages to be made to other areas of cooperation. Advocates of European union notably in the Commission and in France, Italy and Germany soon began to point to the functional logic linking a domestic market to a monetary union. A convincing case could also be made that free movement of people would have deleterious effects unless accompanied by closer police cooperation.

In the late 1980s, the external parameters of European integration also changed dramatically, as the Berlin wall came down and the states of Central and Eastern Europe became independent. There was no inevitability about the EC's integrative response to these events. Without a common adversary to bolster Western European cohesion and solidarity, it would not have been illogical for the EC countries to have given up their concept of a 'smaller Europe' in favour of a broader and looser framework. Yet Franco–German leadership ensured that a different strategy prevailed. Balance-of-fear considerations dictated that Germany pay a price for unification, the price being defined by the French as a reinforcement of the cooperative element in German hegemony. The resurgence of US power under President Bush also helped preserve Franco–German cohesion. Neither of the two countries wished to abandon the strategy of region-state balancing and both feared that a rapid enlargement towards the East might undermine it. Germany was eager to stabilize the Central and Eastern European area

120

and regarded integration in a tight integration structure as the best way of extending cooperative hegemony towards the East. France was determined to prevent Germany from filling the power vacuum which had emerged in Central and Eastern Europe after the Soviet withdrawal.

Reinforcing the core

The first years after the conclusion of the Single European Act were characterized by a certain reinforcement of the Franco–German relationship described by Hubert Vedrine as *à la fois condition sine qua non, moteur et bénéficiaire de la construction européenne.*[2] The relationship was developing a certain momentum of its own with a whole network of advisors and officials oiling its wheels. But the relationship remained ambiguous. The endeavour to relaunch Europe was accompanied by continuing intra-hegemonic rivalry. Germany appeared keen to go beyond economic integration, thereby enhancing its military-political status and at the same time stabilizing its relationship with France. During 1986 Germany approached military leaders in France on several occasions seeking to obtain a right to be consulted regarding the use of France's tactical nuclear weapons. Mitterrand informed Kohl that he could accept consultation but not co-decision.[3] From the German point of view a turning-point was the conclusion of an agreement on 28 February 1986 on nuclear consultations.[4]

In July the following year Teltschik apparently demanded a genuine German *droit de regard* concerning French decisions on nuclear matters. Vedrine asks himself in his memoirs whether Teltschik had a mandate from Kohl to make such demands, calling Teltschik 'a real German nationalist'. On the same occasion German officials proposed the creation of a Franco–German defence council. The French immediately demanded a monetary council in return.[5] The two councils were duly established in the course of 1988. Significantly, in October 1987 Mitterrand had to put an end to nuclear discussions between the German and French military which had continued despite his instructions to the contrary.[6]

Concurrently, Mitterrand was trying to pull Germany into a new European military structure which would provide an outlet for German ambitions, while realizing old French visions. But apparently he was not sure about the reliability of the Germans or about France's ability to control the FRG within a bilateral framework. Thus he told González that in order to make European military integration durable and irreversible, the joint military units had to be enlarged with Italy and Spain.[7] At the G7 summit in Venice in June 1987 Mitterrand and Kohl decided to reinforce Franco–German defence relations. Mitterrand spoke of concluding a new bilateral treaty similar to the Elysée treaty. Kohl declared that he was prepared to set up completely integrated Franco–German military units.

In January 1988 the Federal Republic took over the presidency of the EC. In Story's formulation 'Germany was now gearing up to act as the federator of the EC at least in the monetary dimension'.[8] At the beginning of 1988 France and Germany celebrated the 25th anniversary of the conclusion of the Elysée treaty. On this occasion Kohl said that 'France and Germany must together build the hard core of a European Union'. He 'warmly invited' his European partners to take part in this effort, but added that the two would not let themselves be diverted from carrying the Union forward.[9] The term 'hard core' was new and could be interpreted as signalling a new departure in German policy. It placed France and Germany in a separate category, increasing the distance from the UK.

The push for economic and monetary union

At the same time, a certain momentum for further monetary integration was developing. Balladur, the French minister for economy, finance and privatization under the co-habitation, was leading a battle to reform the EMS. His arguments were essentially technical but the motives were also political – the wish to regain control of the French economy mixed with the traditional goal of using Germany in a global strategy.[10] Balladur sought to introduce greater symmetry in the operation of the EMS, notably in the obligation to defend currencies under attack. Under the EMS regime the FRG was making structural gains through the Deutschmark's undervaluation.[11] The global currency crisis of that year provided Balladur with new arguments for demanding a monetary reform. The Basil-Nyborg agreements of September 1987 went some way towards accommodating Balladur's criticism, but the French were not satisfied. Concurrently, Commission President Delors was pressing for monetary reform as a corollary to the internal market. At Delors' initiative a group of economists led by the Italian Padoa-Schioppa published a report urging greater coordination of monetary policy.[12]

At first the German reaction was reserved.[13] Kohl is reported to have opposed Balladur's plans in off-the-cuff remarks in January 1988.[14] However, the German position soon changed and Germany began to advocate new constitutional negotiations on economic and monetary union. The financial crash of October 1987, which led to acrimonious exchanges across the Atlantic, exposed the FRG's isolation and counselled closer cooperation with the EMS partners.[15] Another factor which forced the Germans onto the defensive was the fact that the French authorities now declared themselves willing to fulfil one of the most important German preconditions for accepting reforms: liberalization of capital movements. At the meeting of economics and finance ministers in February 1988 Balladur welcomed the directive on capital liberalization. But he said that France's acceptance of the directive depended on reforms of the EMS.[16]

In part the softening of the German position may also have been due to pressure from the strongly pro-integrationist foreign ministry which was orchestrating the incoming German presidency and was thus in a stronger position than normal within the German government. The foreign ministry felt the need for a symbolic 'western initiative' to balance its new opening towards Gorbachev's USSR. Finally, the Germans may have reasoned that one could deflect the French pressure and gain time by lifting the debate from the concrete to the constitutional level. In case the German opening were to lead to new treaty reforms, Germany had reason to expect that it would be able to obtain considerable concessions *inter alia* by linking EMU to other issues. Yet, although such short-term considerations were undoubtedly of some importance, they do not constitute a convincing explanation of such a wide-ranging decision as the support for a fully-fledged European Monetary Union.

The German conversion should thus probably be interpreted as a more strategic initiative. At the beginning of the year in a speech to the EP outlining the programme of the incoming German presidency, Genscher had signalled Germany's interest in accelerating the process of economic and monetary union. His arguments are noteworthy. The first two arguments are well-known: the internal market created spillover effects calling for economic and monetary integration and the recent crisis in the international financial markets demonstrated the need for closer monetary cooperation. His third argument is more interesting. Drawing attention to the high degree of convergence around the 'German' economic and monetary philosophy, Genscher adds: '*Die Voraussetzungen dafür* (i.e. for economic and monetary Union, author) *sind gut, vielleicht besser als zu irgendeinem Zeitpunkt in der Geschichte der Gemeinschaft*, and '*entscheidend ist, dass diese Währungsunion zu einer Stabilitätsgemeinschaft wird*'.[17] Here the goal of economic and monetary union towards which Germany – including Genscher himself – had previously expressed considerable scepticism is implicitly portrayed as a long-standing German goal. What he is in fact saying is that Germany ought to seize the opportunity for locking in German economic principles.

On 26 February 1988 Genscher published a paper on the need for monetary union. The paper carried the title *Memorandum on a European Monetary Space and a European Central Bank*. It emphasized the spillover effects of the internal market and the common interest of the Europeans in reducing dependence on the dollar.[18] No doubt the monetary crisis the previous year had made an impact on the German debate, strengthening the position of the foreign ministry and the chancellery vis-à-vis the sector ministries. But as we have seen, Genscher had included the monetary area in his *Dreikönig* speech as early as 1981.

In his memoirs, Genscher describes the new German campaign for monetary integration as in part motivated by a wish to complement the new rapprochement with the East with a reassuring initiative directed at the West Europeans – in other words one of the tactical *sowohl-als-auch* ('both-and') gestures so typical of the West German foreign ministry. But interestingly, he also points out that the domestic reaction to his proposal was 'surprisingly positive' '*insbesondere aus Kreisen der deutschen Wirtschaft*' (especially in circles within the German economy).[19] The German government was essentially coming round to the view that a harmonization of monetary policy, just as harmonization of technical standards, might be beneficial to German industry especially if the new European monetary system mirrored the German system.

France immediately seized what it saw as an opportunity to put its pet project into effect. During the spring of 1988 France and Germany made a joint effort to accelerate the process of monetary integration. Referring to the broad definition of the internal market and basing its efforts on a Commission directive, the German government pressed for a liberalization of capital movements, a proposal adopted in June 1988. Liberalization was to take effect within two years. In a statement on the outcome of the Toronto G7 summmit, Kohl made clear that Germany wanted the Hanover summit to set up a committee on Economic and Monetary Union. Delors and others wanted a committee of experts. Seeking to capitalize on the standing of the German *Bundesbank*, Kohl instead suggested a committee composed of the heads of the central banks with a few experts thrown in. He added that '*es ist selbverständlich, dass die Bundesrepublik Deutschland in diese Diskussion ihre hervorragenden Erfahrungen mit der Bundesbank, mit deren Unabhängigkeit, dezentraler Organization und vor allem mit ihrer Verpflichtung auf die Geldwertstabilität einbringen wird*'.[20]

Taking a middle position between Genscher and the *Bundesbank*, Kohl also called for caution in the handling of this sensitive area, referring to 'preconditions' and 'intermediate steps' in the process of economic and monetary union.[21]

The Hanover summit

At the Hanover summit in June 1988 the first concrete steps in the direction of a European monetary union were taken. Ignoring the pressure of the French, Kohl broke the link between liberalization of capital movements and fiscal harmonization. Liberalization of capital movements would not be conditional. Besides, on Kohl's initiative the summit decided to set up a committee composed of the governors of the central banks assisted by three independent personalities which was to prepare a report on Economic and Monetary Union.[22] Kohl was linking technical reforms to constitutional changes, in the process pulling France in a federal direction.

The established wisdom in the EMU literature is that EMU would be against German interests. This view can be challenged on both economic and political grounds, although granting other countries an influence over German monetary policy obviously involved a risk. Economically, while the existing EMS was certainly beneficial to Germany, protecting it from devaluations by its European partners and keeping the Deutschmark lower than it would otherwise have been, the problem for Germany was that the EMS was fragile. It did not irrevocably lock exchange rates, leaving open the possibility that a country like France might break out of the system. Indeed, Balladur, the French Prime Minister had shown signs of wanting to pursue a more independent economic policy. A full-scale EMU would provide German industry with a rock-solid guarantee against competitive devaluations within the EMU zone. The price would be the sharing of power over monetary policy decisions. But since EMU without German participation was impossible, Germany had an exit option which it could use to extract concessions from its partners in the EC. If a European Monetary System could be shaped according to German wishes, establishing a structural congruence between the German and the EC economic-monetary system, this would moreover give German industry a distinct advantage over the other EC economies. The FRG seemed simply to be heading for a European economic space governed by German economic precepts.[23] The hard question is whether asymmetrical monetary integration was a deliberate German strategy or the outcome of unforeseen developments. Judging from Kohl's statements in 1988, Germany was deliberately aiming for structural asymmetry in the economic sphere. Some sources claim that Genscher's memorandum had not been cleared with the government.[24] Yet in terms of substance Kohl did not seem to differ with his minister. The (public) differences must be interpreted as tactical.

To this should be added the linkage to other areas of EC constitutive politics. Even if German negotiators did not fully succeed in the EMU negotiations, they still stood a very good chance of using EMU to extract concessions from their partners in the political sphere, especially in view of the fact that EMU without German participation was hard to envisage. Apart from these strategic calculations, the foreign ministry in particular felt a need to somehow respond to the growing pressure from France.[25] The setting up of the Delors committee accommodated France without this implying immediate costs for the FRG.

In the Delors committee, Delors appears to have kept a low profile. 'His contribution was small, but we made him famous', is Karl-Otto Pöhl's stinging comment.[26] Karl-Otto Pöhl and his supporters managed to persuade the rest of the committee to adopt a 'fundamentalist' approach which meant focusing on the final shape of the institutions and on the need for a new treaty. Germany would accept nothing less than a fundamentalist model of EMU, Pöhl argued.[27]

What interests the *Bundesbank* were defending is not altogether clear. Realists will expect it to have defended national interests notwithstanding its formal autonomy. It is perfectly possible for a transnational actor like the *Bundesbank* operating in the Delors committee to pay attention to the needs of its home country, although as a member of an epistemic community of central bankers it undoubtedly also acted on the basis of a professional ethos. In the case of comparatively 'weak states' like Germany it is even natural to expect societal actors to assume some of the traditional foreign policy tasks of the state apparatus.

During the second half of 1988 and the first months of 1989 Franco–

German preparations for a new series of constitutive reforms of the EC continued. At a Franco–German meeting in early April 1989 it became clear to the French that Chancellor Kohl not only wanted to consolidate Franco–German and European collaboration following the SEA, but even wanted to accelerate integration. Kohl wanted to initiate talks on further monetary integration at the Madrid summit in June 1989. In addition Kohl wanted new European initiatives in the areas of security and asylum policy. He also indicated that he would like a debate on the establishment of a European police force along the lines of the American FBI to commence during the French EC presidency.[28]

The Delors report was published in April 1989.[29] It called for the creation of a European economic and monetary union in three stages. In the first stage, which the report said should start no later than 1 July 1990, there would be a removal of all barriers to the free flow of goods and services and a single financial system without capital controls. During this stage there would also be closer coordination of economic and monetary policy, the committee of central bank governors would be given a greater role, all currencies would be included in the Exchange Rate Mechanism (ERM) and the structural funds would be expanded to assist weaker economies. The second stage would be transitional and would prepare the way for the third and final stage. In the third stage a European System of Central Banks would be set up, exchange rates being irrevocably fixed.[30]

The rest of the Community received these proposals with polite interest. Not surprisingly, the economic ministries were the most cautious and ECOFIN (the council of economic and financial ministers) soon became the preferred platform of the EMU-sceptics. At an informal meeting of ECOFIN in May 1989 at S'agaro, the EMU-sceptics made some headway. The Benelux countries leaned towards the pragmatic position of the British chancellor. Even Theo Waigel, the German finance minister, seemed to agree with the British. The German and British ministers thus managed to decouple stage 1 from stages 2 and 3.[31]

At the Madrid summit in June 1989, the UK mounted a counter-offensive against the Delors plan. Thatcher argued that the report ought not to be the only basis for discussion, that there should be nothing automatic about the establishment of full economic and monetary union and that there should be no decision now to go ahead with an IGC on monetary union.[32] Signalling a certain flexibility she also announced that the UK would join the ERM 'once the time was right', spelling out five conditions.

At the other extreme, Mitterrand wanted a deadline for stages 2 and 3 to be laid down in Madrid. In this he did not succeed. With the support of Kohl, Thatcher managed to avoid the fixing of deadlines for the second and third phases.[33] Taking the middle ground between France which had the support of Italy, Spain, Belgium and the Commission, and the UK which was supported by Denmark, Kohl came up with a compromise formulation saying that the Delors report defined 'a' process leading to EMU and not 'the' process and that the IGC would only be convened some time after 1 July 1990 after full and adequate preparations. This formulation was accepted by all member states.[34] At the same time, Kohl made it clear that he wanted an intergovernmental conference to decide on transfers of sovereignty to a European System of Central Banks. According to the *Frankfurter Allgemeine Zeitung*, Kohl went further than Delors, who only stated that the process of monetary integration must not be stopped and that the three phases constituted an integrated whole.[35]

French acceleration and German back-tracking

In July 1989 France took over the presidency and accelerated the preparations for EMU. France was determined to secure a commitment to economic and monetary union under its presidency. A committee was set up consisting of representatives from the foreign and European ministries, presided over by the French minister for European affairs. The committee was asked to prepare the agenda for an IGC and produced a report containing a number of questions and answers regarding the second and third stage of EMU. Several member states, notably the UK, did not regard this as sufficient preparation. In November the foreign ministers took note of the report, referring the decision to the European Council.[36]

While committed to the EMU plan the German Chancellor soon began back-tracking as regards the timetable. According to Genscher both Kohl and the ministry of finance remained committed to EMU, but Kohl argued that a rapid convening of an IGC might have a negative impact on his party's score at the parliamentary elections in December 1990.[37] However, overall security considerations were strengthening the hand of the French. On 9 November 1989 the wall separating Eastern and Western Berlin came down.

On 28 November Kohl outlined his 10-point programme on the

future of Germany – without prior consultation with the French. This omission formed part of a wider pattern of growing Franco–German tension. On 18 November the heads of state and government of the EC had met in Paris for a special summit convened by Mitterrand without prior consultation with the Germans. On 22 November Mitterrand had announced that he would be meeting Gorbachev in Kiev on 6 December, a step that provoked some nervousness in the Federal Republic.

In the run-up to the summit Mitterrand managed to obtain the support of the Dutch for a rapid transition to EMU, the Dutch having so far argued for a go-slow approach. The Dutch were now accepting the French view that, for high politics reasons, the EMU project had to be accelerated.[38] This change was important since the Netherlands had so far acted as staunch supporters of the German position in the EC. The Dutch had traditionally fulfilled the function of legitimizing German policy vis-à-vis the smaller members of the Community. However, while the Dutch had tended to ally with Germany on technical and economic issues they now leaned towards the UK and France as the question of Germany's future role in Europe came to the fore.[39]

In the days prior to the Strasbourg summit the temperature in the Franco–German relationship was thus at an all-time low. To make matters worse, Kohl sent Mitterrand a private letter three days before the summit in which he asked that the idea of convening an IGC in the second half of 1990 be dropped. As justification Kohl referred to the negative effect such a decision might have on his party's chances in the parliamentary elections in December 1990. Delors appears to have tried to make Mitterrand understand Kohl's worries.[40] According to the Italian-oriented *Agence Europe* Kohl also demanded that the summit give clear signals regarding the establishment of a political union. He placed special emphasis on the need to strengthen the European Parliament. Such a strengthening would have to take place before the elections to the EP in 1994.[41] In his diary Kohl's advisor, Horst Teltschik, gives an altogether different account describing the letter as '*ein weiterer Schritt auf Mitterrand zu*' (a further step towards Mitterrand).[42] Yet, apart from the fact that the timing of the letter was highly inconvenient, it is difficult to see how new demands in an area where France and Germany were known to be at odds could be described as a conciliatory move.

Despite the tension within the core the Strasbourg summit managed to agree, by 11 to 1, to convene an IGC one year later. The IGC was to last one year.[43] According to the *Frankfurter Allgemeine Zeitung* Kohl had backed down and accepted Mitterrand's timetable in a last-minute telephone conversation.[44] In return, Kohl obtained a concession on the institutional question. The question of institutional reforms would thus be addressed alongside the economic and monetary issues.[45] Mitterrand said at a press conference after the summit that he would have preferred 'not to mix things up', that is he would have preferred to deal with institutional matters like the power of the parliament 'in a second phase' after the conclusion of the treaty changes regarding EMU.[46] According to Teltschik, Kohl also made a plea for granting the European Council new powers of control vis-à-vis the Commission and the European institutions in general.[47] Thus while publicly committed to a federal union in concrete negotiations, Kohl was trying to strengthen the intergovernmental institution where he by virtue of his status and Germany by virtue of its size would be able to wield the greatest influence.

At the margins of the Strasbourg summit Thatcher held two private meetings with Mitterrand at his suggestion. The talks dealt with the issue of German unification. According to Thatcher, Mitterrand was even more concerned than she about the developments in Germany and was very critical of Kohl's ten-point plan. However, unlike Thatcher, he thought there was nothing one could do to stop unification. While broadly agreeing in their analysis, Thatcher and Mitterrand disagreed totally when it came to the question of how to react to growing German power.[48] While Thatcher may have had her own political reasons for exaggerating French animosity towards Germany, Mitterrand's actions also spoke their own clear language.

Political union

During the first months of 1990, plans for additional reforms of the EC were launched. Under the heading of 'political union', issues like the institutional deepening of integration and a common foreign and security policy were put on the EC's official agenda. It is not entirely clear when the idea first surfaced. At the discursive level, it had circulated at least since the beginning of 1989, when Jacques Delors had called for a relaunch of 'political Europe'. As we have seen, Kohl had broached the issue of institutional reform in talks with Mitterrand during 1989.

The pressure for an extension of the IGC agenda thus came mainly from the German side. Teltschik relates how at a trilateral Franco–

German–British conference in Oxford in January 1990, he drew attention to the fact that Kohl had offered France a common foreign policy as early as 1987 and a common *Ostpolitik* in January 1988 – without getting a response from Paris.[49] As described in an earlier chapter, the German side had started pushing for closer Franco–German consultations on the use of the French nuclear weapons immediately after the Single European Act had become effective. Aware of France's keen interest in what they called *l'Europe puissance* (power Europe), which in concrete terms translated into a closer foreign policy and defence integration, the Germans placed the emphasis on these areas in their attempt to persuade the French to embark on a process of political unification alongside the economic and monetary unification.

In February 1990, the French and German leaders met in Paris to discuss German unification. According to the *Frankfurter Allgemeine Zeitung* a high degree of understanding was reached. Thus it was decided to hold an extraordinary summit on German unification on 28 April. As regards EMU Mitterrand, clearly nervous at the prospect of having to negotiate EMU with an already unified Germany, wanted to convene the IGC before December, but expressed understanding for Kohl's domestic political problems.[50] The two leaders also decided to propose the convening of another IGC on political union to run concurrently with the IGC on EMU.

During the second half of February and in March, Kohl's and Mitterrand's advisors set to work trying to flesh out a common approach to 'political union'. Teltschik comments in his diary: '*nach langer Zeit konnten wir Paris wieder zu einer gemeinsamen EG-Initiative bewegen*'.[51] Although it may in part reflect Teltschik's self-congratulatory style and an unconscious tendency to inflate the German role in European politics, the comment fits into a larger pattern of a very active German policy based on a coherent and long-term strategy. In his diary Teltschik thus quotes Kohl as saying in a speech to the *Bundestag* that German and European unification were intertwined and that the process of German unification would function as a 'catalyst' for the acceleration of Europe's integration in the direction of a political union.[52] The statement is interesting in that it places the goal of political union at the level of a national interest alongside German unification.

It is worth drawing attention to the context in which Kohl's statement was made. Had Kohl been addressing, say, the French, the statement would not have been surprising. However here, apart from foreign states with an interest in German unification, he is addressing an audience which, although sympathetic towards European union, can be expected to have been mainly concerned about German unity. A government declaration to parliament on foreign policy can be expected to some extent to try to accommodate the views of the opposition. Kohl's statement thus also shows the extent to which political union was a goal shared by the majority of politicians in Germany.

Although the initiative for the second IGC came from the German side, the French had also for some time been contemplating an initiative on political Europe. However, their definitions of political union differed. To the Germans, political union basically meant a strengthening of the EC institutions, notably the EP, and more frequent use of majority voting. The French were mainly interested in common foreign and security policy, although as we have seen they were far from being alone in wanting reforms in this area.[53] Going back to the Fouchet plan of the early 1960s, the French definition of political union was a confederal structure dealing with foreign policy and security questions.

In a speech in Berlin in early March Dumas, the French foreign minister, spoke of German unification in positive terms. He also talked about the 'determined will to construct Europe's political union'. In this connection he referred to Mitterrand's term 'a community of destiny' between the two countries, interpreting this as including a French commitment to defend German soil and to envisage elements of a common security and defence policy.[54]

Although the atmosphere between Bonn and Paris thus seemed to gradually improve, the Polish question continued to pose problems. France regarded with concern Kohl's unwillingness to guarantee the inviolability of the Polish–German border. Kohl's somewhat legalistic counterargument was that only a unified German parliament could provide such a guarantee. Underlying the sharp French rebuke to Germany over the Polish question was probably the more fundamental worry about the timing of the IGC on EMU. In early March Kohl thus told a press conference in Bonn that although German unification should be part of the whole European architecture, it would not be realistic to 'synchronize the monetary union of the two German states and that of the Community'.[55] Kohl was of course fully aware that synchronization was precisely what Mitterrand wanted.

Mitterrand expressed his support for the Polish demand that the inviolability of the German–Polish border be guaranteed in an international legally-binding treaty prior to German unification. Mitterrand also wanted Poland to be associated with the talks on Germany. Kohl did not react to these statements by Mitterrand. Telephone conversations which Mitterrand had announced would take place the following day did not take place.[56] However, the following day Dumas and Genscher tried to mend fences, declaring that France and Germany were in agreement that Poland should participate in the negotiations on Poland's Western border.

In late March 1990 Kohl held a meeting with Jacques Delors and his commissioners in Brussels. After the meeting he stated that, due to the speed with which German unification was taking place, European integration had to be accelerated. In December a second IGC would have to be prepared alongside EMU. In a veiled criticism of Margaret Thatcher, Kohl said that those who were apprehensive about German unification ought to work for institutional changes in the EC, since such changes would help tie Germany to Europe.[57] The statement is a perfect illustration of the German strategy of cooptation through the granting of voice-opportunity. Yet much like de Gaulle, Thatcher had an optimistic view of her country's alternatives calculating, probably correctly, that her country continued to possess an exit option. Moreover, her style and the style of the political system in which she had been educated was adversarial, not wont to compromise.

In April, eight days before an extraordinary summit in Dublin, Mitterrand and Kohl addressed a letter to their colleagues formally proposing the convening of an IGC on political union. The proposal was endorsed in Dublin, albeit without a specific date being fixed. Several member states, notably Denmark, the UK and Portugal, expressed reservations about a fast move towards a political union.[58] But the majority was in favour of the proposal, although it was widely felt that the concept of political union needed clarification. Having just won the first free elections in the DDR in a resounding victory, Kohl was in a very strong position. The Dublin summit also decided that German unification would take place without renegotiation of the EC treaties and it was decided to increase aid for Central and Eastern Europe. According to Vedrine, Mitterrand surprised everybody at the summit by declaring that he wanted to move towards a system with a *finalité fédéraliste*.[59]

On 22 June 1990 Kohl and Mitterrand met in Bingen-Büdesheim to prepare for the ordinary summit in Dublin in late June. Characteristically, the talk concentrated on the broad direction of EC politics. The two leaders thus agreed that the Dublin summit should make a formal decision on the convening of an IGC on political union, as well as a decision on the timetable of the two IGCs. Teltschik, again perhaps in part with an eye to his domestic audience, does not mince words: '*Sie beschliessen auf dem EG-Gipfel in Dublin eine Entscheidung über die Einrichtung einer Regierungskonferenz zur politischen Union herbeizuführen und den Termin für die Eröffnung dieser Konferenz sowie der zur Wirtschafts- und Währungsunion festzulegen*'.[60] And so the summit did.[61]

Although the French political elite had gradually come round to accepting the fact of German unification seeing that Germany would offer its partners a voice-opportunity, there was little willingness in France to adapt the Community institutions to the reality of Germany's increased population. The institutional parity between France and Germany was expected to continue. Thus one of the most pro-European French politicians, former president Giscard d'Estaing, stated in an interview with *Le Figaro* in July 1990 that France would not ratify a treaty which did not guarantee parity between France and Germany.[62]

Having reached an agreement on procedure in the spring of 1990, France and Germany proceeded to try to harmonize their positions on issues of substance. During a summit in Munich in September Kohl suggested a joint initiative at the IGC on political union. The suggestion had been preceded by preparations at the level of advisors. Teltschik relates how he had approached Attali in early September. Commenting upon Attali's reaction he writes: '*er geht – wie immer – davon aus, dass wir ihm einen Entwurf zuleiten. Wir arbeiten bereits daran*'.[63] It is difficult to determine to what extent Teltschik's account is credible. If the diary has been written in the shadow of events and has not been subjected to major editing *post festum*, it tells us a lot about German and French behaviour. The concentrated and businesslike style suggests that this might have been the case. Of course this does not exclude the possibility that the author has at a later stage added slightly jingoistic formulations aimed at the domestic audience. Assuming that it is largely credible, Teltschik's account of the preparations on political union tells us something about the differences in style and the division of labour between the two leading EU members during the period in question. Unfortunately, we are not in a position to assess Teltschik's characterization of the French negotiating style as reactive. In the concrete context, it is natural to expect the German side to have been the most active, since the Germans were the ones pressing for political union. We can in any case infer from the assertion that the Chancellor's office was eager to be well prepared and one step ahead when entering into negotiations with the French on political union. Teltschik's claim is interesting in that it goes against conventional wisdom which portrays

Germany as a badly coordinated EU negotiator. While this may be the case in everyday politics, it is hardly the case in constitutive politics.

Yet it was easier to persuade the French to accept a statement of intent than to get them to carry it out. Following a meeting between Kohl and Mitterrand on 17–18 September 1990, Teltschik thus congratulates himself and his colleagues in the German government for having achieved a breakthrough with the French in the direction of a common foreign policy.[64] As if as an afterthought, however, he adds the caveat that the question is how many of these undertakings can be implemented.

The common statement from the Munich meeting echoed German thinking, stating that 'the process of European union has been a determining factor in favouring upheavals in Central and Eastern Europe and German unification. This evolution will accelerate the union of Europe'.[65] Although it may simply be seen as an attempt on the part of the EC leaders to take the credit for the Eastern European revolution, while at the same time reassuring Germany's neighbours, the statement fits into a larger picture. It illustrates the German idea of the 'magnetic attraction' of a superior regional 'core' with a centripetal effect in the wider system. The statement brings to mind Karl Deutsch's concept of core, but the use of the concept differs from the Deutschian in that core formation is seen as a strategic concept and not solely as a structural phenomenon. It is possible to draw a parallel to the centripetal effect of the *Zollverein*. To the extent that political loyalty is seen to be based on the quality of the concrete output of a political system, the strategy brings to mind more modern functional arguments.

During the second half of 1990 the presidency passed over to Italy. For Italy the crucial issue at the IGCs was EMU and a strengthening of the European Parliament. The preceding months had seen efforts on the part of the Commission to link monetary union to completion of the internal market. In line with the arguments of the German foreign ministry a Commission document, *Economic and Monetary Union*, published in August 1990, argued that the full potential of the internal market could only be achieved if a common currency were introduced. As pointed out by Sandholz, this neo-functionalist proposition was flawed on two counts. The functional argument was not compelling since currency competition might achieve the same results as monetary integration. Even among central bank directors some treated the spillover thesis with a certain forebearance.[66] The political spillover thesis holds that spillover involves a learning process. But as Sandholz points out, in the case of EMU such a learning process had not had time to occur.[67] From this it does not follow that the efforts of the Commission were fruitless. The point is that the linkage between the internal market and EMU was essentially a political linkage, an element in a strategy of incremental integration.

During the autumn of 1990 the debate concentrated on the timing of the transition to the second and third stage of EMU. Here a 'go-slow' coalition consisting of the *Bundesbank*, the Netherlands and, to some extent also, Luxembourg were lining up against a 'fast-track' coalition consisting of France, Italy and Belgium, supported by the Commission. In the course of the debate, several countries had moved closer to the go-slow coalition. Most importantly the Spanish government proposed to delay the transition to the second stage from 1993 to 1994 and to stretch it until the year 2000.

It had become increasingly clear that no additional regional aid would accompany EMU. As seen from Madrid this deprived EMU of some of its attraction. By the early autumn of 1990 a majority coalition had in fact formed around the German convergence-first view with only France, Italy and Belgium favouring the fast-track approach.[68]

In October with German unification accomplished Kohl made it clear that he could support a transition to the second stage by 1994, as proposed by the Spanish. The way was now cleared for an extraordinary summit in Rome in late October to formally decide that the second stage of EMU would commence on 1 January 1994 despite British opposition. The Italian presidency pushed to a vote the proposal to set a target date for the start of the second stage. The outcome was 11 to 1.[69] The summit also decided the terms of reference of the IGCs which were to begin in December of 1990.[70] However, Kohl still was not prepared to agree to a deadline for the transition to the third stage of EMU. As regards political union the summit decided (once again in the face of British reservations) that '*L'Union est un processus progressif nécessitant une extension des compétences*' (the Union is an ongoing process, a necessary part of which is an extension of its competences). Likewise the 12 agreed on the objective of a common foreign and security policy. The decisions on EMU were to prove fatal for Margaret Thatcher. With the EC now moving from words to deeds, concern grew in the Conservative Party that the UK would be isolated.[71] In November 1990 Thatcher was replaced by John Major as leader of the Conservative Party and Prime Minister.

A week before the ordinary EU summit in December 1990 Kohl and

Mitterrand made public a joint initiative regarding political union. Their letter, which was addressed to the president of the Council, deserves to be dealt with in some detail. It gives an impression of how far the two countries were willing to go at the IGC on political union. It would, however, probably be wrong to interpret the letter as reflecting the negotiating goals of the two countries, since it is possible that for tactical reasons the joint proposal included some of the suggestions made by other member states.[72] However, the IGC having not yet officially started, the two leading countries cannot have had a very clear idea of where their partners would want to put their foot down. Thus the text must be regarded as a reasonably accurate reflection of the Franco–German opening position.

- The letter proposes an extension of the competences of the EC in areas such as environmental protection, health, social policy, energy, research and technology and protection of consumers.
- The letter proposes that certain questions which had so far been dealt with in an intergovernmental framework should be transferred to the Union's sphere of action. Issues like immigration, visa policy, right of asylum, the fight against drugs and international organized crime are mentioned in this context. It is suggested that a council of ministers of the interior and ministers of justice might be created. It is added that the new treaty should include a new provision permitting the transfer of new competences to the Union through a decision of the European Council supported by a majority in the EP.
- The letter mentions several initiatives aimed at strengthening the Community's democratic legitimacy. A genuine European citizenship is proposed and a right of co-decision for the EP is envisaged. It is furthermore proposed that the nomination of the Commission and its President should be confirmed by a majority of the Parliament.
- The two countries propose that the Community be made more efficient. This presupposes first of all a strengthening of the European Council and secondly that qualified majority be made the normal rule for Community matters.
- The letter wants foreign policy cooperation to be extended to all areas. It recommends that the European Council define a number of common action areas such as relations with the USSR and the Conference on Security and Cooperation in Europe. It

is moreover proposed that the European Council may define concrete implementing decisions, which might be subject to majority decisions. Finally, it is proposed that the political union should include a genuine security policy which might in the longer term lead to a common defence.

The letter elicited a quite strong response from the Dutch. In a letter to the Italian presidency, the Dutch Prime Minister and foreign minister criticized several of the Franco–German proposals. Defending classical federalist views they expressed 'serious doubts' about the proposal to strengthen the European Council; they wanted an extension of majority voting and the co-decision procedure with the EP to the foreign policy area and called for a strengthening of the Commission.[73]

Convening the intergovernmental conferences

The 'Rome II' summit in December 1990 officially opened the two IGCs. It also specified the agenda of the negotiations on political union on the basis of the Franco–German letter. The summit conclusions stated that the negotiations on political union would mainly have to deal with democratic legitimacy, common foreign and security policy, European citizenship and the principle of subsidiarity. There was a heated discussion on the role of the European Council, which pitted Mitterrand against Lubbers, the Dutch Prime Minister, who was vehemently opposed to any strengthening of this body.[74]

The first six months of the IGC negotiations were presided over by Luxembourg. The tiny member state opted for a pragmatic approach, not wanting to marginalize the British at this stage of negotiations. At a meeting of foreign ministers Genscher strove four times to deflect Luxembourg from setting too ambitious an agenda for the summit.[75] In their draft treaty presented to the summit in June 1991 Luxembourg suggested that the treaty be split up into three pillars, each governed by different principles. In the run-up to the summit Lutz Stavenhagen from the German chancellery had declared that the summit was unlikely to produce firm commitments but that he expected it to give new impulses to the negotiations. In May Kohl had held a two-day meeting with Felipe González of Spain. González supported the German position whole-heartedly, telling a press conference that 'these two elements (economic and political union, author) are inseparable and must go forward together'. González also supported Germany's wish to coordinate police efforts and create a new police structure at the European level.[76] By contrast, Franco–German relations were rather cool during this period due to differences over the conflict in Yugoslavia. Germany, sympathetic to the Croat cause in particular, wanted to recognize the breakaway republics, whereas France, traditionally close to the Serbs, wanted to continue the efforts to keep the Yugoslav federation unified. France also insisted that minority guarantees had to be fulfilled before the EC could support Croatian, Slovenian and Bosnian–Herzegovinian independence.

The Luxembourg summit in June 1991 held a preliminary debate on the IGCs based on the draft treaty, the Germans commenting afterwards that the proposals regarding political union were still 'too vague'.[77] More satisfactory seen from the German point of view was the fact that the summit in Luxembourg agreed to set up a new European police force and to create a common immigration policy.

In the course of Luxembourg's presidency several countries had submitted drafts for the IGC negotiations. Significantly, the German government had submitted a draft for a complete EMU treaty. Sources close to the negotiations point out that the statutes of the *Bundesbank* were copied 'without much drama'. Nor were there significant differences between the French and the Germans in the preparatory talks in the committee of central banks. The French shared the economic philosophy of the Germans and made no secret of the fact that they were proud of their own achievements. A participant even recalls a certain note of forbearance in the French exchanges with the Germans.[78]

The draft on EMU presaged many of the features of the eventual treaty, notably with regard to the stringent quantitative conditions of entry into the third stage, although well-placed sources point out that during the talks prior to the Maastricht summit the common understanding was that the convergence criteria would be interpreted flexibly.[79]

An intriguing question is whether the German government and the *Bundesbank* coordinated their statements during the preparatory talks on EMU. Cameron argues convincingly that transnational actors were influential in the debate on EMU. What he fails to consider, however, is the possibility that a transnational actor like the *Bundesbank* may act according to a realist behavioural logic. A participant in the negotiations admits that 'the *Bundesbank* seemed to be thinking very much in political terms'.[80] That this should have been the case is not surprising given the fact that on account of its problematic history Germany has tended to some extent to 'privatize' its foreign policy, leaving it to big industry, banks and party *Stiftungen* (establishments) to defend German interests abroad. This pattern seems to some extent to have endured after unification. It is also possible (but less likely) that the *Bundesbank* informally coordinated its actions with the German government so as to maximize Germany's negotiating clout. The government had an indirect link to the bank via the finance ministry, who, together with the bank, undertook preparations for EMU in the council of finance and economics ministers. However, the finance ministry being in the hands of the CSU, it is reasonable to expect there to have been considerable coordination problems between Kohl on the one hand and the finance ministry on the other.

Shortly after the Luxembourg summit the German government in a surprise move invited the UK to take part in Franco–German preparations for an initiative on a common foreign and security policy. Stavenhagen also welcomed Mr Major's new policy of being in the heart of Europe, which he interpreted as a willingness to create a political and not only an economic Europe, and said the German government would not confront the UK with harrowing choices. Finally, he said that Germany was willing to expunge direct references to 'federalism' in the treaty but that the treaty must include 'clear and clean' definitions of different layers of government.[81]

It is probably going too far to interpret the move as reflecting a German wish to replace the bilateral Franco–German partnership with a trilateral leadership structure in the Community. More likely the Germans wanted to highlight the improvement in Anglo–German relations which had taken place following the change of leadership in the Conservative Party in Britain. The personal relationship between Kohl and Major, both middle-ground politicians of the pragmatic type, was said to be excellent. The invitation was also a signal to the British that a more constructive posture would be rewarded. We do not know to what extent the initiative was coordinated with the French. On the one hand, relations between Germany and France were not the best during this period and Bonn may have taken the initiative without consulting the French, wanting to make it clear to France that Germany had alternative options to the close Franco–German partnership and expecting the UK to refuse the offer. On the other hand, there was a chance, however small, that the UK would accept the offer of trilateral talks, and that would have called the bluff. It is therefore most likely that in fact the invitation had been cleared with the French. Both countries knew that the UK held the key to a breakthrough in the crucial defence area. Both also had an interest in weaning the British off their intimate relationship with the USA, as it posed an indirect threat to the plans for a European defence.⌐

The Dutch challenge Franco–German leadership

The Dutch, who took over the EC presidency in July 1991, were more ambitious than their predecessors, wishing to 'federalize' the Community within a reasonably short time-horizon. In this endeavour they counted on German support. The Dutch presidency thus presented a plan for a two-speed Europe in the field of economic and monetary union which had been prepared in collaboration with the German government. Earlier drafts had assumed that the EC as a whole would decide when to start phase three and that members who did not fulfil the criteria would get temporary derogations.

The Dutch now proposed that if by 1996 six or more members wanted to move ahead and had satisfied the convergence criteria over two years, they could start a currency union among themselves. The core would be able to veto admission of other EC members if they judged that these members did not meet the convergence criteria. While close to the position of the German *Bundesbank* and finance ministry the plan drew heavy criticism from southern European members, Italy in particular. But Delors, anxious to keep the southern Europeans on board, also objected to the plan saying that the two-speed idea went against the Community principle that all members shared the same goal.[82] The southern European countries feared that the Dutch were preparing for a system that would exclude countries wanting to take part in a monetary union. The UK by contrast welcomed the plan, as it did not impose a common currency on all members of the Community and implied no coercion to move to the third and final stage. Although apart from the UK only the Germans supported the two-speed plan and modifications had to be injected, the Germans were in a strong position. It is testimony to the German self-confidence that Theo Waigel, the German finance minister, had been 'too busy' to attend ministerial meetings in the IGC for three months.[83] Creating uncertainty as to whether Germany was in or out was an effective way of enhancing Germany's negotiating power.

In September 1991, Mitterrand went to Germany on a three-day visit.

The unofficial purpose of the visit appears to have been to set the record straight regarding Mitterrand's support for German unification. The major part of the visit was thus spent in Berlin, where Mitterrand gave a soothing speech, and in the new *Länder* (German states).[84] During the visit Kohl and Mitterrand managed to renew their joint preparations for the last six months of the IGCs. According to Vedrine they agreed to act bilaterally in the field of defence in order to jolt the Community into action. Vedrine quotes Mitterrand as having said in that connection '*de toute façon, nos partenaires seront vexés, mais tout doit être fait avant Maastricht*'.[85]

In late September Piet Dankert, the Dutch Secretary of State for European Affairs, presented a new draft treaty to his Community partners. Unlike the Luxembourg draft, the Dutch draft proposed a treaty with a single unified structure, a 'tree' as opposed to the Luxembourg 'temple', in Brussels parlance. To compensate for the unified structure, he proposed to strengthen the dispensations. Dankert argued that at the Luxembourg summit at least six members had said they were in favour of a unitary federalist structure. Now the Dutch evidently wanted to pin the federalists down. In part, the explanation for the daring Dutch line should be sought in internal Dutch politics. With the Dutch foreign minister buried to his neck in the ex-Yugoslavian quagmire and Lubbers adopting a detached position, Piet Dankert, a former MEP and committed federalist, managed (albeit briefly) to take control of the Dutch European policy.[86] Despite the high level of ambition of Dankert's proposal it did however reflect fundamental principles in Dutch policy, which set it apart from France in particular.

As seen from The Hague, which voiced a more general small-state concern, it was of vital importance that the supranational institutions reflect a high degree of equality between member states; and that the Commission and the Court be involved in new areas of collaboration like EMU, foreign policy and judicial matters. Wanting to accommodate the confederalists in the UK and France, the presidency proposed a *sui generis* system inside the unified structure. For the time being, decisions in the sensitive areas of foreign and defence policy and judicial affairs would be made by 'the Community and its member states, each retaining their own competences'. But a general review clause was inserted on the understanding that a reassessment would take place later in the 1990s. In the field of foreign policy and defence, the Dutch also moved further than the previous presidency. Thus the defining of a common defence policy would no longer be an option but a commitment. The possibility of majority voting in the field of foreign policy was also left open.[87]

France reacted strongly to the Dutch draft despite the ambitious wording on defence. France was particularly piqued by the federal-oriented approach as regards institutions and decision-making. However the sharpness of the reaction seemed slightly out of proportion. What antagonized the French was probably as much the fact that a small member state was trying to exercise genuine leadership in the EC. Much to the regret of the Dutch even Germany, on whose support the Netherlands had counted, opposed the draft in a meeting in Dresden shortly after its publication. While a number of countries expressed vague sympathy for Dankert's federal ideas only the opponents showed determination. A decisive moment appears to have occurred when H.D. Genscher of Germany, deliberately the last to speak, reached the conclusion that the Dutch vessel would not hold water.[88] The German behaviour seems in part to have been motivated by a pragmatic assessment of what was possible. But it may also have been influenced by the emerging gap between the position of Germany and that of the other member states on the issue of Yugoslavia. This issue raised questions about Germany's ability to defend its interests in a foreign policy set-up governed by majority voting. Finally and crucially, the Dutch initiative revealed that the federal European structure, towards which Germany wanted to move, was asymmetrical.

The impression of a weakening Franco–German leadership was reinforced in the early autumn when Italy and the UK presented a joint text in the field of defence, seeking to harmonize aspirations for a European defence identity with the concern not to damage the framework of the Atlantic alliance. The proposal submitted on 4 October was the outcome of an Italian initiative aimed at including the UK in a European defence effort. The main idea of the proposal was to accord the WEU a dual role as both a component in the defence of the Union (the Italian preference) and a means of reinforcing the European pillar in NATO (the British preference). The fact that Italy had managed to secure British support for a commitment to review the WEU in 1998 must be regarded as a major victory.[89]

The Anglo–Italian initiative immediately improved the atmosphere in the talks on political union. At an informal meeting in Haarzuilen in early October a constructive discussion about foreign and security policy took place. At the meeting it became clear that a majority of member states were in favour of making decisions by qualified majority in foreign policy, with only the UK, Denmark and Greece opposed. Portugal adopted a special stance which provoked an interesting discussion. Not wanting the small countries to be dominated by the big, the Portuguese foreign minister demanded that the 'majority' in foreign policy be calculated on the basis of 'one country one vote'. This view was strongly criticized by several other member states, notably France and, less strongly, Germany. Genscher thus said that while one could envisage majorities constituting a minimum of 8 member states, 'one could not give equal weight to each member state'.[90]

In the run-up to the Haarzuilen meeting H.D. Genscher had outlined the German expectations on political union in an article in the *Nordsee Zeitung*. He expected satisfactory progress on the following points: 1) foreign, security and defence policy 2) a common policy on internal and judicial affairs 3) the rights of the European Parliament and 4) majority voting which he thought should be possible also for foreign and security policy.[91] Some progress having been made on internal and judicial affairs already, the Germans now focused on foreign policy and defence.

In the following weeks the French and German foreign ministers showed signs of wanting to reassert if not take over the leadership at the IGC. At the end of a meeting of foreign ministers on 6 October they first announced that they would hold a meeting on the 11 October on the subject of European political union '*avec tous les collègues qui sont sur la même longueur d'ondes*' (with all the colleagues who are on the same wavelength), as Genscher put it. The initiative, though, seems mainly to have been inspired by the French foreign minister. The Dutch saw it as an attempt to bypass the presidency, as they had not been notified in advance.[92] The purpose of the initiative was mainly to reassert the role of France and Germany in the debate about European defence following the joint British–Italian initiative in this area. France was particularly annoyed by what it regarded as the defection of Italy, which it was used to counting on as being in the French camp. But France and Germany probably also felt that the Dutch were adopting too high a profile for a smaller member state.

Adding a certain amount of drama to the episode, the French and German foreign ministers who wanted at all costs to arrive first at the press conference drove away in the taxi reserved for the President of the Council and the President of the Commission. This provoked what was probably the first car chase in the history of European integration.[93]

The following days saw the customary attempt to apologize without apologizing. But the episode appears to have reflected a more deep-seated frustration on the part of France and Germany. The Bonn daily, *Die Welt*, known to be close to Helmut Kohl, thus wrote in an editorial that 'the EC big powers are fed up with the "presidency of the dwarves"' (successively Luxembourg, the Netherlands and Portugal) ... The Paris invitation ... is a coup'.[94] A spokesman from the French foreign ministry defended the convening of the special meeting in Paris, saying that the Spanish foreign minister would probably take part in the proposed meeting. Dumas said that the meeting was open to all member states wanting the Maastricht summit to succeed. Genscher commented that Bonn and Paris had only wanted to assist the presidency.[95]

The Paris meeting produced a brief joint communiqué, in which the three countries recalled that EMU and political union formed a whole, that the commitment to a common foreign and security policy must include the prospect of a common defence, that qualified majority should be used when deciding on the modalities in setting up the common foreign and security policy, and most importantly that the WEU 'which is an integral part of the process leading to European union, could be given the responsibility of setting up the defence and security policy'.[96]

The episode perfectly illustrates the tension between the formal and the informal leadership structure of the Community, which to all intents and purposes translates into a conflict between the big and small member states. Interestingly, the British foreign minister thus refrained from criticizing the Franco–German–Spanish initiative, calling it perfectly natural, and thereby signalling some agreement with the Franco–German position as regards the need for effective leadership.[97] By contrast, Hans Van den Broek, the Dutch foreign minister, commented that what had happened was a typical example of the development which the Netherlands wanted to avoid: *une entente inter-gouvernementale entre des pays soucieux de former un directoire pour la Communauté.*[98]

On 14 October Kohl and Mitterrand submitted a joint letter to Ruud Lubbers, President of the Council.[99] Picking up some of the ideas already presented in December 1990 (see above), the letter focused on the area of foreign and security policy. It announced the creation of a European corps based on the existing Franco–German brigade and proposed that the WEU be transformed into the EC's defence arm. No restriction would be placed on where the corps might act. By contrast, the Anglo–Italian plan had suggested a European force which would only act outside the NATO area. The idea was that the corps, which would be open to the participation of other EC members, could be made answerable to the WEU. The formation of the corps represented a change in the Franco–German approach to differentiation. Far from merely threatening to form a subsystem, they now actually created a *fait accompli.*

It was furthermore proposed to expand the WEU, to move its secretariat to Brussels, to coordinate its meetings with those of the EC, to set up a permanent WEU group to plan possible deployments and to establish a European armaments agency. Attached to the letter were a number of concrete texts: an article on the general objectives of the treaty; an article on security and defence accompanied by a declaration on the priority areas of foreign policy and security cooperation, the main novelty of which was that it included Middle East policy; and finally a declaration by the WEU member states on cooperation between the WEU and NATO.[100] The Franco–German initiative had been cleared in advance with Scowcroft, President Bush's national security advisor, at a meeting on 4 October, and had subsequently been discussed with the Spaniards, who supported it.[101] According to officials in Bonn, the proposals on defence had been almost entirely drafted in Chancellor Kohl's office.[102]

On 14–15 November 1991 Mitterrand, his Prime Minister and a number of other ministers went to Germany with a view to discussing the IGCs. France and Germany were now apparently in agreement on the basic issues at the IGCs. However, the draft treaty on EMU submitted by the Dutch was the source of some concern. The French and particularly the Germans regarded a Dutch EMU proposal allowing for an opt-out in the monetary area as 'fatal'.[103] The opt-out clause introduced as a face-saving device for Britain had been transformed into a general clause. This risked undermining the very commitment to create a monetary union which Germany and France were determined to push through. At the last meeting of finance ministers before the Maastricht summit, which lasted three days and nights, the UK and Denmark clashed with the other members over the issue. After the Danish minister had given up his support for the general clause, France and Germany supported by Delors eventually managed to have the clause transformed into a singular opt-out for Britain in the form of a binding protocol to the treaty.[104] In general, however, the EMU negotiations were not dramatic. Compared with the difficult discussions on political union, the EMU negotiations, thoroughly prepared by the Delors committee, went relatively smoothly. Five convergence criteria were defined relating to ERM membership and non-devaluation, budgetary deficits as a percentage of GDP, debt as a percentage of GDP, interest rates and inflation rates. The principle of precise criteria of entry into the third phase of EMU had gradually come to be accepted, and a principle of imposing penalties for members guilty of excessive budget deficits had also eventually been decided, but there was agreement that the criteria chosen were to be assessed 'non-mechanically'. There was also some discussion of the Commission's right of initiative, with the large countries agreeing to grant the Commission some limited powers.[105]

Egged on by the Belgians, the Dutch were trying to bolster the Commission's right of initiative and the European Parliament's law-making role in EMU. The Dutch were hereby challenging one of the premises of the German EMU policy which was that the European Central Bank would not only be the central institution in EMU but also free of constraints in its formulation of monetary policy. The Dutch demand for a strengthening of the Parliament across the board and the ensuing debate had revealed that, notwithstanding its rhetoric, Germany was not willing to fight for the European Parliament in all areas.

The general goal of the Dutch was to extend the powers of the Commission, the Court and the Parliament in order to forestall the formation of a monetary directorate of the two or three biggest members. If standard Treaty of Rome rules could be inserted in the EMU treaty, the Council of ministers would need to muster unanimity if wanting to change a Commission proposal. The position of France and Germany seemed to be that they wanted to be able to overrule the Commission on a majority.[106]

Franco–German tension

Notwithstanding the public display of unity, France and Germany were still in disagreement on some important issues relating to both EMU and political union. As regards EMU, the two disagreed on the role of the European Monetary Institute (EMI). Having lost the battle to set up a European Central Bank during the transitional period 1994–97, France and its southern allies had accepted the Dutch compromise of a monetary institute. France now proposed that EMI should have an independent external president and vice-president, whereas the Germans wanted the president to be drawn from the ranks of the central banks. France also wanted EMI to have some foreign reserves at its disposal.[107]

As regards political union Germany was opposed to French demands for an industrial chapter, fearing that France would build French *dirigiste* traditions into the Union. There was also disagreement regarding the powers of the European Parliament, with France adopting a cautious stance. Particularly sensitive was a German demand for an increase in its representation in the Parliament. Kohl wanted an increase of eighteen seats with full voting powers to account for German unification. The issue was very sensitive, infringing as it did the tacit principle of parity which underpinned the dual leadership of France and Germany. Germany had no difficulty rallying the European Parliament to its cause and the German government expressed its support for the Parliament's demand for an increase in the German representation. Vedrine has an interesting comment: '*il est clair que le Chancelier est favorable, mais veut nous donner l'impression qu'on lui a forcé la main*'.[108] In other words, Kohl is seen to be using pressure from the European Parliament as an alibi for presenting new German demands.

In mid November Mitterrand unsuccessfully confronted Kohl, saying that the German demand risked provoking fear of a German Europe. Kohl was only willing to accept that the representation of the other big member states be increased as well, but less than the German. Faced with Kohl's intransigence Mitterrand along with Andreotti from Italy considered proposing the creation of a senate where the member states would have equal representation. The controversy reflected an enduring uneasiness in the Franco–German relationship, the roots of which were German unification. A German official told a British newspaper in late October that 'Franco–German relations had been so bad since last year that we simply had to get them back to where they had been. To this day Mitterrand has not understood unification ... The French have a nuclear weapon that does not have range enough to hit Poland but that can hit Germany. We don't like that. The bilateral force proposal was one way of improving our ties'.[109] Germany's economic problems in the wake of unification further complicated Franco–German cooperation. Decisions on the joint Hermes space shuttle thus had to be postponed because of Bonn's inability (or refusal) to find more money on its budget.[110]

Despite these underlying problems the two leaders remained strongly committed to the goal of European union. The parallel debate with the USA on the future of European defence undoubtedly helped weld the two European states together. At the end of the November summit the two leaders both tried to whip up a crisis atmosphere, Kohl talking about a 'historic opportunity' and 'the risk of setting back European integration for more than a generation' and Mitterrand saying that a 'failure to reach agreement in Maastricht would be the beginning of the downfall of the Community and mark the return of competitive nationalism'.[111]

In the meantime, the UK tabled a series of amendments seeking to water down the preamble to the proposed treaty. The amendments were aimed at removing from the preamble the words 'federal goals' as well as the commitment to a single currency. The move provoked a heated exchange with the German foreign minister and the Dutch presidency.[112] The Germans were now getting somewhat anxious about the British position. The problem was that, whereas on the issue of new competences problems could be solved if need be by granting the UK an opt-out, on the issue of institutions, which was crucial to Germany, variable geometry was not an option. Major was therefore invited to Bonn in November to discuss possible compromises ahead of the summit. During the talks, Kohl referred to the goal stipulated in the Single European Act according to which 'the Rome treaties should be preserved and the totality of the relations between member states should be transformed into a European Union'. However, he was willing to offer concessions. First of all, since Major could only accept granting the Parliament a right of co-decision in the area of the internal market, Kohl proposed to extend the Parliament's rights in two phases. Similarly, in the field of judicial and internal affairs, Kohl envisaged a phased approach. The British side apparently refused to commit itself to specific decisions in the future, but was prepared, if need be, to include revision clauses.[113]

The Maastricht Treaty

The Maastricht summit in December 1991 had to wrap up a wide range of technical and highly political items in a single reform package. Whereas EMU was well-prepared and benefited from a coherent input from the community of European central bankers, political union was little less than an umbrella concept. The summit took place against the backdrop of an emerging conflict in former Yugoslavia. The German foreign minister thus used the summit to 'announce' his government's intention to recognize the breakaway republics Croatia, Slovenia and

Bosnia-Herzegovina.[114] While at times the summit was highly dramatic, eventually agreement on a new treaty was reached. The most difficult issue proved to be not the institutional changes, which had for the most part been settled in advance, but the social chapter on which John Major refused to give ground. Britain's status vis-à-vis EMU had also essentially been settled before the summit. The solution consisted of granting the British an individual opt-out clause as agreed by the finance ministers. But in the social sphere Major refused to accept an opt-out, evidently wanting to be seen to export the Thatcherite free market model to Europe. Eventually, Chancellor Kohl assisted by Ruud Lubbers, the President of the Council, and Delors and his advisor, Pascal Lamy, broke the deadlock by proposing to separate the social chapter from the treaty and add a social protocol to the treaty.[115] The implication was that not the UK but the eleven would opt out. The idea was, however, that they would use the EC institutions. The social deal was subsequently sold to Mitterrand during a night break. This effectively pre-empted other leaders, who had been expecting a more modest opt-out for Britain alone.[116]

Paradoxically, in previous rounds of negotiations during the summit the UK had blocked attempts to grant MEPs a right of veto. Social policy would now be decided according to a procedure dictated by the UK, even though the UK would not take part in social policy decisions!.[117] The UK also managed to water down the preamble to the treaty and were successful in including subsidiarity clauses. Notwithstanding these considerable achievements, the British role was essentially reactive. The agenda had been set by others, apart from the Anglo–Italian initiative on defence.

The other difficult dossier was EMU, notably the wording describing the transition to the third phase, and it consumed a lot of time at the summit. Eventually, France and Italy, supported by a very active Commission President, pushed through the so called 'automaticity clause' according to which the third stage would automatically take effect in 1999 in the case that a majority of member states did not qualify in 1997. Sources close to the negotiations emphasize that Kohl, too, was totally committed to the automatic transition. However, tactically it would have been unhelpful for Kohl to have led the push for the automaticity clause. Mitterrand and Andreotti were therefore given the task of proposing it. According to one highly-placed official 'this saved EMU'.[118]

An analysis of proposals submitted by Germany to the IGC on EMU reveals that Germany played a highly influential role in the negotiations.

The section on coordination of economic policy and supervision of member states in Germany's 'comprehensive proposal' on EMU submitted to the EMU conference on 26 February 1991 corresponds closely to the formulations in the treaty in these areas. Yet the German text had also proposed that the decision on the transition to the second and third stages of EMU be taken unanimously.[119] On this important point the German government was overruled. A later proposal had proposed that Article 2 of the treaty concerning the goals of the Community should include a formulation to the effect that the Community's goal was to promote 'closer relations between the member states *in parallel with* (author's emphasis) economic and monetary integration'.[120] This must be interpreted as an attempt to formalize the parallelism between EMU and political union and underlines the German commitment to political union. This demand was also rejected by the Maastricht summit. The German texts on EMU had been very specific, the Germans evidently wanting to 'lock in' a number of principles and rules central to their own economic order and to a liberal-capitalist system. The German proposals on EMU tended to focus on first principles. This was the case in other areas of the treaty as well. Germany thus submitted a proposal on 'fundamental rights'.[121]

Not all of the proposed formulations found their way to the treaty. One German amendment to Article 102a thus proposed that the treaty should forbid 'indexation and escalation clauses based on prices or wages, or on the evolution of the exchange rates of foreign currencies of non-member states and clauses having the same effect'.[122] Escalation clauses would, however, be permitted under exceptional circumstances. Another formulation in the same proposal refers to the free choice of consumers and free price formation within the context of a free and undistorted competition. Such formulations may seem superfluous, even verbose, but for the Germans they made good sense. The price for granting other states a voice opportunity over German monetary decisions was the specification of the rules and principles on the basis of which this influence could be exercised. The more specific the commitments in the Maastricht Treaty, the less leeway other member states would have in trying to influence German policy. Fortunately, from the German point of view, most other member states in the EC seemed to regard the German model as attractive and worthy of emulation and export.

The principles enshrined in the Maastricht Treaty must also be seen in the context of Eastern enlargement. The fact that new members had to accept the Union's previous decisions (the principle of *acquis*) in fact gave the Union and in particular Germany a tremendous opening to diffuse its values and principles as well as its legislation.

The chapter on foreign policy and security largely corresponded with a German proposal submitted earlier in November 1990 in which Germany had suggested an evolutionary process towards majority voting on foreign policy. Interestingly, the proposal had included a formulation saying that '*die Variante "opting out" oder "Nichtteilnahme" wird dem Gemeinsamkeitsprinzip nicht gerecht*' (the variant 'opting out' or 'non-participation' is not compatible with the principle of community).[123] The latter formulation was not included in the treaty.

The new co-decision procedure constituted a more unequivocal victory for Germany. The new Article 189b mirrored Germany's own arrangement for consultations between the two chambers of parliament, which granted a conciliation committee (*Vermittlungsausschuss*) a central role.[124]

After the summit Kohl stated that the summit had been an 'unqualified success for his teams'. He continued: 'We have made certain that German conceptions, German interests and German intentions were fulfilled with respect to economic and monetary union'. The European Central Bank would 'correspond directly to German measurements, perhaps adhering to even more stringent criteria than those applying to the independent German *Bundesbank* ... That is a *tremendous success*' (author's emphasis).[125] Conceding that not all his wishes had been fulfilled on political union he added 'but we are getting what we wanted – irreversible progress towards economic and monetary union'.[126] There were also setbacks. Due to French opposition Kohl did not obtain the eighteen new seats in the European Parliament which he had wanted, but he expressed his confidence that he would eventually get them.

Kohl's reasons for praising the new treaty were spelt out in greater length in a speech to the CDU in October 1992. Kohl started out recalling the basics: '*Wir waren zu allen Zeiten die Hauptnutzniesser dieses sich einigenden Europas*'. And further: '*Für die Exportnation Deutschland ist der Zusammenschluss Europas von entscheidender Bedeutung*'. Kohl also stressed the need for a balance between EMU and political union: '*entweder tritt zur Wirtschafts- und Währungsunion die Politische Union hinzu – dann wird das von dauer sein, weil in diesem Falle eine Balance hergestellt ist – oder aber die Wirtschafts- und Währungsunion gilt nur auf Zeit, und geht dann wegen Interessengegensätzen auseinander*'.[127] This was another case of strategic spillover. From the perspective of cooperative hegemony political union was the price that had to be paid in order to coopt secondary states. The primary goal – EMU – could not be realized unless integration was extended to other areas.

On the EMU chapter Kohl said that '*hier haben sich alle anderen in Richtung der deutschen Gesetzgebung über die Bundesbank bewegt*'.[128] Bjørn Engholm, the SPD leader, was less enthusiastic, commenting that 'there was no great leap forward. Not enough progress was made to ensure more rights for the European Parliament', whereas the Confederation of German Industry regretted that there had not been equal progress in political and economic union, a fact that might eventually damage the chances of success for both.[129] The reaction is interesting, first of all, because the powerful Confederation seems quite satisfied with the EMU chapter and secondly, and more importantly, because it argued in political and not only economic terms, which supports our proposition that in Germany foreign policy has to some extent been 'privatized'.

The key question is why the Germans advocated political union with such fervour. The strategy of cooperative hegemony once again provides a clue. First of all, in James Sperling's formulation, in exchange for economic hegemony 'Germany has acquiesced to political union to allay fears of a hegemonial Germany without however sacrificing its leadership role'.[130] In large part political union was thus the concession to the smaller member states needed to prevent balancing behaviour. Seen in this light, the de-territorialization represented by the European Parliament was the most important aspect of political union. Yet political union would also re-distribute power between states. It was part of a gradual strategy aimed at institutional asymmetry. Although on most issues of everyday politics MEPs vote according to ideological preferences, on more important issues national affiliation appears to play a role. A strong European Parliament will thus indirectly favour Germany because of the country's population strength. Yet, the commitment to a strengthening of the European Parliament cannot be explained solely in instrumental terms. To understand the special emotional attachment of the German political elite to the European Parliament, one must recall the special role played by the Frankfurt parliament in the process of German unification in the last century. The Paulskirche assembly (also called the *Professorparlament*) was a leading force in the national unification movement of 1848. In the German perception (national) unification and democratization are thus processes which are intimately linked. It comes naturally to the educated German to regard the democratically elected supranational assembly in Strasbourg as the

prime force for unity. That the experience of 1848 is part of Kohl's mental map is confirmed by the speech given by him in 1992 to a CDU party meeting. In the context of a defence of the EP performance against critics in his party Kohl says that '*um die wirkliche Dimension der Aufgabe zu begreifen, muss man die deutsche Geschichte betrachten und sich etwa das Parlament der Paulskirche von 1848 ansehen. Sie können auch den Bismarckschen Reichstag nennen*'.[131] The statement is also interesting in a wider sense, as an indication that Germany's political class regards European integration as a process of federalization on a par with Germany's own unification in the last century.

Political union also means a common security and defence policy. Such a policy will indirectly augment Germany's influence by gradually removing (or reducing the value of) the special prerogatives and status which France and the UK possess (nuclear weapons in particular). It will also balance new and perhaps more daring German initiatives in its Eastern policy. Finally, it will spread the burden of coping with the challenging problems in Central and Eastern Europe.

All in all, the Maastricht Treaty added significantly to the asymmetry of the EC system, mainly in the economic and monetary area, but also to some extent in the political area.[132]

France also had reason to be satisfied with the outcome, not only because of the automaticity clause in the EMU chapter but also because of (albeit limited) progress on foreign policy and defence. However, the French success was less spectacular than the German. In part this was due to the fact that in this area, unlike in the monetary area, the British did not seek an opt-out. It was hardly a coincidence that the British weight was felt most clearly in the area which the French accorded the greatest importance. A common defence policy was only made a long-term objective, although the WEU had been recognized as the Union's defence organization. An essential feature of the new structure of the Union was that the three pillars would be capped by the European Council.[133] Likewise, in the area of EMU France had managed to reduce the role of the Commission and the EP to a largely advisory one. Significantly, Article 103 in the Maastricht Treaty which deals with economic policy leaves it to the European Council to draw a 'conclusion' on overall economic policy (based on a report from the Council); the Commission is only permitted to make 'recommendations' (as opposed to 'proposals') and the Parliament is to be 'informed'.[134] As seen from the (very ambitious) perspective of the federalist states, notably Italy and the Netherlands, the outcome of the Maastricht negotiations was thus a disappointment of historical dimensions, one official noting in despair that 'this was the last chance to create a federal Europe'.[135] The federalist plans for a unified structure with the Commission and the Parliament at the apex which the Dutch had aimed for appeared to have been buried. Yet federalists could draw a certain comfort from the fact that the European Parliament had been strengthened, majority voting extended and EMU put on a fast track. EMU alone represented a huge transfer of sovereignty away from member states, although not altogether on the terms wanted by the Dutch.

John Major claimed that the real victor at Maastricht had been Britain. Subsidiarity had been introduced to curb centralization. Majority voting on foreign policy had been reduced to marginal changes. The WEU would remain an independent organization linked to both NATO and the EU and Britain had obtained opt-outs in the most sensitive areas. Britain had indeed done quite well in Maastricht. But in two crucial areas, it had failed to slow down the union process: EMU looked set to become a reality with all the consequences flowing from that and the institutional system had been reformed, the main changes being the co-decision procedure granting Parliament real powers in a number of legislative areas and the extension of majority voting. Besides, to some extent the British victory looked more like a truce. Thus in the defence area the treaty foresaw a new round of negotiations within five years.

Cooperative hegemony and the case of the Maastricht Treaty

The directional leadership role of France and Germany comes out quite clearly from the account of the process leading to the Maastricht summit. With few exceptions, France and Germany managed to set the agenda. The two countries were of course helped by the fact that the Commission President was a Frenchman, and a very effective one at that. Delors played an important role in launching the discussion on EMU in 1986–87, in close coordination with Mitterrand and the Italians. From 1988 Germany gradually assumed a more important role in the debate, unblocking the road towards EMU at the Hanover summit in 1988. The crucial decision to convene an intergovernmental conference with a view to changing the treaties was essentially made by Mitterrand and Kohl in bilateral talks, with Mitterrand trying to accelerate the pace of the EMU process.

As regards political union, the role of France and Germany as directional leaders was also apparent, although it must be qualified. The UK and Italy intervened to exercise intellectual leadership in the foreign policy and defence areas. A British observer uses this example to make the general point that two big countries are always able to exercise leadership in the EU and that there is nothing special about Franco–German leadership.[136] The joint letter of December 1990 set the agenda of the negotiations on political union at a time when the IGC had not yet been convened. If one compares the outcome of the IGC with the content of the letter, one is struck by the similarity. The EC's competences had been extended; the areas of immigration policy, asylum, visa policy and the fight against drugs and organized crime had been transferred to the Union; a European citizenship had been introduced and the European Parliament had been granted a right of co-decision; it had furthermore been decided that the EP should confirm the nomination of a new Commission; qualified majority voting had been extended though it had not, as Germany and France had wanted, been made the normal rule of decision; foreign policy cooperation had been extended to all areas and the notion of common action areas had in principle been accepted. The idea that implementing decisions might be taken by majority voting also reappears in the Franco–German letter (see p. 137). The final treaty thus broadly reflected the Franco–German compromise negotiated at the start of the negotiations, except for the proposal to permit the European Council to transfer new competences to the Union if supported by a majority in the European Parliament. The joint letter of October 1991 had had a narrower focus, sending a signal to the other members that foreign policy and in particular defence were areas on which France and Germany placed particular priority.

Undoubtedly, the importance of the directional leadership in the EU at a given point in time depends to a certain extent on which country holds the presidency. Ireland held the presidency in the first half of 1990 and was clearly bypassed by Kohl and Mitterrand. The Dutch presidency on the other hand exercised a more active leadership, provoking strong reactions from France. The struggle between the Dutch presidency and the Franco–German duo in the autumn of 1991 is particularly illustrative of the underlying tension in European politics between intergovernmental power-politics and the elements of a domestic order. Characteristically, France and Germany were particularly anxious to retain the directional leadership in the high politics areas of foreign policy and defence, whereas in the EMU discussions the Dutch leadership was less directly challenged. During the final stage of negotiations,

France and Germany once again asserted themselves. Kohl and to a lesser extent Mitterrand thus played a crucial role in wrapping up the final agreement on the social dimension.

It is typical for France and Germany to try to shape the outcome by convincing other members (and each other) of the final outcome at an early stage in the negotiations.[137] The Franco–German *acquis* will then in part be renegotiated in the course of the negotiations in the light of inputs from other member states, with the UK holding a key position as 'barrier'. A minor country like the Netherlands appears indirectly to have played a not insignificant role by virtue of the fact that Germany regards Dutch acceptance of its ideas as important in its attempt to sell these ideas to other smaller members.

Officials close to the process point out that there is an important image aspect to the joint Franco–German initiatives. Reaching agreement time and again proved painful, especially during the period after German unification. Yet it was crucial to both leaders to be seen to be acting together and to be seen to be in control of European politics. The external aspect of Franco–German behaviour in EU constitutive politics is thus of great importance.[138] France and Germany can in diplomatic terms broaden their power base by acting together. At the same time, European posturing cuts a certain amount of ice with the voters, notably in France, though the saliency of foreign policy remains in general rather limited.

Tactical differentiation was used on at least one occasion, as seen in the convening of a separate meeting in Paris with only France, Germany and Spain attending. This meeting produced some nervousness in the UK and probably helped pave the way for a solution on defence acceptable to Paris and Bonn. At the same time, the creation of the Eurocorps reflected a move towards strategic differentiation, which presented the rest of the Community with a *fait accompli*. Kohl's reference to France and Germany as constituting a hard core reflected a hardening of the German position vis-à-vis the UK. The arrival of John Major seems, however, to have led to a certain softening of the German stance.

There were differences in style within the Franco–German leadership. Thus small states found it much more difficult to make pre-cooked deals with Germany than with France. The reason is the fragmented and pluralistic political system in Germany, in which no-one at the lower levels seems to be in control. Everyone is waiting for a *Weisung* (instruction) from above, which in one observer's view points to the continuing existence of a semi-authoritarian political culture in Germany.[139] Whereas the German political system may produce an embarrassing lack of coordination, it would be incorrect to draw the conclusion that this always has a negative effect on Germany's influence. Bulmer and Paterson point out correctly that 'sectorized policy may not be simply a matter of dissipating the efforts of German European policy. It may prove to be a policy resource'.[140] The point is that a quite effective division of labour may develop, with sectoral ministers and the *Bundesbank* feeling free to take a firm policy line and the Chancellor hiding behind a declaratory pro-integration stance but at the same time able to use domestic pressures as an alibi for adopting a tough stance when appropriate. In general it is difficult to take seriously the argument that Germany's constitutive EU policy should be constrained by domestic politics, since the major parties agree on the main lines of EU policy and the general public is largely disinterested in EU policy, with EMU as a partial exception. Even as regards EMU it should be remembered that the influence of the German electorate is in any case indirect given the fact that referenda are not used in Germany. As we have seen, a French advisor confirms this impression of instrumental use of domestic politics in European policy by the German executive. Finally, the cacophony of voices emerging from Germany leaves the Chancellor with a high degree of latitude and makes it difficult for other member states to predict German actions.

To what extent were the bargains concluded biased in favour of Germany? Most importantly, as we have seen, there is a significant degree of structural asymmetry in the Maastricht Treaty. The monetary structure and the principles governing future European monetary policy are essentially copied from the German system. There remains a certain amount of uncertainty as to the political control France and its allies will be able to bring to bear on aspects of EMU decisions, but Germany seems determined not to enter EMU until its demands are fulfilled. The fact that Germany has an exit option, although it is hardly ever referred to explicitly, puts it in a very strong bargaining position. To this should be added the likely spillover effects of EMU which can be counted as indirect German bargaining achievements.

The co-decision procedure with its conciliation procedure similarly mirrors the arrangement in the *Bundestag*. The Maastricht Treaty also, albeit more modestly, gives regions a greater say. Subsidiarity is of less importance but could also be interpreted as reflecting an attempt to establish congruence between the structure and principles of the Union and the German federal system. However, it should be stressed that at least prior to Maastricht subsidiarity remained a vague rhetorical term. The use of subsidiarity could also be interpreted as an exercise in reassurance typical of a cooperative hegemon.

How should one interpret the opt-outs granted to the UK and Denmark? A member state with an opt-out could be said to accord defensive power greater importance than offensive power in a given policy area.[141] This choice may reflect general features of a country's foreign policy, but it may also simply reflect a rational calculation of the chances of exercising offensive power in a given area. Member states with opt-outs obtain surplus autonomy at the price of a smaller voice-opportunity. Basically, opt-outs represent a setback from the point of view of the cooperative hegemon in that opt-outs reflect a refusal to let oneself be coopted. The granting of opt-outs is a sign that the threat of exclusion has failed. Exit-prevention fails, raising the spectre of balancing. The possibility of opt-outs in European integration visualizes the continued existence of national alternatives to participation in the integration system, which enhances the negotiating power of secondary states. Moreover, to the extent that opt-outs become more widespread the area of shared commitments shrinks, making it more difficult to play nested games and create linkages. In this general sense, the opt-outs in the Maastricht Treaty must be interpreted as setbacks for Germany and France. However, the value of opt-outs can be argued to differ, depending of whether we are talking about a balancing state or a secondary state. Effective balancing is difficult to envisage without a considerable amount of offensive power. By opting out of EMU the UK thus deprived itself of offensive power, making it easier for Germany and France to set the agenda for EMU. On the other hand, effective balancing may be incompatible with (full) participation in certain policies of economic integration, if such policies create highly asymmetrical interdependence and whittle away at the autonomy of the member state in question. For secondary states, on the other hand, defensive power is more important and opt-outs therefore less costly, notwithstanding the goodwill costs. These goodwill costs will vary depending *inter alia* on the credentials of political leaders in secondary states.[142]

In the theoretical part of the book we suggested a number of mechanisms typical of the strategy of cooperative hegemony. Some of these mechanisms were indeed applied during the Maastricht negotiations. Perhaps the most glaring example was Germany's role in the negotiations on the structural funds, which were increased very significantly at Maastricht. Anderson puts it succinctly 'As the EC's wealthiest member and *de facto* paymaster, Germany footed the bill for the structural funds, yet could expect to receive only a trifling share of the outlays'.[143] This is a classical case of the triumph of Germany's long-term over its short-term interests. The side-payments in terms of financing of the structural funds essentially overcame the objections of Ireland and the southern members to the treaty. Expansive gradualism was also evident. Germany managed to secure British acceptance of an increase in the legislative powers of the EP by introducing the reform in stages. Similarly, the review clause in the Maastricht Treaty ensured that the debate on e.g. foreign policy and defence integration would be reopened at a later stage. The strategic use of spillover came out clearly in speeches by Hans-Dietrich Genscher. Regional identification was less important, perhaps due in part to the weak position of the West Europeans vis-à-vis the USA in the aftermath of the Gulf war.

Our approach has been to analyse constitutive politics in isolation from 'normal politics'. In real life, as we have seen, such a separation rarely exists. The case of the EC's policy towards the conflict in Yugoslavia demonstrates how a major issue in normal politics inevitably spills over into constitutive politics. Overriding constitutive issues may also impinge on negotiations in the field of normal politics. This once again seems to have been the case as regards the conflict in Yugoslavia. France essentially sacrificed its preferred policy on the Yugoslav conflict in order to secure what was seen as the vital support of Germany for the Maastricht Treaty. Normal politics issues of a high politics nature are particularly likely to intervene in constitutive debates. EU–USA relations belong in that category. A case in point is the debate on the SDI project in the mid-1980s, which momentarily put a spoke in the wheel of the Franco–German cart. Another is the GATT negotiations, which intervened in the Maastricht and also the Edinburgh negotiations.

Notes

1. The *Economist* called the treaty a smiling mouse.
2. 'at one and the same time indispensable condition, motor and beneficiary of European construction', Hubert Vedrine, *Les Mondes de François Mitterrand*, Paris: Fayard, 1996, p. 403.
3. *Ibid.*, p. 405.
4. Hartmut Bühl, 'Deutsch–Französische Sicherheitspartnerschaft', *Dokumente*, Heft 5, 46. Jahrgang, October 1990, p. 373.

5. Vedrine, *op. cit.*, p. 413.
6. Vedrine, *op. cit.*, p. 414.
7. Vedrine, *op. cit.*, p. 413.
8. Jonathan Story and Marcello De Cecco, 'The Politics and Diplomacy of Monetary Union: 1985–1991', in Jonathan Story (ed.), *The New Europe. Politics. Government and Economy since 1945*, Oxford: Blackwell, 1993, p. 328.
9. Quoted in Roger Morgan, 'France and Germany as Partners', in Patrick McCarthy (ed.), *France–Germany 1983–1993. The Struggle to Cooperate*, London: Macmillan, 1993, p. 101.
10. Here I differ slightly with Karsten Skjalm, who in his excellent analysis of the EMU process stresses the domestic political motives. See also David Cameron, 'Transnational Relations and the Development of European Economic and Monetary Union', in Thomas Risse-Kappen (ed.), *Bringing Transnational Relations Back In*, Cambridge: Cambridge University Press, 1995, pp. 37ff.
11. Story and de Cecco, *op. cit.*, p. 344.
12. Cameron, *op. cit.*, p. 43.
13. Charles Grant, Delors. *Inside the House that Jacques Built*, London: Nicholas Brealey Publishing, 1994, p. 119.
14. Cameron, *op. cit.*, p. 46, who quotes a *Financial Times* correspondent.
15. Story and de Cecco, *op. cit.*, p. 330.
16. Karsten Skjalm, *Det Europæiske Valutasamarbejdes Politiske Økonomi*, Aarhus: Institut for Statskundskab, Aarhus University, 1995, p. 232.
17. 'The preconditions for (EMU) are good, perhaps better than at any other time in the history of the Community and the crucial thing is that this monetary union becomes a community of stability'. The speech is printed in *Europa-Archiv*, Folge 6, 1988, pp. D 149ff.
18. Vedrine, *op. cit.*, p. 400.
19. Hans-Dietrich Genscher, *Erinnerungen*, Berlin: Siedler Verlag, 1995, p. 388.
20. 'It is obvious that in this discussion the Federal Republic will refer to its outstanding experiences with the *Bundesbank*, with its independence, decentralised organisation and most importantly with its commitment to monetary stability.'
21. The statement is printed in *Europa-Archiv*, Folge 14, 1988, pp. D 388ff.
22. Vedrine, *op. cit.*, p. 418. The conclusions of the summit are printed in *Europa-Archiv*, Folge 16, 1988, pp. D 443ff.
23. James Sperling, 'A Unified Germany, a Single European Economic Space, and the Prospects for the Atlantic Economy', in Carl F. Lankowski (ed.), *Germany and the European Community*, New York: St. Martin's Press, 1993, p. 199.
24. Interview, August 1997.
25. Interview, March 1997.
26. Quoted in Grant, *op. cit.*, p. 123.
27. Grant, *op. cit.*, p. 122.
28. *Le Monde*, 6 April 1989, p. 4.
29. The report is printed in *Europa-Archiv*, Folge 10, 1989, pp. 283–304.
30. Cameron, *op. cit.*, pp. 49ff.
31. *Le Monde*, 14 June 1989, p. 6.

32. Margaret Thatcher, *The Downing Street Years*, London: HarperCollins, 1993, pp. 750ff.
33. Skjalm, *op. cit.*, p. 238.
34. Cameron, *op. cit.*, p. 54.
35. *Frankfurter Allgemeine Zeitung*, 27 June 1989, p. 2.
36. Cameron, *op. cit.*, p. 55.
37. Genscher, *op. cit.*, p. 390.
38. Skjalm, *op. cit.*, p. 242.
39. Interview, Brussels, June 1996.
40. According to Teltschik, quoted in Grant, *op. cit.*, p. 141.
41. *Agence Europe*, 8 December 1989.
42. Horst Teltschik, *329 Tage*, Bonn: Siedler Verlag, 1992, p. 68.
43. Vedrine, *op. cit.*, p. 446; Cameron, *op. cit.*, p. 55.
44. *Frankfurter Allgemeine Zeitung*, 11 December 1989, p. 3.
45. Teltschik, *op. cit.*, p. 72.
46. According to *Agence Europe*, 10 December 1989, pp. 15–17.
47. Teltschik, *op. cit.*, p. 71.
48. Thatcher, *op. cit.*, p. 796.
49. Teltschik, *op. cit.*, p. 106.
50. *Frankfurter Allgemeine Zeitung*, 17 February 1990, pp. 1–2.
51. 'after a long time we were once again able to induce Paris to a common EC-initiative', Teltschik, *op. cit.*, p. 176.
52. Teltschik, *op. cit.*, p. 228.
53. Vedrine writes that he himself took care of preparing a plan on common foreign and security policy. See Vedrine, *op. cit.*, p. 138.
54. Teltschik, *op. cit.*, p. 164.
55. *Agence Europe*, 2 March 1990.
56. *Le Monde*, 14 March 1990, p. 4.
57. *Frankfurter Allgemeine Zeitung*, 24 March 1990, p. 1.
58. *Frankfurter Allgemeine Zeitung*, 30 April 1990, pp. 1–2.
59. Vedrine, *op. cit.*, p. 439.
60. 'they *decided* (author's emphasis) to bring about a decision at the EC summit in Dublin on the convening of an IGC on political union and to lay down a timetable for the opening of this conference as well as the conference on EMU', Teltschik, *op. cit.*, p. 283.
61. Teltschik, *op. cit.*, p. 287.
62. *Frankfurter Allgemeine Zeitung*, 31 July 1990, p. 4.
63. 'As always he assumes that we will prepare him a draft. We are already working on one', Teltschik, *op. cit.*, p. 356.
64. Teltschik, *op. cit.*, p. 369.
65. *Agence Europe*, 19 September 1990, p. 4.
66. Interview, August 1997.
67. Wayne Sandholz, 'Choosing Union: Monetary Politics and Maastricht', *International Organization*, Vol. 47, no. 1, Winter 1993, p. 21.
68. Cameron, *op. cit.*, p. 66.
69. Stephen George, *An Awkward Partner. Britain in the European Community*, Oxford: Oxford University Press, 1994, p. 228.

70. Cameron, *op. cit.*, p. 69.
71. Interview, September 1997.
72. The letter is printed in *Le Monde*, 9–10 December 1990, p. 4. See also Vedrine, *op. cit.*, p. 459.
73. *Conf-UP 1725/91 annexe 2.*
74. Interview, March 1996.
75. The *Independent*, 25 June 1991.
76. *Reuter Library Report*, 2 May 1991.
77. *Ibid.*
78. Interview, August 1997.
79. Interview, August 1997.
80. Interview, August 1997.
81. The *Guardian*, 5 July 1991.
82. Grant, *op. cit.*, p. 183.
83. *Grant, op. cit.*
84. *Financial Times*, 20 September 1991.
85. 'in any case our partners will be annoyed, but everything must be done before Maastricht', Vedrine, *op. cit.*, p. 466.
86. Interview, March 1997.
87. *Agence Europe*, 26 September 1991.
88. Interview, March 1997.
89. See *Agence Europe*, 5 October 1991.
90. *Agence Europe*, 8 October 1991.
91. Quoted in *Agence Europe*, 5 October 1991.
92. *Le Monde*, 8 October 1991, p. 7.
93. *Financial Times*, 10 October 1991, 'hurt feelings, burnt rubber'.
94. Quoted in *Reuter Newswire*, 10 October 1991.
95. *Le Monde*, 10 October 1991.
96. *Agence Europe*, Europe Documents no. 1737, 17 October 1991.
97. *Le Monde*, 13–14 October 1991.
98. 'an intergovernmental understanding between the countries wanting to form a *directoire* in the Community', quoted in *Le Monde*, 9 October 1991, p. 5.
99. The letter was printed in *Le Monde*, 17 October 1991, p. 4.
100. *Financial Times*, 16 October 1991; *Agence Europe*, 17 October 1991, pp. 3–4.
101. Vedrine, *op. cit.*, p. 466.
102. *Financial Times*, 14 November 1991.
103. *Frankfurter Allgemeine Zeitung*, 14 November 1991.
104. Grant, *op. cit.*, p. 184.
105. *Agence Europe*, 26 November 1991.
106. *Financial Times*, 30 October 1991.
107. *Financial Times*, 30 October 1991.
108. 'it is clear that the Chancellor is favourably disposed, but wants to give us the impression that his hand has been forced', Vedrine, *op. cit.*, p. 469.
109. The *Independent*, 25 October 1991.
110. *Financial Times*, 13 and 14 November 1991.
111. *Financial Times*, 16 November 1991.
112. *Financial Times*, 15 November 1991.

113. *Frankfurter Allgemeine Zeitung*, 29 November 1991, p. 2.
114. The expression 'announced' was used by one interviewee.
115. The *Independent*, 12 December 1991.
116. Mitterrand, perhaps because of his illness, appears to have been somewhat detached during the negotiations, leaving Elisabeth Guigou to take the French chair now and then. Interview, March 1997.
117. *Financial Times*, 12 December 1991.
118. Interview, March 1997.
119. *Gesamtvorschlag der deutschen Delegation.* UEM/29/91. 26 February 1991.
120. Artikel 2, 3A; *Änderungsvorschlag der deutschen Delegation.* UEM/89/91.
121. *Fundamental rights and human rights*, German delegation, CONF – UP 1767/91.
122. *Title VI: economic and monetary policy, amendments proposed by the German delegation*, UEM/62/91, 10 September 1991.
123. *Deutsche delegation. Sprechnotiz für die Sitzung der persönlichen Beauftragten der Minister am 8.11.1990 in Brüssels*, SN 4611/90.
124. See also the German proposal regarding co-decision submitted on 19 February 1991, European Committee of the Danish Parliament, bil. 185.
125. Obviously, the observer has to make allowance for Kohl's need to sell the treaty to the German public. Yet Kohl's statement is very strong and contains a coherent and persuasive argument in defence of the EMU chapter.
126. *Daily Telegraph*, 12 December 1991.
127. 'We were at all times the main beneficiary of this integrating Europe' (And further) 'for the German export nation the unification of Europe is of decisive importance' ... 'either political union is added to EMU – then it will be a durable arrangement because a balance will have been created – or EMU only lasts for a period of time, and then breaks up because of conflicting interests'.
128. 'here all the others have moved in the direction of the German laws regarding the *Bundesbank*', ' "Wir gewinnen mit Europa", Grundsatzrede auf dem 3. Parteitag der CDU in Düsseldorf am 27 Oktober 1992', in Helmut Kohl, *Der Kurs der CDU. Reden und Beiträge des Bundesvorsitzenden 1973–1993*, Stuttgart: Deutsche Verlags-Anstalt, 1993, pp. 430ff.
129. *Daily Telegraph*, 12 December 1991.
130. Sperling, *op. cit.*, p. 209.
131. 'in order to understand the real dimension of the exercise one must look at German history, for instance the Paulskirche parliament from 1848. One could also mention the Bismarck *Reichstag*', ' "Wir gewinnen mit Europa", Grundsatzrede auf dem 3. Parteitag der CDU in Düsseldorf am 27. Oktober 1992', in Helmut Kohl, *Der Kurs der CDU. Reden und Beiträge des Bundesvorsitzenden 1973–1993*, Stuttgart: Deutsche Verlags-Anstalt, 1993, p. 440.
132. Although sharing my view that German policy basically has to be assessed in instrumental terms, Anderson and Goodman disagree with my assessment of EMU, arguing that the benefits of EMU were clear but remote and that EMU involved risks for Germany. However 'the political leadership in Bonn took these risks in stride because of the overwhelming importance assigned to political union', Jeffrey J. Anderson and John B. Goodman, 'Mars or Minerva?

A United Germany in a Post-Cold War Europe', in R. Keohane, J. Nye and S. Hoffmann (eds), *After the Cold War. International Institutions and State Strategies in Europe 1989–1991*, Cambridge, Mass.: Harvard University Press, 1993, pp. 53 ff.

133. Interview, March 1996.
134. See Peter Biering and Klavs A. Holm, *EU – det samlede traktatgrundlag*, Copenhagen: DJØF's forlag, 4. udg, 1996, p. 59.
135. Interview, March 1996.
136. Interview, September 1997.
137. Interview, March 1996.
138. Interview, March 1996.
139. Interview, March 1996.
140. Simon Bulmer and William E. Paterson, 'Germany in the European Union: Gentle Giant or Emergent Leader?', *International Affairs*, Vol. 72, no. 1, 1996, p. 20.
141. See the interesting discussion in Hans Mouritzen, *Finlandization*, Aldershot: Gower, 1988.
142. Interview, September 1997.
143. Jeffrey J. Anderson, *A United Germany in Europe: Hard Interests and Soft Power*, Paper delivered at the 1995 Annual Meeting of the American Political Science Association, Chicago, 31 August–3 September 1995, p. 20.

9 Barriers to hegemony: the ratification crisis

The Danish 'no'

In the absence of a strong formal leadership the task of crisis management in an organization will be carried out by the informal leadership. In the EC France and Germany assumed this role in the early 1980s, and they did so again during the crisis following the Danish 'no' to the Maastricht Treaty in June 1992. At the beginning of 1992, there were no signs of impending drama in the EC. The first months of 1992 were dominated by German initiatives aimed at fleshing out the Franco–German plans for a European defence corps and the discussion of issues arising out of the Maastricht summit. Thus Germany invited all members of the WEU 'seriously interested' in setting up such an entity to attend a brainstorming session in Bonn on 19 and 20 February. Spain and Belgium expressed interest, whereas the UK and the Netherlands were very sceptical.[1]

In April the two countries announced that they would establish a joint naval squadron expanding their bilateral military cooperation.[2] The following month a joint Franco–German defence delegation met UK defence officials to try to allay fears in London that the attachment of German units to a 35,000-strong Eurocorps would come into conflict with NATO planning. The German argument was that the main effect of the corps would be to bind French conventional forces more closely to NATO forces. In a reaction to the talks the German embassy in London described the talks as 'constructive'.[3] In May the British government for the first time accepted that the controversial joint Franco–German corps might be among the forces made available to the WEU. At the same time, the British defence secretary insisted that NATO should have first call on troops in the event of a crisis.[4]

In May 1992 at a two-day summit in La Rochelle, Kohl and Mitterrand signed a treaty on the Eurocorps. They stated that the corps would be fully operational in 1995.[5] The corps would consist of separate national units, the Germans having rejected a French proposal to fully assign troops to the corps in peacetime.[6] In a comment on speculation about the consequences of a 'no' at the forthcoming Danish referendum on the Maastricht Treaty the two leaders made it clear that they would press ahead with the Maastricht Treaty regardless of how the Danes voted. They also said they welcomed the membership candidacies of Austria, Sweden and Finland, these countries having shown their willingness to accept the Community as it was, adding that these countries would reinforce the Union economically and politically.[7]

In preparation for the Lisbon summit in late June the Commission had prepared a report on the consequences of enlargement. Unveiling some of the thinking behind the report, Jacques Delors made some statements in April 1992 regarding the need to streamline the Union and to reduce the powers of the small states which were to reappear in Danish newspapers, where they fanned the protests against the treaty. Amongst other things Delors mentioned that 'the President of the Commission would become president for the entire Community and chair a cabinet government for Europe'.[8]

The outcome of the Danish referendum on 2 June 1992 was a 'no'.[9] The difference between the 'yes' and the 'no' votes was only 46,000 votes. The outcome unleashed an immediate crisis in the EC. The Maastricht Treaty had now to all intents and purposes fallen, since Article 236 of the Treaty of Rome stipulated that treaty changes required unanimity. Despite the mixed news having emerged from Copenhagen during the weeks prior to the referendum, the result nevertheless came as a shock to France and Germany. The more so since their Danish ministerial colleagues had ensured them that Denmark would vote yes, referring to polls taken during the months before the referendum. A number of hesitant supporters appear to have changed their minds at the last moment.

The risk as seen from Paris and Bonn was now that the whole package deal negotiated in Maastricht might come unravelled with severe consequences for European stability. True to their earlier promises, the two leaders declared that although they regretted the Danish 'no', 'their determination to realize the European Union was unswerving'. Commission President Delors was less diplomatic, warning of 'consequences not only for the Community but also for Denmark and the Danes'. Most blunt was the Portuguese foreign minister, who held the presidency and whose timetable for the last month would now be ruined: 'we can't have a member state which does not accept the fundamental goals of the Community (as contained in Maastricht) continuing to be a member of the Community; it could have another status, another relationship with the EC'. Interestingly, even the British foreign minister, Douglas Hurd, defended the Maastricht Treaty saying that 'the Danish vote was not a reason to stop others going ahead'.[10]

The reactions partly reflected European geopolitics, but the issue also had repercussions for the enlargement of the Community. Portugal had few historical or cultural ties to Denmark, whereas for Germany Denmark was so to speak the entrance gate to the Nordic region. Given the fact the Germany was – mainly for economic reasons – keenly interested in the accession of the EFTA countries, it had to treat the issue of the Danish 'no' in a way which did not create bad feelings in the rest of the Nordic region, as this might jeopardize the Nordic enlargement. Throughout the crisis, the Danish foreign ministry thus had the (correct) impression that Germany was more willing than France to listen to Denmark.[11] This explains the relatively moderate tone of the Franco–German comment on the referendum. On the following day, Mitterrand decided to call a French referendum on the treaty, hoping to drown the tiny Danish 'no' in a big French 'yes'.

On 4 June the EC foreign ministers, assembling for an emergency meeting in Oslo on the fringe of a NATO meeting, declared unanimously that the Maastricht ratification process would continue. The underlying message was that Denmark, not the EC, had a problem. The case of the Danish 'no' is thus of more general interest. First of all it makes visible the inherent contradictions between the rule of law and the rule of power in the EU. *De jure*, the Maastricht Treaty had fallen on 2 June; *de facto*, it apparently had not. Secondly, and related to that, it shows that in formal terms the EU's constitutive politics contain a democratic element of minority protection in that each state in the Union must ratify changes in the constitutive treaties before such changes can take effect.[12] This is not a common procedure in federations. Only Canada has a similar constitutive procedure, which goes to show the extraordinary decentralization of the European federal structure. Thirdly, the Danish 'no' in June 1992 may in part have been provoked by perceptions of too marked an asymmetry in the EC. Although analyses of the referendum result do not suggest that fear of big-power dominance was widespread among the Danes, it is possible that the issue tipped the balance among undecided voters. Certainly the statements by Delors on the consequences of enlargement had produced some public uproar, as had the Franco–German message to Denmark to the effect that the Maastricht Treaty would be implemented regardless of how the Danes voted. The announcement of the Euro-corps in May may also have caused concern among the Danish voters, many of whom were known to have anti-militaristic attitudes. The first Danish 'no' thus illustrates the risks involved in the core countries adopting too high a profile or moving too fast towards the goal of an asymmetrical federation. The Dutch reaction to the Franco–German attempt to assume the leadership in the IGC on political union in October 1991 essentially reflected the same underlying anxiety about regional hegemony.

The reaction of the other member states to the Danish 'no' sent a signal to the other members and to prospective new members, as well as to the citizens of the Union, that if the provisions of the treaty collided with the political interests of the core, the interests of the core would prevail. At a more general level this illustrated the fragility of the federal guarantees in the EU. The episode also illustrated a fundamental weakness in the strategy of differentiation: how could the core remain cooptative, if it had to exclude? Put differently, would membership of the core remain attractive to a peripheral country, once this country had been treated badly by the core? A related question was to what extent the regional core possessed the means necessary to discipline the outsiders.

The monetary crisis and the French referendum

Meanwhile, tension was growing within the EMS, with Germany smarting from the problems of unification. The German government essentially decided to pass on the costs of financing unification to the other European countries, raising interest rates instead of raising taxes. The immediate effect was to produce tension in the EMS, but at the same time the German unilateralism highlighted the need for closer European monetary coordination. At a meeting of EC finance ministers in Bath in early September 1992 the French, Italian and not least the

British ministers tried to make their German counterpart lower interest rates in order to take off some of the pressure on their currencies. The *Bundesbank* refused, arguing that the currencies of the three countries were overvalued.[13]

Speculation against the three currencies continued until 15 September 1992, when Helmut Schlesinger, the president of the *Bundesbank,* told the German *Handelsblatt* that in his view a devaluation of the lira and the pound might be imminent. The following day the lira and the pound fell through the EMS floor. Bernard Connolly, former head of the Commission's office for monetary affairs, claims that in the days before the two currencies were forced out of the EMS, Germany and France had struck a deal according to which Italy was to be forced out of the ERM, whereas the *Bundesbank* would defend the parity between the franc and the Deutschmark.[14] A few days later France and Germany published a joint declaration, in which the *Bundesbank* and the *Banque de France* stressed that the two banks would defend the franc with all means at their disposal. The fact that the *Bundesbank* defended both the franc, the Danish krone, the Dutch guilder and the Belgian franc (but not the lira and the pound) during the following months indicated that the Bank was indeed in the process of creating a two-speed Europe, signalling which currencies it was willing to support. It is significant that despite a very high foreign debt, greatly overshooting the EMU target of 60 per cent of GDP, the Belgian franc was among the currencies enjoying a privileged status. This suggests that the *Bundesbank* did not assess the various countries from a purely economic perspective and may have acted in tacit understanding with the German government. Certainly, from a political point of view, Belgium belonged to the countries with close political ties to the two leading countries in the Union.

The ratification problem was of course essentially political but it soon began to interact with the economic problems in Europe. The Danish 'no' had weakened the markets' confidence in EMU. John Major's solidarity with the Danes and the strength of the anti-Maastricht forces in the Conservative Party added to the nervousness of the markets. The British reaction was strong. Michael Heseltine, not a Euro-sceptic, was blunt: 'I don't think there is any serious doubt that the remarks attributed to the president of the *Bundesbank* triggered the turbulence which led us to suspend our membership of the ERM'.[15]

We still do not have a clear picture of what happened in September 1992. A well-placed observer argues that politicians and the press unduly dramatized the episode. His assessment is that, whereas Italy was in fact

forced out of the EMS, it is more doubtful whether the British were
forced to exit. He does, however, share the view that Belgium was
accorded special treatment for political reasons.[16] This suggests that
although the *Bundesbank* may not directly harmonize its views with the
government, it either shares the government's basic views on European
policy or anticipates them. This assessment of the British exit does not
seem convincing. It is difficult to avoid the impression that John Major's
hesitancy to ratify the Maastricht Treaty was an element in the monetary
crisis between the UK and Germany. One should also recall Major's
ambitious strategy of attaining Deutschmark-like currency stability,
which the Germans can be forgiven for having interpreted as an overt
challenge to German monetary supremacy.[17] David Marsh, a specialist
on Germany with the respected *Financial Times*, claims that Kohl, during
a one-hour telephone conversation with Major, told Major firmly that
'Britain's credibility would take a further dive unless it went ahead with
ratifying the treaty'. There may also have been a personal dimension to
the clash. Kohl probably felt he had been let down by Major, whom he
had helped obtain opt-out clauses in Maastricht. But the Anglo–German
clashes on European policy should probably be seen in a wider context.
There had been recurrent skirmishes on the policy towards Yugoslavia;
the British were opposed to German demands for a permanent seat on
the UN Security Council; and Nazi caricatures had appeared in the
more jingoistic part of the British press. The culmination of the Anglo–
German crisis was a German plan – promptly abandoned – to officially
support a ceremony to commemorate the first flight of Hitler's V2
rocket.[18]

With the UK and Italy outside the ERM, the fate of EMU now
depended on France, President Mitterrand having decided to call a
referendum on the treaty on 20 September 1992. Already the British
were calling for a rethinking of EMU as well as for changes in the
Maastricht Treaty. A senior diplomat in Brussels said that a 'no' vote in
France would leave the Community 'like a chair with three legs'.[19] As
anxious to get a 'yes' as his French partner, Kohl appeared on French
television to reassure the French voters. In the end the pro-Maastricht
side won a slim victory, but at a cost.

Firstly, the French debate with its reference to German demons
caused some concern on the German side. Marie-France Garaud, a
leading no-campaigner, described her fear of Germany's 'empire of
money' asking: 'is it necessary that we enter this empire as junior
partners?'. But it was the pro-camp which made the most use of the

171

German card. Pierre Beregovoy, the Prime Minister, said that unification made it necessary 'for Germany to be solidly tied to the European wagon'.[20] A German political observer reassured himself that 'they have to convince chauvinist French voters'.[21]

Secondly, Mitterrand, renowned for his casual approach to economics, told his countrymen during a televised debate that the powers of the new European Central Bank would be balanced by a strong economic council. The Germans regarded this as a reinterpretation of the treaty.

Thirdly, the narrow victory for the pro-side unleashed renewed speculative pressure, this time against the franc. Seen from Bonn, the attack on the French franc was also an attack on the Maastricht Treaty. An ERM and an EMU without France was of no interest to Germany. The German *Bundesbank* therefore made an all-out effort to defend the franc, succeeding together with France in defending the parity.[22] By contrast, Spain and Ireland, having come under attack, had to re-impose exchange controls.

Concern about the stability of a future monetary system prompted the former president of the *Bundesbank*, Karl Otto Pöhl, to suggest the formation of a 'mini-EMS' consisting of countries with strong currencies. He suggested that Germany, France, the Benelux countries and Denmark might be joined by Austria and Switzerland. By including the Swiss the proposal broke the link between EMU and political union, by which Kohl set so much store, and it cannot have pleased the Chancellor, who incidentally had fired Pöhl because of disagreements over German monetary union.

On 22 September 1992 immediately after the French referendum, Kohl and Mitterrand met in Paris for a mini-summit, expressing their firm commitment to ensuring that European monetary and political union would not be halted.[23] Two days later Jacques Delors said, in a thinly veiled reference to the growing UK opposition to Maastricht, 'if some countries are looking for alibis for delaying the treaty, it may well be that others take the lead . . . this cannot be ruled out'.[24] Referring to sources in the chancellery, the German magazine *Der Spiegel* reported that a Franco–German central bank project already existed on paper. The plan was to base the new Central Bank in Frankfurt. The bank's president was to be a Frenchman. The officials in the chancellery commented, however, that it was a rescue plan, not a priority.[25]

In a surprise move indicating that German loyalty to the French was far from absolute, all the main parties in Germany including the CDU-CSU signalled that the *Bundesbank* would need to have a final say on the introduction of the common currency. Apart from reflecting domestic political anxiety about the terms on which Germany would be giving up its Deutschmark, the move also amounted to a *de facto* opt-out clause for Germany – unilaterally declared. Although members of the *Bundestag*'s European committee made a point of stressing that this did not constitute a second ratification of the treaty, the decision broke the automaticity on transition to the third stage of EMU which France regarded as the essence of the Maastricht Treaty.[26]

In what must be regarded as a show of force on the part of Helmut Kohl, the informal network of Christian Democratic leaders in the Community met in Brussels at the end of September and issued a firm statement in support of the German position. The *Bundesbank* had been blameless for the immolation of sterling; the pound must be formally devalued if the UK wanted to rejoin the ERM; and there would be no question of reforming the system along the lines suggested by Britain.[27]

A meeting of EC finance ministers on 28 September appeared to repair part of the damage done to European monetary cooperation, if not to Anglo–German relations. Norman Lamont, the British Chancellor of the Exchequer, gave the Germans an indirect apology, but his ministry later said that his remarks had only related to press comments for which he had no responsibility. A statement was issued from the meeting in which the ministers affirmed their faith in the European monetary system, describing it as a 'key factor of economic stability and prosperity in Europe'. The statement also declared in words that were sure to please the British that 'everyone present emphasized their opposition to the concept of a two-speed Europe'. Although the UK claimed not to have been isolated, arguing that it had support in Italy and Spain, an Italian official said that 'we're not blaming the *Bundesbank*, like some countries I could mention'.[28]

The Anglo–German 'war of words' as it was called in the press did leave scars in Britain, and not only in Conservative quarters. It is interesting that the left-leaning *Guardian*, not normally on the anti-EC and anti-German side, published an article on 2 October 1992 in which it drew comparisons between the currency war and the post 1871-period arguing that 'once again there are signs of German assertiveness and arrogance'.[29]

The British were not alone in being worried. In early October the Dutch Prime Minister, Ruud Lubbers, sent what was meant to be a private letter to John Major expressing concern about the Franco–

German axis and the position of the small countries within the European Community. The content of the letter was revealed to the *Daily Telegraph* by a British official who had seen it. Although Lubbers' office subsequently denied having expressed such concern, his spokesman indirectly confirmed the report by the *Telegraph* saying that it had been a 'private letter' between the two leaders.[30]

Apart from threats of exclusion, France and Germany also used additional side-payments in their attempt to save the Maastricht Treaty. An extraordinary summit in Birmingham on 16 October 1992 was called to discuss the principle of subsidiarity and democratization of the EU institutions, both issues being regarded as important to the EU-sceptics in Europe.[31] However, there would be no re-opening of the treaty negotiations, Kohl pointed out, only *eine interpretierende Erklärung* (an interpreting statement). Kohl also spoke about *Regelungswut* (regulatory fury) in the Commission, and did not rule out that some of the competences residing in Brussels should be recalled to the states or regions.[32] But during a meeting in Paris a few days before the summit, Germany, France and Spain agreed that EMU and political union should be ratified and implemented without changes. No joint Franco–German text had been prepared, allegedly because such a text would provoke suspicion among other member states. The German side pointed out that in their view the declaration from Birmingham should highlight three principles: 1) the principle of subsidiarity, 2) greater transparency in the decision-making process and 3) democratic controls by national parliaments and the EP.[33] The problem was how to agree on a supplementary declaration with binding effect without this implying a change in the treaty. Provided a reopening of the treaty negotiations and a 'domino effect' in the sense of demands for new additions could be avoided, the supplementary declarations were not unwelcome to the German government which had been criticized in the *Bundestag* as well as publicly for not having obtained sufficient concessions in precisely this area. The French, alarmed by the high 'no' vote, also had an interest in reassuring voters. The crucial difficulty consisted in inserting a 'political fire-belt' making it abundantly clear to Maastricht opponents and sceptics in the UK that it would be pointless to press for genuine changes in the treaty. Much therefore depended on finding a legal form which would satisfy the Danes and British without sharpening their appetite.

In early December Kohl and Mitterrand met in Bonn to prepare for the Edinburgh summit on 11 and 12 December. On the eve of the summit the omens for a successful summit or indeed for the survival of the Maastricht Treaty were not good. There was still uncertainty as to whether one would find a solution to the 'Danish problem'. Beleaguered by French peasants, Mitterrand was looking for support from Germany and the rest of the Community on the issue of the GATT round, a support the free market Germans would only give at a price. He also wanted Germany to confirm its support for the French franc, a demand that it was easier for Germany to accommodate. Apart from the political implications, a French devaluation would of course also have had unpalatable effects on the German economy, which is closely linked to the French economy, and it might have forced Germany to cut interest rates more than they would have liked.[34] In return for these French demands, Kohl wanted the summit to agree to making the eighteen extra members of the European Parliament taken in after unification full voting members, and he was eager to make decisions on enlargement.[35]

However, there was also cause for some optimism. France and Germany had weathered the storm caused by currency speculators and made progress in the defence area during the autumn. Bonn officials said that they were pleased with a Franco–German agreement to place their future army corps under NATO command for common alliance defence and peace-keeping missions outside the NATO area.[36]

At the summit in Edinburgh, Denmark obtained a special opt-out in four areas – currency, defence, citizenship and judicial and internal affairs – the skilful British diplomats deserving most of the credit for this success. The legal formula chosen was a 'decision by the Council', a novelty in EC jurisdiction but one that was capable of solving the political problem at hand. Three factors explain the willingness of the other member states (including Portugal) to compromise on the issue. First of all, as referred to earlier, the Germans very much interpreted the Danish issue in the context of the EFTA enlargement. Secondly, the British government linked its own ratification of the treaty to a satisfactory solution to the Danish problem. Thirdly, the Danish Prime Minister and foreign minister, both staunch supporters of the Maastricht Treaty, had accumulated some goodwill in Bonn and other European capitals. In other words, it is not possible to draw the conclusion from the Danish episode that in the case of a small country rejecting a constitutive bargain, the core will always try to find a way of keeping the country in the Union. This will depend on the context and the country.

The breakthrough on the Danish issue broke the ice, clearing the way for solutions to a number of other problems, including the difficult budgetary issue, where the UK might have blocked decisions. Germany was granted its eighteen new full members of the Parliament and a declaration on subsidiarity and transparency was agreed to. Trying to assist John Major in his fight against the Maastricht opponents at home, Jacques Delors' commission had announced its intention to withdraw around 20 directives including ones on harmonization of tobacco advertising, summer time, and the living conditions of animals in zoos.[37]

The German Constitutional Court intervenes

In May 1993 Denmark held a second referendum, this time on the Maastricht Treaty with exceptions and additions. This time the outcome was a comfortable 'yes'. The British government followed suit ratifying the treaty in early August 1993 after the House of Commons and the House of Lords had given its consent. In the meantime the treaty had also aroused controversy in Germany. A number of independent economists attacked the EMU chapter, arguing that the guarantees of the new Central Bank's independence and of the primacy of the goal of price stability were insufficient. At the same time, they also warned that a hasty realization of the EMU plan might lead to growing social tensions in the Union. Their arguments were countered by the three largest banks in Germany, which defended the treaty, arguing that the treaty contained the necessary guarantees.[38] This debate did not directly threaten Germany's adherence to the Union, referenda having no place in the German constitution.[39] However, the public debate found an echo in Parliament. With reference to the public debate on EMU, the main parties in the *Bundestag* decided to make German participation in the third stage of EMU dependent upon a separate decision in the two chambers of the German parliament.

Critics of the Maastricht Treaty also had the option of seeking assistance from the Constitutional Court in Karlsruhe. A group of citizens led by the former Commission employee, Manfred Brunner, thus decided to sue the government. On 12 October 1993 the German Constitutional Court passed a verdict on the compatibility of the treaty with the German constitution. Given the fact that a referendum was not an option, the verdict in a sense became an *Ersatzreferendum* (substitute referendum). The verdict which became the source of much comment at home and abroad contained a number of points, three of which deserve to be stressed. First of all, the court argued that a supranational order must respect democratic principles. Since there is no European people, the court argued, democratic legitimacy resides in the nation-states. The court thus argued that the EU was not a federation but a special political order which it called a state union (*Staatenbund*). It added, however, that it followed from the requirement of democratic legitimation that as the EU extended its competences, the powers of the European Parliament had to be similarly strengthened. Secondly, the court stated that Germany's signing of the Maastricht Treaty did not subject it to any automatic movement towards EMU. This view was diametrically opposed to the French view, and in fact amounted to a unilateral German re-negotiation of the Maastricht Treaty, since it was not challenged by other member states or the European Court of Justice. Thirdly and finally, the court challenged the right of the supra-national institutions to undertake expansive interpretations of EU law. EU legislation had to be clear and unequivocal.[40] This was a setback for the political elite, which had, as we have seen, based its integration strategy on a policy of integration by stealth. The strategy of cooperative hegemony had hit some rather solid, domestic barriers, some of which were located within the hegemonic state itself!

On 3 November 1993 the German government eventually ratified the Maastricht Treaty. Having been the first to talk about union, the Germans were the last to ratify the union treaty.

Notes

1. *Financial Times*, 6 February 1992.
2. *Financial Times*, 23 April 1992.
3. *Financial Times*, 13 May 1992.
4. *Financial Times*, 15 May 1992.
5. *Financial Times*, 23 May 1992.
6. *Financial Times*, 21 May 1992.
7. *Financial Times*, 23 May 1992.
8. According to *The Times*, 15 June 1992, which quotes 'rumours'.
9. The Danish 'no' and its implications are analysed in Nikolaj Petersen, ' "Game, Set and Match' '. Denmark and the European Union from Maastricht to Edinburgh', in Teija Tiilikainen and Ib Damgaard Petersen (eds), *The Nordic Countries and the EC*, Copenhagen: Copenhagen Political Studies Press, 1993.
10. *Financial Times*, 4 June 1992.

11. Interview, April 1997.
12. In this respect, the EU resembles the United States under its first constitution, the Articles of Confederation of 1777. In the Articles amendment of the original compact was subject to consent by all states. See Ivo Duchacek, *Comparative Federalism: The Territorial Dimension of Politics*, New York: Holt, Rinehart and Winston Inc., 1970, p. 157.
13. See Carsten Grønbech, *En realpolitisk tolkning af ØMU-projektet*, unpublished M.A. thesis, Institute of Political Science, University of Aarhus.
14. Quoted in Grønbech, *op. cit.*
15. The *Independent*, 19 September 1992.
16. Interview, August 1997.
17. *Financial Times*, 3 October 1992.
18. *Financial Times*, 3 October 1992.
19. The *Independent*, 19 September 1992.
20. The *Independent*, 1 September 1992, p. 6.
21. *Financial Times*, 5 September 1992. See also *Le Monde*, 4 September 1992, p. 9.
22. *Financial Times*, 9 October 1992.
23. *Financial Times*, 23 September 1992.
24. *Financial Times*, 25 September 1992.
25. *Le Monde*, 29 September 1992.
26. See *The Times*, 25 September 1992.
27. The *Sunday Telegraph*, 27 September 1992, p. 8.
28. *The Times*, 29 September 1992.
29. The *Guardian*, 2 October 1992, p. 25.
30. *Dialog. Reuters. 1168757*, European Community Report, 5 October 1992.
31. *Frankfurter Allgemeine Zeitung*, 22 September 1992, p. 1.
32. *Frankfurter Allgemeine Zeitung*, 24 September 1992, p. 2.
33. *Frankfurter Allgemeine Zeitung*, 13 October 1992, p. 4.
34. *Sunday Telegraph*, 6 December 1992, p. 41.
35. *Reuter Newswire*, 4 December 1992.
36. *Reuter Newswire*, 4 December 1992.
37. *The Times*, 9 December 1992.
38. See Thomas Pedersen, 'Europa – Tysklands "anden Nation"', in Henning Gottlieb and Frede P. Jensen (eds), *Tyskland i Europa*, Copenhagen: SNU, 1995, pp. 79ff.
39. This was intended as a guarantee against populist politics with which Germany has sad experiences.
40. See Thomas Pedersen, *op. cit.*, pp. 78ff.

10   Geopolitical asymmetry: the post-Maastricht era

Enhanced structural asymmetry: the stability pact

The Maastricht Treaty contained a number of holes which had to be filled, notably in the EMU area. Germany proved particularly adept at filling such holes. A well-placed observer points out that 'when the five EMU criteria were formulated, it was not the impression that they should be understood literally and very precisely. The criteria were targets that were presumed to be liable to political interpretation. Gradually this has changed on German initiative and without much resistance from other countries'.[1] This tightening was justified by reference to domestic political pressure. Domestic pressures clearly played a role, notably the growing EMU scepticism in the CSU. Yet despite the polls showing considerable opposition to EMU amongst German voters, the issue only rarely became an electoral issue in Germany, and when it did the opposition party, the SPD, was generally punished by the voters.

In other respects as well, the *de facto* Maastricht 'renegotiation' continued. Referring to the need to reassure the German population that the new European currency would be as strong and as stable as the Deutschmark, the German government proposed the conclusion of a so-called stability pact as a supplement to the Maastricht Treaty. The pact would transform the entry criteria for the third phase of EMU into permanent obligations binding member states. Reflecting positions adopted by German negotiators during the IGC, these new demands constituted a renegotiation of the treaty. During the negotiations on the

179

pact, which ended in the conclusion of the pact in December 1996 at the Dublin summit, Germany furthermore managed to institute tough rules relating to the imposition of fines. In a concession to France, which wanted the goal of job creation to be given a higher priority the name of the pact was eventually changed to a 'growth and stability pact'. The content of the German proposal was, however, only changed at the margins.

German decision-makers also stressed the spillover effects of EMU. In a speech delivered in Schwarzwald in Switzerland in March 1995, Hans Tietmeyer, the *Bundesbank* president, said *inter alia* that '*das Spannungsverhältnis zwischen einer supranationalen Währungspolitik und anderen weiterhin national kontrollierten Politikbereichen ist nicht zu übersehen*'.[2] Tietmeyer particularly drew attention to the need to harmonize tax systems. Others argued that EMU would of necessity generate a strong pressure for much larger transfers from the EU budget to weaker areas in the Union as well as a pressure for stronger parliamentary control over the Union's economic policy.

The advent of Jacques Chirac as President of France raised questions about the continuing commitment of France to the EMU project. In part to placate EU critics in his own party, Chirac adopted a more assertive policy style vis-à-vis Germany than his predecessor. Only in October 1995 did Chirac unequivocally commit himself to EMU. The nuclear tests conducted in 1995 underlined this new style, at the same time sending a signal to Germany that France remained in a category of its own amongst the European powers by virtue of its independent nuclear capability. Chirac's decision to reform his country's conventional forces creating a 'leaner but meaner' French army on a par with 'the best in the world, notably the British army' also caused some concern in Germany.[3] Was France trying to overtake Germany in NATO? The decision was supplemented with efforts to upgrade Franco–British defence collaboration notably in the nuclear field.[4] Kohl reacted to Chirac's posturing by engaging in a strong public defence of EMU, warning France not to abandon the Maastricht road. Although after a period of uncertainty France basically resumed its previous pro-EMU policy, the Franco–German relationship appears to have suffered considerably from the nuclear test episode. The victory of the socialists in the 1997 elections to the National Assembly led to a brief period of uncertainty, but at the Amsterdam summit later in June, a minor addition to the stability pact referring to job creation managed to restore calm in Franco–German relations, at least in public.

Strategic differentiation: the *Kerneuropa* proposal

During 1994, the year after the Maastricht Treaty had taken effect, France and Germany made public new ideas indicating a shift of emphasis in their grand strategy. The paper on a *Kerneuropa* (core Europe), technically an internal discussion paper in the CDU, sketched out a two-pronged strategy: it proposed institutional reforms which should make the Union more effective, while at the same time reshaping the institutions so as to give the big powers more power. In addition it proposed the formation of a stable core of particularly committed EU members.[5] The German plan which contained a mixture of federalist reforms and strategic differentiation was essentially a response to two different challenges. First of all, German political leaders were anxious as to whether France would remain loyal to the institutionalist strategy which Germany advocated. The *Kerneuropa* plan with its notion of an avant-garde within the Union was flattering to French ears recalling old Gaullist ideas. However, it was widely seen to be rigid. Secondly, the *Kerneuropa* plan was a German response to the barriers to hegemonic leadership which had become visible in connection with the Danish 'no' to the Maastricht Treaty. But the problem was wider. Given the well-known hesitancy of the neutral EFTA members: Sweden, Finland and Austria, in the field of defence integration, the problem of 'small state obstruction' could be expected to grow in the future. The timing of the German proposal supports the interpretation that the problems that accompanied the EFTA enlargement was one of the causes of the German re-thinking.

France saw eye to eye with Germany as regards the need to find ways of bypassing sceptical member states. Yet the French idea of differentiation differed from the German. France envisaged a number of overlapping circles of cooperation with France and Germany at the centre. In the monetary area, it did not wish to exclude Italy, a major market for its exports. In the defence area, it regarded Britain as a natural member of the inner circle of integration in part as a counterweight to Germany but also as an invaluable asset in a future European defence entity. France thus preferred a looser version of strategic differentiation. This is reflected in the proposal published by the then Prime Minister, E. Balladur, on 30 August 1994 in a conversation with *Le Figaro*. Here he sketched out a European architecture built around three 'circles'.[6] Although France and Germany were meant to play the dominant role within it, the inner circle would not be closed and exclusive.

Rather the two countries would form the centre of a number of over-lapping circles. Interestingly, France was thus less enthusiastic about strategic differentiation in the 1990s than in the 1980s. It clearly feared that it might be unable to measure up to Germany in a tighter frame-work.

In March 1995, Jacques Chirac presented his own version of a 'concentric circle Europe'. Like Balladur he distinguished between three circles: 1) the Union 2) the outer circle of partners: given the German influence in an enlarged Union Chirac seemed to want to balance the Eastern enlargement with a consolidation of the Medi-terranean policy and 3) an inner circle of 'reinforced solidarity'.[7]

The notion of a core Europe appears to have been influenced by the EMU negotiations.[8] The indirect formation of a core through strict entry criteria seemed an effective and discreet way for Germany to exercise leadership, and an EMU core might serve as the basis and as a model for a more general asymmetry within the Union.[9] Significantly, it had been endorsed by the EC as a whole and thus legitimated a differentiated Europe. At the same time, the core Europe concept was sweet music in the ears of the German *Bundesbank* and helped accom-modate the EU sceptics in the CSU. In a small core, Germany would find it easier to impose its views.

In his interesting study of the *Kerneuropa* strategy Deubner, a researcher at the influential think-tank *Stiftung Wissenschaft und Politik*, known to have close ties to CDU circles, outlines one possible road which such a strategy may take. Deubner's core consists of five countries, Germany and France and the Benelux countries. His proposal envisages that these countries should adopt common positions in a range of areas, notably the more sensitive ones, and that they should form caucuses in all EU institutions.[10] Deubner describes his proposal as an answer to a widespread concern in Germany that it might lose control of EU affairs as a consequence of large-scale enlargement. Yet, given the fact that Germany has close economic and cultural ties with a number of the new and likely future members of the EU, this pessimism seems exaggerated. Elsewhere in his book Deubner concedes that in the future France will become less interesting to Germany, whereas countries like Finland and Austria will gain in importance.[11] One thus detects a certain inner tension in the book's overall argument, which suggests that the *Kern-europa* plan also contained a more strategic aspect.

In the real world, strategic differentiation suffered from certain weaknesses which became ever more visible during the second half of the 1990s. This was obvious in the case of EMU. One problem was that the cost of remaining outside the core proved to be rather small in economic terms. The UK and Denmark both had flourishing economies and Italy's devaluations posed a severe threat to French industry in particular. The German thinking seemed to be first that the members of EMU would constitute a caucus within the Union, and secondly that EMU would have strong spillover effects prompting integration in other areas like taxation and that the effect would be a further loss of political influence for the outsiders. Yet the difficulty was that whereas the economic cost of outsider status was visible, the political cost, for instance in terms of a loss of goodwill was much less visible to the general public which at the end of the day would (indirectly) decide on membership. Moreover, as long as the EMU core remained small, the goodwill cost would be limited. If, however, the EMU core were to be large, the goodwill cost would be big.[12]

In his seminal speech to the Catholic University in Leuven on 2 February 1996, Chancellor Kohl also touched upon the issue of differentiation: '*es darf nicht sein, dass das langsamste Schiff auf Dauer das Tempo des Geleitszugs bestimmt*' (the slowest ship cannot be allowed to permanently decide the speed of the convoy). Member states which were not willing or able to undertake certain integration steps must not be able to prevent others from pressing ahead. The practical implication was of course an erosion of the formal right of veto, which each member state possessed on constitutive matters. The speech, which was meant to be a response to John Major's speech in Leiden earlier the same year, in which Major had made a plea for a Europe of diversity, also carried other interesting messages. Kohl applied a subtle version of the threat of exit saying that '*Die Politik der europäischen Einigung ist in Wirklichkeit eine Frage von Krieg und Frieden im 21. Jahrhundert*' (the policy of European unification is in reality a question of war and peace in the 21st century). This might be read as an admittedly rather stark rehearsal of the old theme of European reconciliation. Yet, the continuation is more ambiguous. The speech is also meant as a warning. Kohl adds '*ich weiss, einige möchten dies nicht gerne hören. Meine* Warnungen *mögen eine* unangenehme *Wahrheit enthalten*' (author's emphasis) (I know some will not like to hear it. My *warnings* may contain an *unpleasant* truth). And later: '*fehlt der Schwung zur Fortsetzung des Einigungswerks, dann gibt es nicht nur Stillstand, sondern auch Rückschritt* (if the momentum to continue the work of unification stops then there will not only be stagnation but also retrogression). Kohl goes on to quote Thomas Mann, not his remark on the European

183

Germany, but the more equivocal *'wir sind deutsche Europäer und europäische deutsche'* (we are German Europeans and European Germans).[13]

Enhanced cooperation – or flexibility

The first concrete proposal regarding strategic differentiation was made in a joint letter by President Chirac and Chancellor Kohl to the President of the European Council, Felipe González, published on 6 December 1995 shortly before the summit on 15–16 December. In their letter, the two leaders propose the inclusion in a new treaty of a general clause, permitting states who are able and willing to do so to establish an enhanced cooperation, provided they respect the single institutional framework of the Union.[14]

A joint letter by the German and French foreign ministers, published in *Le Figaro*, the *Financial Times* and the *Frankfurter Allgemeine Zeitung* on 29 March 1996, that is on the day the new IGC was convened in Turin, outlines the general goals of the two countries in the context of the IGC.[15] The letter first of all refers to the need for a more efficient union. It mentions the need to make the Commission more cohesive; the need for greater use of majority voting in the Council as well as the need to pay attention to the weight of each member state in the Council; it also calls for the EP to be more closely involved in EU politics. Secondly, it stresses the need for reforms which will enable the Union to defend its interests abroad. In this connection the idea of a new office of foreign policy spokesman for the Union is mentioned. Thirdly, the letter refers to the need for a flexible Europe, allowing a smaller group of member states to push ahead with integration. In this connection it is stressed that no-one should be excluded. Finally, the letter speaks in rather vague terms about a Europe closer to the citizens. Interestingly, the German wish for closer cooperation on pillar 3 issues (judicial and internal affairs) is only referred to in one sentence. The hegemonic leadership aspirations of the two countries are highlighted by the letter's closing remarks: *'wir sind überzeugt, dem* allgemeinen Interesse Europas (author's emphasis) *zu dienen, wenn wir wie beschrieben vorgehen und uns hochgesteckte Ziele setzen'* (we are convinced that we are serving the *common interests of Europe* when we proceed as described and set ourselves ambitious goals).

In the autumn of 1996 France and Germany presented a quite detailed eight-page proposal with the title 'enhanced cooperation/

flexibility'.[16] The proposal described how smaller groups within the Union, intent on deepening integration, could be granted the right to push ahead with integration. The crucial point of the proposal was that the grouping embarking on closer cooperation would determine the criteria of admission. Moreover, new members joining such a cooperation would have to accept the core's *acquis*. The proposal would in a sense formalize and institutionalize the directional leadership of France and Germany, since the two countries could, if it were to be accepted, justify their special role in the Union with reference to the treaty.

The smaller member states generally gave the German and French ideas a cool reception without however altogether turning them down. Their calculation seemed to be that the two countries would build their 'mini-Europe' outside the Union unless they were allowed to set it up inside it. This was probably a miscalculation since the German view clearly was that the core had to be institutionalized and thus legitimated.

The Amsterdam Treaty

In the negotiations prior to the Amsterdam summit the small countries assisted by Italy managed to obtain a number of concessions consisting of conditions for the setting up of closer cooperation schemes (now termed *intégration renforcée*) and the involvement of the Commission. Gulliver was to have his movements severely restricted. Most of these conditions were included in the Amsterdam Treaty concluded in June 1997: the setting up of sub-groups for closer integration must only be used as a last resort, must be aimed at furthering the objectives of the Union, must respect the principles of the treaty and the single institutional framework and must concern at least a majority of member states. They must not affect the *acquis communautaire* nor the competences, rights, obligations and *interests* (author's emphasis) of member states not participating. However, while they must be open to all member states, there were strings attached: they would be open 'provided that they comply with the basic decision and with the decisions taken within that framework'. Thus the Franco–German fingerprints were also clearly visible.

The rules of authorization vary depending on the area. In pillar 1, authorization requires a qualified majority unless a country objects with reference to important national interests. The same procedure applies in pillar 3 (judicial and home affairs). As regards pillar 2, the Maastricht

Treaty already contains a paragraph permitting differentiation. However, the essential point in the Franco–German proposal was left untouched: other members of the Union would only be admitted to subgroups of reinforced integration provided they accepted both the basic decision setting up the sub-group and the subsequent decisions of the group (*l'acquis*).

The Amsterdam Treaty fulfilled most but not all of the Franco–German expectations outlined in the joint letter of March 1996. From the German point of view the main achievements were the flexibility clause, the enhanced use of majority voting, the extension of the co-decision procedure and the (phased) transfer of a number of pillar 3 issues relating to judicial and internal affairs to pillar 1. The price was German concessions to small and minor member states, as well as to the French socialists, on sectoral issues and overall principles. The Amsterdam summit saw an energetic effort on the part of a powerful coalition of left-of-centre governments to strengthen the social and environmental dimension of the Union and to codify human rights, including transparency and non-discrimination. The ideological as opposed to the power-political dimension was thus quite prominent in the new treaty, although as regards employment policy the treaty specified that joint efforts in this area had to be compatible with the overall economic policy, which of course had to be seen in the light of EMU. The effort to bring the Union closer to the citizens partly reflected the renewed strength of the Social Democrats in the majority of member states. In part it reflected an acceptance on the part of centre-right governments as well as the Commission that the Union had to be made more human and more relevant to ordinary citizens if it was to retain legitimacy. The lesson of the Danish and French referenda had not been forgotten. And the fact that the new treaty also had to pass referenda added to the caution.

The preamble to the treaty was extended to include the principles of sustainable development and a high level of employment and transparency. A new employment chapter was inserted in the treaty and it was agreed that members grossly violating the principles of democracy may have their membership rights (partly) suspended.

As regards institutional issues, on the other hand, France and Germany exercised the decisive influence, although they encountered strong opposition when it came to changing the distribution of power in the institutions. The main achievements of the two countries at Amsterdam was thus the chapter on flexibility (France and Germany), the enhanced powers of the Parliament (Germany) and the reforms in the foreign policy and defence area (France and Germany). On the Parliament, the coverage of the co-decision procedure was extended. On defence, the formulation in the Maastricht Treaty on the 'long-term creation of a common defence policy' was replaced by the formulation 'the gradual creation of a common defence policy'. A small step was also taken in the direction of further integration between the WEU and the EU. By way of compensation the UK obtained additional guarantees against an undermining of NATO. Foreign policy cooperation was reinforced mainly through the creation of a new post of General Secretary of the Council with special responsibility for foreign policy. Some 25 years after Henry Kissinger asked in vain for a telephone number on which to reach 'Europe', the USA was at least given a name. There was also some movement on decision-making. The principle of constructive abstention was introduced, as was a new concept of common strategy. Common strategies in areas of common interest, while defined by the European Council by unanimity, could from now on be implemented by qualified majority voting. However, to balance this change the UK inserted an 'emergency clause' to the effect that a country opposed to majority voting on an issue might block a decision, which would force the majority to refer the matter to the European Council.

Although the Amsterdam Treaty was billed as a response to the challenge of Eastern enlargement, little was achieved in this area except for the laying down of general principles and the setting of a future agenda. The Amsterdam Treaty was more a follow-up to Maastricht than a forward-looking response to enlargement. The treaty linked Eastern enlargement to two rounds of future reforms. The first would take place once the first members were admitted and would involve a reduction in the size of the Commission (with the big members giving up one of their Commissioners), balanced by a re-weighing of the votes in the Council to compensate the big states. The second reform, which would involve a general overhauling of the institutional system, would occur once the Union's membership superseded 20.[17] In the months following the Amsterdam summit France, Italy and Belgium made clear that they interpreted the agreement as laying down tough institutional conditions for admitting Central and Eastern applicants, a sign that enlargement would cause enduring tension within the EU, not least between Germany and France.

The new Blair government in the UK arrived in Amsterdam armed with all the self-confidence that a landslide inspires. Tony Blair thus did very well at Amsterdam breaking some British taboos on the Parliament and majority voting which immediately earned him sympathy from Helmut Kohl, while obtaining an opt-out on border control and managing to block major reforms in the foreign policy and defence areas. The Blair government also put an end to the infamous British opt-out on social policy.

Geopolitical and institutional asymmetry

The admission of new members to the EU has always been a high politics issue. Throughout the history of the EU linkages have been made between admission of new members and the core's wish to deepen integration.[18] Often these linkages have been defensive, aimed at protecting the integration system as such. But underlying this discussion has been another discussion relating to the way enlargements might affect the inter-state balance of power in the Union. The geopolitical aspect was salient in connection with the British accession, Britain being a big power with views far removed from those of France and (to a lesser extent) Germany. The fact that it took Britain ten years to join the EC was not due to any incapacity on Britain's part to fulfil the Community's technical requirements for membership, but reflected France's determination to protect and consolidate its privileged position in the EC before the door was opened to Britain. The balance-of-power problem was less salient in connection with the Greek and Iberian accession, in part because these states were either small or already had close links with one or both of the leading countries, as was the case with González's Spain. With the accession of the three EFTA countries, and the prospect of the admission of a number of Central and Eastern European countries, however, the question of power re-appeared in a big way.

The key problem was that the EFTA and Eastern enlargements threatened the parity on which Franco–German leadership in Europe was based. The EFTA enlargement may have implied some indirect financial benefits for France, but in terms of geopolitics and culture the EFTA enlargement would benefit Germany, not France or its allies in the south of Europe.

When it came to the Central and Eastern countries, geopolitics and culture were once again largely on the side of the Germans. Enlargement towards the East would benefit the Germans disproportionately, whatever the intentions of the German government. With a planned effort to penetrate Central and Eastern Europe, the benefits might be even larger. German economic influence in this area is already very high. Heather Grabbe from the Royal Institute of International Affairs has made some revealing calculations on German economic activity relating to the Central and Eastern Europeans, that is Bulgaria, the Czech Republic, Estonia, Hungary, Latvia, Lithuania, Poland, Romania and Slovakia.[19] In 1989 Germany accounted for 36.05 per cent of exports to these countries. In 1995 the figure had risen to 51.43 per cent. France's share fell from 9.83 per cent in 1989 to 5.84 per cent in 1995 and the UK's from 7.79 per cent in 1989 to 5.47 per cent in 1995. As far as FDI (foreign direct investments) is concerned Germany again leads among EU member states, although here the lead is smaller. The share of German FDI into the Czech Republic, Hungary and Poland was thus 21 per cent in 1995, closely behind the US share of 22.6 per cent. France and the UK account for 7.1 and 4.5 per cent, respectively.

There are, however, some mitigating aspects to a prospective Eastern enlargement as seen from Paris. France has close political ties to at least two of the applicant countries, Poland and Romania, the latter countries being members of the *Francophonie.*

Yet the overall picture is one of enhanced power asymmetries within the EU as a consequence of enlargement. The American case provides an interesting parallel. Deudney describes how the expansion of the American union led to a redistribution of power between advocates and opponents of slavery. Until the 1850s great compromises involving *inter alia* the 'pairing' of new slave states and new 'free soil states' prevented open conflict, but in the 1850s the establishment of slave states fell behind. The absence of an ultimate veto protecting minorities was thus one of the factors leading to the Civil War.[20]

It was obvious that Germany was deliberately trying to use enlargement to strengthen its position within the Union. On 13 October 1994, that is a year after the Karlsruhe verdict, Chancellor Kohl stated that '*für mich als Deutschen ist der Gedanke inakzeptabel, dass die Westgrenze Polens und der Tschechischen Republik auf Dauer die Ostgrenze der Europäischen Union sein sollte*'.[21] Foreign Minister Kinkel was more blunt in his government statement after the completion of the enlargement negotiations with the EFTA applicants, characterizing the Northern enlargement of the EU and Austria's accession as '*ein wesentlicher Schritt auf dem Weg . . . die Balance* (author's emphasis) *in Europa wiederherzustellen*'.[22] Such statements, which to many Germans were only stating the obvious, could not but provoke a furore in France. In March 1994 the French ambassador in Germany, François Scheer, thus criticized the dominant role of Germany in the enlargement negotiations in an interview with journalists in Bonn and added a more general concern about Germany's Eastern policy.[23] The growing tension between the north and south in the Union had come into the open at the Corfu summit in 1994, when the German foreign minister used very strong language when faced with Spanish intransigence on the enlargement issue.[24] The heated exchange on EFTA enlargement should be seen in the context of a more assertive leadership style on the part of the German government. Thus Kohl effectively vetoed Ruud Lubbers' candidacy for the Commission presidency despite Lubbers having the support of a majority of member states.[25]

From the French point of view there were basically two possible responses to the challenge of geopolitical asymmetry. They could try to stop it or they could re-shape the institutional structure to improve France's chances of coping successfully with Northern and Eastern enlargement. Since the first option was hardly realistic, as long as France wanted to preserve its partnership with Germany, preparations had to be made for the second option. Here the concentric circle model was a natural response, given France's traditional reticence about federalist schemes.

For Germany the strategic game was altogether different. For the Germans Eastern enlargement was not a 'natural disaster' as much as a development patiently anticipated. As we have seen, the German strategy had always been to create a European house spacious enough to put a roof over 'the unification of the German peoples', as Kohl phrased it. Just as in the 1950s the ECSC had legitimated the Federal Republic, dressing it up for a return to the family of democracies, the European Union would shelter a unified German *Kulturnation* (cultural nation) against the storm of anti-German sentiment. If the whole of Central and Eastern Europe plus Scandinavia could be made a part of the Union this would significantly strengthen Germany's power within it. Geopolitical asymmetry could be linked to a strategy of institutional asymmetry. Germany's institutional strategy was therefore focused on fashioning a governing structure which would transform the German *Kulturnation*'s population and coalitional strength into political assets. A first expression of this strategy was to be the proposal for a so-called 'double majority' in the Council, according to which a proposal would only be adopted if it could assemble both a majority of states and a majority of citizens in the Union. The point was that whereas one of the criteria satisfied the small members and the other all the big states, only Germany could expect to benefit on both counts, as it possessed both population strength and coalitional strength.

The main advantage of geopolitical asymmetry is its low visibility. This gave Germany an advantage in comparison with France (and the UK). The German advocacy of enlargement could be backed up with an impressive array of normative arguments, whereas France (and the UK) had to rely on the much more visible and risky option of institutional asymmetry. Chirac was aiming for a re-weighing of the votes in the Council and an upgrading of the role of the Council of ministers and the European Council. He also envisaged the election of a president of the European Council for a period of three years, an idea first broached by Giscard d'Estaing.[26] It was obvious to all, including the small members, that the Eastern enlargement would require some institutional adaptations. The introduction of more majority voting was thus relatively uncontroversial. The re-weighing of votes in Council was a different matter. First of all, this demand did not take into account the fact that the population strength was already broadly reflected in the composition of the European Parliament, the powers of which were strengthened in the Amsterdam Treaty. Secondly, the demand was based on the dubious premise that small members tend to gang up against the big. This is rarely the case, except perhaps for IGC negotiations, but here decisions are taken with unanimity.

The EU's Eastern enlargement will not only affect the balance between France and Germany, it may also lead to more general changes in the European political order. It is apparent that on the important issue of institutional adaptations to enlargement the UK basically shares the view of France and Germany. In fact, the British along with the Spanish may adopt a tougher stance than France and especially Germany on the institutional issue, as their influence is more dependent on formal representation than on informal coalition-politics. British observers express strong views on the issue, one observer arguing that the weight of the small members in Council should at least be halved and that one must think in terms of an EU security council consisting of the six big member states (the UK, France, Germany, Italy, Spain and Poland). In a similar vein, the presidency could be organized as rotating group presidencies with the big members each leading a group.[27] Given the scale of the Eastern enlargement and the sensitivity of the institutional issue, it may thus pave the way for a more complex political order in Europe with elements of *directoire* alongside the German-inspired cooperative hegemony.

Cooperative hegemony in the post-Maastricht era

The post-Maastricht era saw attempts to enhance the asymmetry of the EU, but this endeavour was hampered by growing intra-hegemonic tension as well as by clashes between big and small member states over the distribution of power within EU institutions. First of all, in continuation of previous policy, Germany tried to strengthen the congruence between the German and the European system of governance. A central element in this endeavour was the gradual tightening of the convergence criteria. Secondly, with the initiative on a *Kerneuropa* in 1994 as a starting-point, Germany embarked upon a new strategy aimed at strategic differentiation within the EU. Essentially, this strategy reflected a wish to circumvent the opposition of the UK and some small members to further integration. This concern was echoed by French initiatives on a 'Europe of concentric circles'. There were, however, considerable differences between the German and French notions of strategic differentiation. In addition, using EMU as a model and basis, the Kohl government seemed to be trying to create an inner circle (*ein fester Kern*) within the integration system where Germany could more easily impose its directional views.

Thirdly, the prospect of a very considerable increase in the membership of the Union with its attendant consequences for the balance of power prompted a debate on a reshaping of EU institutions. For Germany, enlargement towards the East opened up prospects for exploiting geopolitical and cultural asymmetries institutionally. Germany thus used the prospect of large-scale enlargement offensively to push for reforms that would enhance the institutional asymmetry of the Union, whereas French thinking assumed a more defensive character. The geographical enlargement of the Union generated new intra-hegemonic tension testing the tactical and strategic acumen of the Germans.

The novelty of the post-Maastricht era compared to the previous period was the emphasis on strategic differentiation and the related push for institutional asymmetry. The creation of the so-called 'euro-x' caucus inside ECOFIN confirmed that trend. Whereas structural asymmetry is an indirect form of hegemonic leadership, institutional asymmetry implies a more overt attempt to influence the regional integration system. It is therefore only logical that the degree of acceptance of the cooperative hegemony amongst the smaller EU member states should have declined during this period. However, institutional asymmetry and the cooperative hegemony that it represents remain a more indirect way of exercising great power influence than unilateral hegemony.

The post-Maastricht era also saw a change in the German leadership style within the EU, although to some extent this change reflected a change in the international and European agenda with new issues of vital importance to Germany coming to the fore.[28] What Volker Rühe has called *die Kultur der Zurückhaltung'* (the culture of reticence) was gradually abandoned.[29] The influential Michael Stürmer, head of the think-tank *Stiftung Wissenschaft und Politik* and close to the CDU/CSU government, probably catches the new mood in the political elite well: '*es zeigt sich, dass das alte Prozessmanagement unter dem Leitstern der Gemeinsamkeit seine Grenzen erreichte. Die Bundesrepublik muss, um ihre Interessen zu wahren, Führung entwickeln'*.[30] German academics were now saying aloud what had discreetly been practised for years, with Stürmer calling for '*zunehmende Internationalisierung nationaler Interessen'* (increasing internationalization of national interests).[31]

Notes

1. Interview, August 1997.
2. 'The tension between a supranational monetary policy and other policy sectors still under national control cannot be overlooked.' The speech is printed in *Internationale Politik*, 6/1995, pp. 86ff.
3. Anne-Marie Le Gloannec, 'Europe by Other Means?', *International Affairs*, 73/1, 1997, pp. 89ff.
4. See Stuart Croft, 'European Integration, Nuclear Deterrence and Franco–British Nuclear Cooperation', *International Affairs*, 72/4, 1996.
5. Karl Lamers and Wolfgang Schäuble, *Reflections on European Policy*, 1 September 1994, CDU/CSU Fraktion des Deutschen Bundestags, Überlegungen zur Europäischen Politik.
6. *Le Figaro*, 30 August 1994. See also Balladur's comments on the idea at a press conference following the EU summit in Essen on 10 December 1994; see *Internationale Politik*, 1/1995, pp. 110ff.
7. Christian Lequesne, 'Die Europäische Politik von Jacques Chirac: Auf dem Weg zu einer Notwendigen Klärung?', *Aus Politik und Zeitgeschichte*, 21 July 1995, p. 32.
8. Christian Deubner, *Deutsche Europapolitik: Von Maastricht nach Kerneuropa?*, Baden-Baden: Nomos Verlag, 1995, p. 183.

9. This is the assessment of German scholars expressed in conversations in February 1997.

10. Deubner, *op. cit.*, pp. 184ff.

11. Deubner, *op. cit.*, p. 118.

12. Some of these points were put to me in an interview in August 1997.

13. Kohl's Leuven speech is printed in *Internationale Politik*, 8/1996, pp. 82ff.

14. The letter is printed in *Internationale Politik*, 8/1996, p. 80.

15. The letter is printed in *Internationale Politik*, 8/1996, pp. 108ff.

16. See the joint memorandum by the French and German foreign ministers printed in *Europe Documents no. 2009*, 29 October 1996.

17. *Draft treaty of Amsterdam; conf/4001/97*, 19 June 1997.

18. See Thomas Pedersen, *European Union and the EFTA Countries. Enlargement and Integration*, London: Pinter, 1994; Line Hagn-Meincke and Charlotte Kinimond Hassø, *Udvidelse af EU – en integrationsskabende faktor?*, Copenhagen: DJØF, 1996.

19. See Heather Grabbe and Kirsty Hughes, *Enlarging the EU Eastwards*, London: Pinter/Royal Institute of International Affairs (1998).

20. Daniel H. Deudney, 'The Philadelphia System: Sovereignty, Arms Control, and Balance of Power in the American States-Union Circa 1787–1861', *International Organization*, Vol. 49, no. 2, Spring 1995, p. 218.

21. 'for me as a German the thought that the Western border of Poland and the Czech Republic should remain the Eastern border of the Union is not acceptable', see *Bulletin (Presse- und Informationsamt der Bundesregierung)*, Nr. 89/1993, p. 1006.

22. 'an important step in the direction of restoring the *balance* in Europe', see *Das Parlament*, no. 11, 18 March 1994, p. 2.

23. Renata Fritsch-Bournazel, 'Paris und Bonn: Eine Fruchtbare Spannung, *Europa-Archiv*, Folge 12, 1994, p. 343.

24. Spanish sources quote Kinkel as having shocked not only the Spanish but also a number of other personalities by saying to the Spanish minister that he was going to break his back unless he gave a green light for enlargement. Interview, September 1994.

25. Interview, March 1996. Lubbers appears to have been the victim of a vendetta on the part of Kohl, who never forgave him for his critical remarks on German unification and the Polish issue nor, one suspects, his letter to John Major warning about Franco–German dominance in the EU.

26. Lequesne, *op. cit.*, p. 33.

27. Interview, September 1997.

28. For instance there is no way of knowing how the German government would have reacted to a Serb–Croat conflict had it erupted in the late 1970s.

29. Quoted by Michael Stürmer in 'Deutsche Interessen', in Karl Kaiser and Hanns W. Maull (eds), *Deutschlands Neue Aussenpolitik. Band 1. Grundlagen*, Munich: R. Oldenburg Verlag, 1995, p. 58.

30. 'it has become clear that the old process management under the lodestar of common interest (has) reached its limits. The Federal Republic must develop leadership, in order to defend its interests', *ibid.*, p. 59.

31. *Ibid.*

11 Europe's cooperative hegemony

This study has challenged the liberal-pluralist interpretation of European integration, suggesting an alternative overall interpretation centring on the proposition that a high degree of regional institutionalization is compatible with the continuing importance of power politics and the pursuit of relative gain. A traditional hegemonic perspective focusing on material capability and unilateral behaviour cannot account for European integration. It takes an ideational realism to explain the peculiarities of informal leadership in Europe. Big states with a limited capacity for unilateral action may opt for a soft hegemonic strategy emphasizing institutionalization. We have called this strategy cooperative hegemony. A central aspect of this strategy is the policy of cooptation. Departing from Stephen Walt's assumption that states balance fear and not superior capability, it is reasonable to expect 'weak' great powers to look for strategies that might help prevent balancing behaviour. The grand strategy of cooperative hegemony may be combined with various political orders. But we have pointed to asymmetrical federation as one goal that cooperative hegemons may pursue. We have moreover outlined a brief typology of federal asymmetry, indicating ways in which cooperative hegemons may seek to mobilize bias in regional systems. Finally, we discussed a number of dynamics of hegemonic integration.

The concrete analysis of the EU's intergovernmental conferences in 1985 and 1991 confirms our expectation that France and Germany provided directional leadership by generally managing to set the overall agenda of the IGCs. However, the proposition has to be modified. Italy and the UK both exercised occasional leadership. Italy thus played an important role in bringing about the IGC that led to the Single European Act. The analysis of the results of IGC negotiations more unambiguously confirmed our expectation that Germany and France would be able to control the outcome. In both 1985 and 1991 the outcomes of the constitutive negotiations broadly reflected the joint negotiating positions of the two countries. In fact, Franco–German influence was even greater than expected in that the two countries' control extended beyond the area of high politics. France, however, was less successful than Germany and *inter alia* had to bow to the German pressure for a strengthening of the powers of the Parliament. More generally, our account modifies the established view according to which France has been leading the process of European unification. German decision-makers have been more initiating in EU constitutive politics than normally assumed. Their motives are more difficult to establish but certainly appear to have had an important power-political dimension. The concessions made to secondary members almost exclusively consisted of side-payments in the low politics area. There were indications, however, that the admission of a number of new small states would lead to a costly increase in the aggregate amount of side-payments, while making it less easy for the dual leadership to impose its views in the high politics and institutional areas.

Cooperative hegemony implies power-sharing and side-payments. Our proposition that the cooperative hegemon would regard the area of constitutive high politics as a hegemonic domain while being willing to make concessions in other areas has thus been broadly confirmed. Defence and monetary politics, both belonging to the category of constitutive high politics, were areas in which Germany and France tried to impose their views, when necessary bypassing the official EU leadership. In part, they used differentiation of the integration system to assert leadership. As the Union enlarged and Germany acquired a greater freedom of action, one saw an evolution from tactical differentiation to strategic differentiation and institutionalized asymmetry culminating in the Amsterdam decision which permitted a smaller group of members to push ahead with integration on certain conditions.

Europe's cooperative hegemon also exercised power by means of socialization. It was customary for German and less frequently French leaders to portray opponents of deeper integration as disturbers of the European peace, with Kohl's speech in Leuven being a prominent example. At the same time, the two countries – but France in particular

– cast themselves in the role of defenders of European civilization against foreign challengers.

The explanatory reach of the theory of cooperative hegemony probably transcends the borders of Europe. The theory of cooperative hegemony may be applied to different regions and different political orders. The theory thus has a comparative potential that ought to be developed. Cooperative hegemony may also co-exist with other strategies in a complex grand strategy. Thus Clinton's USA and Kohl's Germany could be argued to be applying the strategy of cooperative hegemony to varying degrees and in varying forms. Both use institutions in their hegemonic projects, the USA using NATO and APEC to coopt potential challengers such as Germany and China, and Germany using the EU with its system of cooptative, concentric circles to prevent balancing in Europe. However, there are conspicuous differences between the Clinton and the Kohl approach. The European hegemonic approach is much more institutionalized than the American and relies more heavily on economic and political resources, an expression of Germany's comparative weakness as a hegemon. The USA under Clinton, while pursuing a cooperative hegemonic approach, retains the fall-back option of unilateral and coercive military action in foreign policy.

In the European case the cooperative hegemonic strategy has aimed at federal asymmetry and has been pursued by a dual leadership with Germany playing a more prominent role than generally assumed. Our account showed clearly the tensions within the dual leadership. The intra-hegemonic problems are often solved at the cost of small-state influence. But they also create opportunities for smaller states, allowing them to act as mediators. While the concrete analysis has identified a coherent and long-term German grand strategy relating to European integration, it has also highlighted the growing tension within Europe's dual core caused first by German unification and subsequently by the ongoing process of geographical enlargement. The intra-hegemonic tension in Europe's core lends some credence to the proposition of neo-realists like Mearsheimer, who stress the disintegrating effects of resource inequality. Yet, as we have seen, the dual core survived unification. A crucial question is what has kept the dual core together in the face of disintegrative, structural pressure.

The customary neo-realist answer is that the unipolar international power structure creates a strong incentive for European big powers to merge. To some extent our study confirms that such a structural pressure exists. If one compares the 1985 IGC to the 1991 IGC it becomes apparent that the sector with the greatest international implications, that is defence, played a greater role in the IGC discussions in 1991 than in 1985. The sometimes hostile involvement of the USA in the European debate during 1990–91 appears overall to have had an integrative effect. Likewise, the three major initiatives aimed at closer monetary integration (the Werner plan, the EMS and EMU) all coincided with major turbulence in Euro–Atlantic monetary relations and in all three cases the external dimension of monetary integration was accorded great importance. Thus we do regard external balancing of unipolarity and the opportunities it creates for regional identification as part of the explanation for continuing Franco–German cooperation, although in the case of Europe and the USA, normative bonds serve as a brake on European assertiveness. It is noteworthy that those integration areas which have attracted the greatest attention in Germany and France have been monetary and defence policy, areas with a high international saliency and significant international repercussions.

Yet the systemic factor is hardly the most important one. Franco–German integration seems to thrive even in the absence of systemic pressures. And France has moved closer to NATO at a time when one would expect it to have led a crusade against the USA. A glance at the Amsterdam Treaty also reveals that the defence chapter is rather modest. The neo-realist proposition of intra-regional balancing is to some extent confirmed by the study. We noted that France's change of policy in 1984 was in part motivated by security concerns about Germany. Yet balancing assumed a special form in Europe. The dominant state in the West European region defined the terms of balancing by pre-emptively offering its neighbours a voice-opportunity in decisions affecting its domestic and foreign policy. The most important reason for the survival of Franco–German collaboration in the post-Cold War era is thus Germany's offering France a share in its evolving regional hegemony *and* the opportunities for regional hegemonic rule, which such a continental leadership offers both countries. Put differently, (German) strategy has been more important than (Waltzean) structure. Interestingly, the German propensity to reassure its neighbours is to some extent echoed by American reassurance of its European allies. One may perhaps talk about a layered cooperative hegemony in the West. Just as the USA has on the whole refrained from overtly trying to dominate Western Europe, has tried to coopt Germany and thus has prevented the hostile merging of Europe – with the Reagan period as the crucial exception that helped give birth to the Single European Act – so Germany has, since 1989, offered France a partnership and a mission which has made underlying changes in the bilateral power balance easier to accept. In this sense, cooperative hegemony challenges Robert Gilpin's theory of hegemonic transition with its emphasis on the inevitability of armed conflict.[1]

How do we explain the special German strategy of cooperative hegemony? Although this study has not analysed German strategic thinking and behaviour in great depth, a general pattern is clearly visible. The twin factors of geography and ideas deserve to be stressed. Cooperative hegemony is a logical strategic response to an exposed geopolitical location. Japan's much greater reluctance to engage in regional institutionalization suggests that geography is one determinant behind Germany's support for European integration. Yet the same geopolitical challenge may elicit quite different strategic responses. Historically, Germany has interpreted the lesson of geopolitics quite differently, although it is important to note the parallels between the Bismarck strategy, the Stresemann strategy and the Kohl strategy. The role of ideas is thus more important than geography. The German political elite has learned from historical experience, not to the extent of abandoning *Realpolitik*, but in the sense of picking the more sustainable strategic response. German politicians of an earlier epoch had, as it were, left stones on the path enabling the Federal Republic to find its way out of the forest. German politicians in the post-war period also acted within the confines of causal beliefs rooted in German history.[2] During the first decades of the integration experiment German decision-makers relied very much on Stresemann's principles. Adenauer continued Stresemann's policy of building up trust and Genscher's *sowohl-als-auch* reflex had a distinct Weimar flavour. From the second half of the 1980s, however, Germany under Kohl's ever more self-confident leadership seemed to be gradually abandoning the neo-Streseman guidelines and swinging round to a policy which bore a certain resemblance to the non-military aspects of Bismarck's German unification policy. Differentiation became a key element in the German strategy and the pursuit of asymmetry became more pronounced. One thus detects shifts of emphasis under the broad strategic umbrella of cooperative hegemony.

Another secret of the German success in establishing itself as the Union's leader was the Federal Republic's more recent tradition of cooperative federalism developed after the Second World War. The EC and later EU appeared and could be presented as simply another layer in a layered, federal system. German negotiators also arrived in Brussels well trained in consensus-oriented negotiations, in practice the most common bargaining style in the EC. By contrast, British politicians have received their training in a much more adversarial political system and are not used to solving problems through constitutional change. At the same time, paradoxically, by constructing a new consensual reality in which coercion had no place, German-influenced networks of academics and policy-makers removed a number of obstacles to the realization of the economic and political elite's more traditional goals.

A key element in the strategy of cooperative hegemony was the tactic of expansive gradualism. This tactic contained two elements. One was that, in a reformulation of the classical federalist strategy according to which federal institutions were to be created in a single constitutional decision made by a constitutional assembly, the Germans divided the great federal leap forward into a number of manageable jumps. In addition the German federal strategy was much more materialist than, for instance, the American. It counted on mobilizing popular support for integration by means of concrete achievements. The facts were expected to speak for themselves. The federal doctrine was wedded to the idea of the attraction of a core country or core area in a way that may have been inspired by the German experience in the last century. German hegemonic thinking after the Second World War thus centred on economic and ideological power and not least on the virtues of a long-term strategy and a 'political war of attrition'.

On balance the political aspects of hegemony were probably even more important than the ideological. This gradualism not only reflected pragmatic considerations but also a far-sighted self-restraint in the exercise of power. The goal of an ever closer union effectively concealed the transfer of power to Germany which was expected to be the cumulative effect of the various constitutive changes.

The British strategy towards European integration is also best understood from a hegemonic perspective. It consisted of a mixture of anti-hegemonic balancing and selective engagement, with occasional cooptation in an informal *directoire*. From a theoretical point of view the interesting thing about British EU policy is the extent to which it challenges the basic premise of the German strategy – that exit is not an option. Even Britain often found it difficult to resist the pull of the regional core, responding with integrative gestures to Franco–German threats of exclusion from a regional core. Yet, while seeking to avoid

200

isolation, the UK was hesitant to embrace the more binding commitments in areas like monetary policy and notably judicial and internal affairs. Europe's strategic set-up is of course not static. Eastern enlargement looks set to modify the political order in Western Europe. And not only do the UK and Germany see eye to eye on the issue of enlargement. The debate about institutional adaptations to enlargement also creates a new cleavage in European politics, placing the UK alongside France and Germany. The emerging leadership structure in Europe is likely to continue to be based primarily upon cooperative hegemony, but it will probably contain a larger element of *directoire*.

How did the secondary members respond to the Franco–German attempt to lead? In general, confrontational counter-strategies were rare. Band-wagoning and cooptation were the normal pattern, which seemed to vindicate the German strategy. In part this was due to German economic influence within an integrated economic system. Deliberate side-payments played an important role. Although the question has not been researched in this study, one suspects that asymmetrical economic interdependence also affected political discourse in the smaller European states, in many cases producing adaptation to core views so as to avoid cognitive dissonance. A distinction must, however, be made between the larger secondary states, the minor states and the small states just as allowance must be made for strategic discretion. It was typical for the larger secondary states such as Italy and Spain to be quite concerned whenever confronted with signs of exclusive differentiation. In most cases, however, France and Germany managed to prevent protests by co-opting the two countries either on a bilateral basis or in a extended core structure. France and Germany have adopted a similar stance vis-à-vis Poland, the largest country among the current applicant states.

Minor member states such as the Netherlands in a sense posed a bigger problem. As we have seen, apart from the UK the Dutch were among the strongest opponents of Franco–German bilateralism. The problem was that as a minor, but not small, member with a high seniority, the Dutch were too unimportant to be offered significant concessions and too important – and ambitious – to simply accept their fate as pawns in the European chess-game. Traditionally, the Dutch and the Germans had been allies sharing a broad federalist aspiration. From the 1980s this alliance eroded somewhat, as it became increasingly clear that Germany's version of federalism was asymmetrical, as opposed to Dutch symmetrical, federalism. The moment of truth occurred in the early autumn of 1991 when the Dutch presidency felt that it was being let down by Hans-Dietrich Genscher at the foreign affairs council in Dresden.

It should be added that federal asymmetry has not been a panacea for Germany. Concentration of power did not always produce band-wagoning behaviour, though this was the typical pattern. The Danish and British opt-outs represented a setback for the strategy of cooperative hegemony. Thus differentiation had only a limited effect in the case of Britain and Denmark and it remained uncertain how great a leverage the hard EMU core would have over the rest of the Union. This also points to the more fundamental problem that, unlike unilateral hegem-ons, cooperative hegemons cannot afford free-riding on a large scale.

We noted an evolution over time in which the German willingness to share power with France and smaller states diminished somewhat espe-cially after unification, without, however, at any time showing signs of disappearing. The premise of France's game of chicken with Germany – that Germany would pay a high price for avoiding open confrontation – seemed to be eroding. It was not altogether clear whether Germany would stick to cooperative hegemony as its primary strategy in the future. There was a risk that the very success of this strategy would lead to its demise in the sense of whetting Germany's appetite. But it was more probable that success would in strategic terms lead to more of the same, especially since the strategy of cooperative hegemony was broad enough to allow significant changes in leadership style. A tendency towards German unilateral reassertion within the EU co-existed – and to some extent interacted – with another trend. Geographical enlarge-ment created a need for institutional reform. Yet the voice-opportunity and special rights granted to the smaller powers proved difficult to change and indeed the very strategy of cooperative hegemony seemed less workable in the context of a greatly enlarged Union. At the end of the 1990s there were signs of emerging deadlock in constitutive negotia-tions. With a steady influx of new member states with a peripheral status, most of them poor, the cumulative cost of side-payments to ensure the support of these countries for continuing integration might prove very high. The emergence of a strong informal coalition of German-leaning countries and parties would probably only partly offset this trend. In these circumstances, there was also a risk that the German voters would lose patience with their EU partners and demand a new and more unilateral foreign policy line.

The personal prestige of Kohl still ensured that Germany did well at the Amsterdam summit but how would a new leader fare? Was Germany once again overestimating its power? If so, what would be the domestic reaction once this became clear? On closer inspection, such German worries to the extent that they existed were probably exaggerated. Kohl himself would probably answer that the quality and performance of future German leadership was not that important. EMU would do the job. It was advertised by Kohl as an 'irreversible' act of union. Indeed, the merging of monetary assets would be harder to undo than say the coordination of non-proliferation policy. What was to be made irreversible was not only European stability, it was also, albeit indirectly, German primacy.

In its European strategy Germany has generally stressed the less visible forms of federal asymmetry, preferring structural asymmetry and geopolitical asymmetry to the more risky push for institutional asymmetry. The plans for a hard core and the underlying notion of strategic differentiation are a notable exception. This version of federal asymmetry had been endorsed by the German CDU/CSU in 1994, but as we have seen, it had already been suggested by Kohl immediately after the adoption of the Single European Act as a way of marginalizing Margaret Thatcher's Britain.

France on the other hand has no other option than pursuing institutional asymmetry with the attendant costs. Its intermittent efforts to attain structural asymmetry had not been very successful, although it had managed to diffuse French administrative culture in the Commission. France was loath to accept any changes in the intra-hegemonic set-up as a consequence of German unification, but in the end had to give way. Yet the intra-hegemonic tension endures, with France demanding new institutional concessions as compensation for the (anticipated) asymmetry caused by enlargement.

The domestic political consequences of federal asymmetry in neighbouring countries is an imponderable that Germany has found it difficult to foresee and control. Chirac's debacle in the 1997 parliamentary elections illustrated this clearly. A vicious circle developed, in which the hardening of the policy of cooperative hegemony in Germany tended indirectly to fuel domestic discontent in France, which further hardened the German position. The net effect was to produce growing tension in the Franco–German duo. Particularly in the EMU negotiations Germany seemed to some extent to distance itself from earlier norms of dual leadership. Spurred on by its success in creating a growing structural asymmetry in the emerging European economic system, the Kohl government seemed at times to neglect the task of legitimating its rule. Instead of embedding the imposition of a German model in a wider global vision, German leaders (notably Theo Waigel of the CSU) at times indulged in self-congratulatory hectoring. Worrying from the point of view of European stability, there were also signs of a decreasing German ability – and willingness – to offer financial side-payments. With Eastern enlargement pending this was not a good omen.

While we detect a clear trend towards greater German self-assertion in the EU and notably in relation to France, this trend coincides with the Kohl era. Thus it is not easy to separate national assertiveness from personal and party political leadership style. There are indications that in the course of his long tenure as Chancellor and senior political figure in EU councils Kohl developed a somewhat dominant leadership style.[3]

A new and somewhat more fragile balance appeared to be emerging at the centre of Europe in which Germany assumed indirect primacy in the economic-monetary sphere and increasingly also in the political sphere, with France trying to retain leadership in the security and defence areas. With the devaluing of the French *force de frappe* (strike force) and France's return to a reformed NATO the latter role has become more and more difficult to maintain, although France keeps a residual independence in the nuclear area, the value of which may yet prove to be considerable.

The tendency over the last decade has been for the Franco–German collaboration to become more and more institutionalized both internally and vis-à-vis the Union. The move towards flexibility reflected a Franco–German attempt to circumvent sceptical member states and at the same time to institutionalize and thereby legitimate Franco–German leadership. This transformation of strategic differentiation into institutional asymmetry showed how cooperative hegemons are able to overcome the barriers of national ratification procedures. In part the Danish 'no' thus proved counterproductive for the small member states in that it paved the way for new constitutive procedures weakening the Union's minority protection. As part of a push for asymmetry this indicated a growing polarization between big and small member states in part caused by growing intra-hegemonic tension. The risk seemed to be that small members would have to pay the price for Franco–German unity – and European stability. Yet, by the late 1990s, the Franco–German axis was still functioning and there seemed as yet little prospect that it would change role from motor to detonator.[4]

Theoretical implications

From a theoretical point of view, our analysis supports the view of Stephen Brooks and others that Waltzean neo-realism makes simplified assumptions about state behaviour. The price of parsimony may be to reduce the scholarly debate to an intelligent debate about the self-evident. Specifically, our analysis of Germany's integration strategy indicates that states may pursue long-term goals and do not necessarily subordinate such goals to short-term security requirements, as Waltz would have it.[5] The preliminary theory presented in this volume suggests a number of conditions which may impel big states to opt for cooperative hegemony and links this grand strategy to the institutional strategy of federal asymmetry. However, the study explicitly rejects the view that strategy may be inferred from structure. The closest we can get to predicting strategic behaviour is to formulate a range of typical responses to a given objective constellation. A historical perspective must be added to our theoretical analysis to account for the peculiarities of state strategies. Ideational realism thus in a sense rediscovers history, escorting it back to the discipline of international relations in an orderly fashion.[6]

Ideas seem to have important effects on foreign policy. This is most clearly indicated by the continuity in the thinking in German foreign policy – and European policy – in the post-Cold War era. It may be objected, however, that the nature of this effect has not been determined by our argument. As Jachtenfuchs points out, the really interesting question in relation to the debate about the future role of Germany and Japan is whether the currently prevailing foreign policy ideas will endure and continue to withstand structural pressures, or whether we are simply dealing with a typical time-lag between structural change and strategic thinking.[7] Seen from this perspective, ideational analysts do not yet possess the empirical evidence necessary to test or falsify their theory. This criticism is important but not damaging. First of all, it is always going to be difficult to specify, when 'mental lags' can be expected to have lost importance. The argument about lags easily becomes an excuse for not taking the ideational proposition seriously. Secondly, our proposition that ideas matter does not hinge upon the case of German strategy after unification alone. It has also *inter alia* been shown that there are striking parallels between contemporary and earlier German grand strategies, with the Nazi period as the big pattern-breaker.

Our analysis also indicated that overall high politics and politics in general are more important determinants of behaviour in European integration than are economics. Political factors cannot explain all the features of EU politics, but politics in the realist sense can explain the most important features. Overall, EU politics combine three behavioural logics – the logic of power-politics, the logic of governance, and the logic of ideology. The logic of power-politics is about the re-distribution of power between member states. This, as we have seen, is the dominant logic in constitutive politics. The logic of governance is the integration logic that derives from common problems, which call for common solutions, for instance because of negative externalities and advantages of scale. Environmental problems are a case in point. The logic of ideology in integration is articulated mainly by political parties, who try to use the supranational political system to realize ideological programmes. For instance social democratic parties in the EU try to impress their employment-oriented agenda upon the EU. We would expect normal politics in the EU to be characterized by a mixture of the three logics but with the logic of governance and the logic of ideology playing an important role. The normal politics of the EU operate within a complex multi-level system with transnational party groups, supranational actors and interest groups playing a major role. Over time the fact that a range of non-state actors get a stake in an integration project undoubtedly tends to stabilize it, enhancing the costs of exit for all members, though not to the same degree. One may also speculate that over time this 'mobilization' of new non-state actors potentially tends to shift the balance away from the power-politics logic in integration politics and towards the logics of governance and ideology.

Our analysis of the EU's constitutive politics over the period from 1983 to 1993 shows clearly the continuing importance of power-politics, albeit in a new version. German and French leaders were very concerned about relative gains and characteristically devoted a lot of time to high politics issues like defence. The analysis has also broadly confirmed our expectation that political leaders at the highest level are the primary actors in European integration, the Delors Commission being a partial exception. Contrary to the view espoused in much contemporary EU research, the role of top-level political leaders has been strengthened in recent years. The new and frequent use of the institution of the IGC has strengthened the power of national heads of state and government, in the process producing a shift of power within national administrations.

The use of constitutive bargains also affected the inter-state balance of power. To the extent that the major powers find it easier to control negotiations in less formalized frameworks like the European Council and the IGCs, this is a further aspect of federal asymmetry that should not be overlooked.

Different normative conclusions may be drawn from our analysis. Should the emphasis be placed on 'hegemony' or on 'cooperative'? Is the cup half full or half empty? Some will emphasize the cooperative aspects of contemporary European power politics and stress the security risks involved in any attempt to rock the EU boat. They will also point to the benign features of European politics that emerge from a comparative historical analysis and to the multi-dimensional nature of contemporary European politics. Others will draw attention to the gulf between words and deeds, between formal rules and *de facto* influence in European politics. They will also stress that soft power strategies can be very effective. When asked about alternatives they will make a plea for global governance and a rediscovery of level-headed functionalism. To a certain extent the answer depends on the standards of evaluation one applies. Pragmatists are likely to be impressed by the level of peaceful co-existence achieved in Europe. Idealists are likely to be disappointed by the stickiness of power-political motives. This study cannot, of course, settle that debate. What it tries to do is to offer new tools and new material that may help improve the quality of the ongoing debate.

Notes

1. Robert Gilpin, *War and Change in World Politics*, Cambridge: Cambridge University Press, 1981.
2. Judith Goldstein and Robert E. Keohane (eds), *Ideas and Foreign Policy: Beliefs, Institutions and Political Change*, Ithaca, N.Y.: Cornell University Press, 1993.
3. This assessment is *inter alia* based upon statements from a well-placed observer. Interview, March 1996.
4. The expression 'detonator' is borrowed from Helen Wallace in Roger Morgan and Caroline Bray (eds), *Partners and Rivals in Western Europe: Britain, France and Germany*, Aldershot: Gower, 1984.
5. Stephen B. Brooks, 'Dueling Realisms', *International Organization*, Vol. 51, no. 3, Summer 1997, p. 450.
6. See also the interesting recent debate on the relationship between international relations and diplomatic history, e.g. Colin Elman and Miriam Fendius Elman, 'Diplomatic History and International Relations Theory: Respecting

Difference and Crossing Boundaries', *International Security*, Vol. 22/1, Summer 1997.
7. Marcus Jachtenfuchs, 'Ideen und Internationale Beziehungen', *Zeitschrift für Internationale Beziehungen*, 2. Jg., Heft 2, 1995, p. 421.

References

Adenauer, Konrad, *Erinnerungen 1945–1953, Bd. I*, Frankfurt am Main and Hamburg: Fischer Bücherei, 1967 (1965).

Adenauer, Konrad, *Erinnerungen 1955–59. Bd. III*, Frankfurt am Main and Hamburg: Fischer Bücherei, 1969 (1967).

Anderson, Jeffrey J., 'The State of the (European) Union', *World Politics*, no. 47, April 1995.

Anderson, Jeffrey J., *A United Germany in Europe: Hard Interests and Soft Power*. Paper delivered at the 1995 Annual Meeting of the American Political Science Association, Chicago, 31 August–3 September 1995.

Anderson, Jeffrey J. and Goodman, John B., 'Mars or Minerva? A United Germany in a Post-Cold War Europe', in Robert O. Keohane, Joseph S. Nye and Stanley Hoffmann (eds), *After the Cold War. International Institutions and State Strategies in Europe 1989–1991*, Cambridge, Mass.: Harvard University Press, 1993.

Ash, Timothy Garton, *In Europe's Name*, London: Vintage, 1994.

Attali, Jacques, *Verbatim I, 1983–1986*, Paris: Fayard, 1993.

Biering, Peter and Holm, Klavs A., *EU – det samlede traktatgrundlag*, Copenhagen: DJØF's forlag, 4. udg, 1996.

Bismarck, Otto von, *Werke in Auswahl. Zweiter Band. Das Werden des Staatsmannes 1815–1862. Zweiter Teil: 1854–1862*, Darmstadt: Wissenschaftliche Buchgesellschaft, 1963.

Bonvicini, Gianni, 'The Genscher–Colombo Plan and "The Solemn Declaration on European Union" (1981–1983)', in Roy Pryce (ed.), *The Dynamics of European Union*, London: Croom Helm, 1987.

Breckinridge, Robert E., 'Reassessing Regimes: The International Regime Aspects of the European Union', *Journal of Common Market Studies*, Vol. 35/2, June 1997.

Brooks, Stephen B., 'Dueling Realisms', *International Organization*, Vol. 51, no. 3, Summer 1997.

Bühl, Hartmut, 'Deutsch–Französische Sicherheitspartnerschaft', *Dokumente*, Heft 5, 46. Jahrgang, October 1990.

Bulmer, Simon and Paterson, William E., 'Germany in the European Union: Gentle Giant or Emergent Leader?', *International Affairs*, Vol. 72, no. 1, 1996.

Burgess, Michael, *Federalism and European Union*, London: Routledge, 1989.

Buzan, Barry, Jones, Charles A. and Little, Richard (eds), *The Logic of Anarchy*, New York: Columbia University Press, 1993.

Buzan, Barry, Kelstrup, Morten, Lemaître, Pierre, Tromer, Elzbieta and Waever, Ole, *The European Security Order Recast: Scenarios for the Post-Cold War Era*, London: Pinter, 1990.

Buzan, Barry and Little, Richard, 'Reconceptualizing Anarchy. Structural Realism Meets World History', *European Journal of International Relations*, Vol. 2/4, 1996.

Cameron, David, 'Transnational Relations and the Development of European Economic and Monetary Union', in Thomas Risse-Kappen (ed.), *Bringing Transnational Relations Back In*, Cambridge: Cambridge University Press, 1995.

Carlsnaes, Walter, *Ideology and Foreign Policy: Problems of Comparative Conceptualization*, Oxford: Basil Blackwell, 1987.

Carr, William, *A History of Germany, 1815–1945*, 2nd edition, London: Edward Arnold, 1979 (1969).

Charlton, Michael, *The Price of Victory*, London: BBC, 1983.

Corbett, Richard, 'The 1985 Intergovernmental Conference and the Single European Act', in Roy Pryce (ed.), *The Dynamics of European Union*, London: Croom Helm, 1987.

Count Coudenhove-Kalergi, *An Idea Conquers the World*, London: Hutchinson, 1953.

Cowles, Maria Green, 'Setting the Agenda for a New Europe: The ERT and EC 1992', *Journal of Common Market Studies*, Vol. 33/4, December 1995.

Croft, Stuart, 'European Integration, Nuclear Deterrence and Franco–British Nuclear Cooperation', *International Affairs*, 72/4, 1996.

Crone, Donald, 'Does Hegemony Matter? The Reorganization of the

Pacific Political Economy', *World Politics*, no. 45, October 1992–July 1993.

Davies, Norman, *Europe. A History*, Oxford: Oxford University Press, 1996.

Deubner, Christian, *Deutscher Europapolitik: Von Maastricht nach Kerneuropa*, Baden-Baden: Nomos Verlag, 1995.

Deudney, Daniel H., 'The Philadelphian System: Sovereignty, Arms Control, and Balance of Power in the American States-Union Circa 1787–1861', *International Organization*, Vol. 49, no. 2, Spring 1995.

Deutsch, Karl, *Political Community in the North Atlantic Area*, Princeton: Princeton University Press, 1957.

Duchacek, Ivo, *Comparative Federalism. The Territorial Dimension of Politics*, New York: Holt, Rinehart and Winston Inc., 1970.

Elman, Colin and Elman, Miriam Fendius, 'Diplomatic History and International Relations Theory: Respecting Difference and Crossing Boundaries', *International Security*, Vol. 22/1, Summer 1997.

Evans, Peter B. and Jacobsen, Harold K., *Double-Edged Diplomacy*, Berkeley and London: University of California Press, 1993.

Fawcett, Louise and Hurrell, Andrew (eds), *Regionalism in World Politics*, Oxford: Oxford University Press, 1995.

Friis, Lykke, *Den tyske magt*, Copenhagen: Politiske Studier, 1994.

Friis, Lykke, 'Germany as a Soft Great Power?, in Birthe Hansen (ed.), *European Security – 2000*, Copenhagen: Copenhagen Political Studies Press, 1995.

Gaddis, John Lewis, 'International Relations Theory and the End of the Cold War', *International Security*, Vol. 17/3, Winter 1992/93.

Gaddum, Eckart, *Die Deutsche Europapolitik in den 80er Jahren*, Munich and Vienna: Ferdinand Schöningh, 1994.

Gamble, Andrew and Payne, Anthony (eds), *Regionalism and World Order*, London: Macmillan, 1996.

Geipel, Gary L., 'The Nature and Limits of German Power', in Gary L. Geipel (ed.), *Germany in a New Era*, Indianapolis: Hudson Institute, 1993.

Genscher, Hans-Dietrich, *Erinnerungen*, Berlin: Siedler Verlag, 1995.

George, Alexander L., 'Knowledge for Statecraft: The Challenge for Political Science and History', *International Security*, Vol. 22/1, Summer 1997.

George, Stephen, *An Awkward Partner. Britain in the European Community*, second edition, Oxford: Oxford University Press, 1994.

Gerbet, Pierre, 'Le Rôle du Couple France–Allemagne dans la Création et le Développement des Communautés Européennes', in Robert Picht and Wolfgang Wessels (eds), *Motor für Europa?*, Bonn: Europa Union Verlag, 1990.

Gilpin, Robert, *War and Change in World Politics*, Cambridge: Cambridge University Press, 1981.

Goldstein, Judith and Keohane, Robert O. (eds), *Ideas and Foreign Policy: Beliefs, Institutions and Political Change*, Ithaca, N.Y.: Cornell University Press, 1993.

Grabbe, Heather and Hughes, Kirsty, *Enlarging the EU Eastwards*, London: Pinter/Royal Institute of International Affairs, 1998.

Grant, Charles, *Delors. Inside the House that Jacques Built*, London: Nicholas Brealey Publishing, 1994.

Greenwood, Sean, *Britain and European Integration Since the Second World War*, Manchester and New York: Manchester University Press, 1996.

Gretschmann, Klaus, *European Monetary Integration: EMU between the Common Good, National Interests and Regime Formation*, Esbjerg: The Torkild Kristensen Institute, Working Papers, 18/1997.

Grieco, Joseph M., 'The Maastricht Treaty, Economic and Monetary Union and the Neo-Realist Research Programme', *Review of International Studies*, Vol. 21, 1995.

Grieco, Joseph M., *Systemic Sources of Variation in Regional Institutionalization in Western Europe, East Asia, and the Americas.* Paper prepared for delivery at the Annual Meeting of the American Political Science Association, Chicago, 31 August–3 September 1995.

Grønbech, Carsten, *En realpolitisk tolkning af ØMU-projektet*, unpublished M.A. thesis, Institute of Political Science, University of Aarhus.

Grunberg, Isabelle, 'Exploring the "Myth" of Hegemonic Stability', *International Organization*, Vol. 44, no. 4, Autumn 1990.

Haas, Ernst B., *The Uniting of Europe*, London: Stevens and Sons Ltd, 1958.

Haas, Ernst B., *Beyond the Nation State*, Stanford: Stanford University Press, 1964.

Haas, Ernst B., 'The Uniting of Europe and the Uniting of Latin America', *Journal of Common Market Studies*, Vol. 5/1967.

Haas, Ernst B., 'The Study of Regional Integration: Reflections on the Joy and Anguish of Pretheorizing', in Leon L. Lindberg and Stuart Scheingold (eds), *Regional Integration: Theory and Research*, Cambridge Mass.: Cambridge University Press, 1971.

Haas, Peter M., 'Introduction: Epistemic Communities and International Policy Coordination', *International Organization*, Vol. 46, no. 1, Winter 1992.

Hagn-Meincke, Line and Hassø, Charlotte Kinimond, *Udvidelse af EU – en integrationsskabende faktor?*, Copenhagen: DJØF, 1996.

Hallstein, Walter, *Europe in the Making*, New York: Norton & Company, 1972.

Hamilton, Daniel, 'A More European Germany. A More German Europe', *Journal of International Affairs*, no. 46, Summer 1991.

Hansen, Birthe, *Unipolarity – A Theoretical Model*, Copenhagen: Institut for Statskundskab, Working Paper no. 10, 1993.

Hellmann, Günther, *'Einbindungspolitik'. United Germany and the Promise of Foreign Policy Continuity*. Paper prepared for the 36th Annual Convention of the International Studies Association in Chicago, 21–25 February 1995.

Hellmann, Günther, 'Goodbye Bismarck? The Foreign Policy of Contemporary Germany', *Mershon International Studies Review*, Vol. 40, Supplement 1, April 1996.

Hirschmann, Albert, *Exit, Voice and Loyalty*, Cambridge, Mass.: Harvard University Press, 1970.

Hoffmann, Stanley, *The European Sisyphus. Essays on Europe 1964–1994*, Boulder: Westview, 1995.

Hoffmann, Stanley, 'Obsolescent or Obsolete? The Fate of the Nation-State and the Case of Western Europe', *Daedalus*, Vol. 95, Summer 1966.

Hueglin, Thomas O., 'Europe's Ambiguous Federalism: A Conceptual and Analytical Critique', in Alan W. Cafruny and Carl Lankowski (eds), *Europe's Ambiguous Unity*, London and Boulder: Lynne Rienner Publishers, 1997.

Ikenberry, G. John, 'The Future of International Leadership', *Political Science Quarterly*, Fall 1996.

Ikenberry, John G. and Kupchan, Charles A., 'Socialization and Hegemonic Power', *International Organization*, Vol. 44, no. 3, Summer 1990.

Jachtenfuchs, Marcus, 'Ideen und Internationale Beziehungen', *Zeitschrift für Internationale Beziehungen*, 2. Jg., Heft 2, 1995.

Jachtenfuchs, Marcus, 'Democracy and Governance in the European Union', *European Integration Online Papers*, Vol. 1, 1997.

Jackson, Lears T.J., 'The Concept of Cultural Hegemony: Problems and Possibilities', *American Historical Review*, Vol. 90, no. 3.

Jacobsen, John Kurt, 'Much Ado about Ideas. The Cognitive Factor in Economic Policy', *World Politics*, no. 47, January 1995.

James, Scott C. and Lake, David A., 'The Second Face of Hegemony: Britain's Repeal of the Corn Laws and the American Walker Tariff of 1846', *International Organization*, Vol. 43, no. 1, Winter 1989.

Jenkins, Roy, *European Diary*, London: Collins, 1989.

Joffe, Joseph, ' "Bismark" or "Britain"?', *International Security*, Vol. 19, no. 4, Spring 1995.

Johnston, Alistair Iain, 'Thinking About Strategic Culture', *International Security*, Vol. 19, no. 4, Spring 1995.

Kaelberer, Matthias, 'Hegemony, Dominance or Leadership? Explaining Germany's Role in European Monetary Cooperation', *European Journal of International Relations*, Vol. 3, no. 1, March 1997.

Keatinge, Patrick and Murphy, Anna, 'The European Council's Ad Hoc Committee on Institutional Affairs (1984–85)', in Roy Pryce (ed.), *The Dynamics of European Union*, London: Croom Helm, 1987.

Keohane, Robert O. (ed.), *International Institutions and State Power: Essays in International Relations Theory*, Boulder: Westview, 1989.

Keohane, Robert O. and Hoffmann, Stanley, 'Conclusions', in William Wallace (ed.), *The Dynamics of European Integration*, London: Pinter, 1990.

Keohane, Robert and Nye, Joseph S., *Power and Interdependence: World Politics in Transition*, Boston: Little & Brown, 1977.

Keohane, Robert O., Nye, Joseph S. and Hoffmann, Stanley (eds), *After the Cold war: International Institutions and State Strategies in Europe 1989–1991*. Cambridge, Mass.: Harvard University Press, 1993.

King, Gary, Keohane, Robert O. and Verba, Sidney, *Designing Social Inquiry. Scientific Inference in Qualitative Research*, Princeton: Princeton University Press, 1994.

Krasner, Stephen, 'Structural Causes and Regime Consequences: Regimes as Intervening Variables', in Stephen Krasner (ed.), *International Regimes*, Ithaca, N.Y.: Cornell University Press, 1983.

Krasner, Stephen, *Structural Conflict*, Berkeley: University of California Press, 1985.

Krosigk, Friedrich von, 'A Reconsideration of Federalism in the Scope of the Present Discussion on European Integration', *Journal of Common Market Studies*, Vol. 9, no. 1, April 1968.

Krüger, Peter, *Die Aussenpolitik der Republik von Weimar*, Darmstadt: Wissenschaftliche Buchgesellschaft, 1985.

Lake, David A., 'Leadership, Hegemony and the International Economy: Naked Emperor or Tattered Monarch with Potential?', *International Studies Quarterly*, Vol. 33, no. 4, 1993.

Lake, David A., 'Anarchy, Hierarchy, and the Variety of International Relations, *International Organization*, Vol. 50, no. 1, Winter 1996.

Lamers, Karl and Schäuble, Wolfgang, *Reflections in European Policy. 1 September 1994*, CDU/CSU Fraktion des Deutschen Bundestages, Überlegungen zur Europäischen Politik.

Lankowski, Carl F., *Germany and the European Community*, New York: St Martin's Press, 1993.

Layne, Christopher, 'From Preponderance to Offshore Balancing: America's Future Grand Strategy', *International Security*, Vol. 22, no. 1, Summer 1997.

Le Gloannec, Anne-Marie, 'Europe by Other Means?', *International Affairs*, 73/1, 1997.

Lequesne, Christian, 'Die Europäische Politik van Jacques Chirac: Auf dem Weg zu einer Notwendigen Klärung?', *Aus Politik und Zeitgeschichte*, 21 July 1995.

Leslie, Peter M., *Asymmetry and Integration: The Emergence of Regional Hegemonic Systems*. Paper prepared for presentation at the Annual General Meeting of the Canadian Political Science Association, University of Calgary, 12–14 June 1994.

Lijphart, Arent, 'Typologies of Democratic Systems', *Comparative Political Studies*, Vol. 1, no. 1, April 1968.

Lindberg, Leon and Scheingold, Stuart, *Europe's Would-Be Polity*, New Jersey: Prentice-Hall, 1971.

Lutz, Heinrich, *Zwischen Habsburg und Preussen. Deutschland 1815–1866*, Berlin: Siedler Verlag, 1985.

Mahbubani, Kishore, 'The Pacific Impulse', *Survival*, Vol. 37, no. 1, Spring 1995.

Malnes, Raino, 'Leader and Entrepreneur in International Negotiations: A Conceptual Analysis', *European Journal of International Relations*, Vol. 1, no. 1, 1995.

Markovits, Andrei S. and Reich, Simon, *The New Face of Germany: Gramsci, Neo-Realism and Hegemony*, Graduate School of Public and International Affairs, University of Pittsburgh, Working Paper Series 28.

Martin, Lisa L., 'Institutions and Cooperation. Sanctions during the Falklands Islands Conflict', *International Security*, Vol. 16/4, Spring 1992.

Mastanduno, Michael, 'Preserving the Unipolar Moment: Realist Theories and US Grand Strategy after the Cold War', *International Security*, Vol. 21/4, Spring 1997.

Mazzucelli, Colette, *France and Germany at Maastricht. Politics and Negotiations to Create the European Union*, New York: Garland Publishing, 1996.

McCarthy, Patrick (ed.), *France–Germany 1983–1993. The Struggle to Cooperate*, London: Macmillan, 1993.

Mearsheimer, John J., 'Reply', *International Security*, Vol. 15, no. 2, Fall 1990.

Mearsheimer, John J., 'The False Promise of International Institutions', *International Security*, Vol. 19, no. 3, Winter 1994/95.

Milward, Alan S., *The European Rescue of the Nation-State*, London: Routledge, 1992.

Mitterrand, François, *Reflections sur la Politique Etrangère de la France*, Paris: Fayard, 1986.

Monnet, Jean, *Mémoires*, Paris: Fayard, 1976.

Moravcsik, Andrew, 'Negotiating the Single European Act', in Robert O. Keohane and Stanley Hoffmann (eds), *The New European Community. Decisionmaking and Institutional Change*, Boulder: Westview, 1991.

Moravcsik, Andrew, 'Negotiating the Single European Act', *International Organization*, Vol. 45, no. 1, 1991.

Moravcsik, Andrew, 'Preferences and Power in the European Community: A Liberal Intergovernmentalist Approach', *Journal of Common Market Studies*, Vol. 31, no. 4, December 1993.

Morgan, Roger, 'France and Germany as Partners', in Patrick McCarthy (ed), *France–Germany 1983–1993. The Struggle to Cooperate*, London: Macmillan, 1993.

Morgan, Roger and Bray, Caroline (eds), *Partners and Rivals in Western Europe: Britain, France and Germany*, London: Gower, 1986.

Morgenthau, Hans J., *Politics Among Nations: The Struggle for Power and Peace*, fifth revised edition, New York: Alfred A. Knopf, 1978 (1948).

Mouritzen, Hans, *Finlandization*, Aldershot: Gower, 1988.

Naumann, Friedrich, *Mitteleuropa*, Berlin: Georg Reimer, 1915.

Nordlinger, Eric A., *Isolationism Reconfigured*, Princeton, New Jersey: Princeton University Press, 1995.

Nye, Joseph S., *Peace in Parts*, New York: University Press of America, 1987 (1971).

Nye, Joseph S., *Bound to Lead*, New York: Basic Books, 1990.

Ohmae, Kenichi, *The Borderless World*, London: Fontana, 1991.

Ougaard, Morten, 'Dimension of Hegemony', *Cooperation & Conflict*, Vol. XXIII, 1988.

Pedersen, Thomas, 'EF – en supermagt i svøb? Vesteuropæisk sikkerhedspolitisk samarbejde udenfor NATO', unpublished dissertation, Copenhagen, 1989.

Pedersen, Thomas, 'Political Change in the European Community: The Single European Act as a Case of System Transformation', *Cooperation & Conflict*, Vol. 1, 1992.

Pedersen, Thomas, *European Union and the EFTA Countries. Enlargement and Integration*, London: Pinter, 1994.

Pedersen, Thomas, *Three Faces of European Governance*, Institute of Political Science, Aarhus University, 1995.

Pedersen, Thomas, 'Europa – Tysklands anden Nation', in Henning Gottlieb and Frede P. Jensen (eds), *Tyskland i Europa*, Copenhagen: SNU, 1995.

Pedersen, Thomas, 'Sub-systems and Regional Integration – the Case of Nordic and Baltic Cooperation', in Susanna Perko (ed.), *Nordic–Baltic Region in Transition*, Tampere: Tampere Peace Research Institute, 1996.

Pedersen, Thomas, 'Structure or Strategy: The Case of French European Policy after the Cold War', in Georg Sørensen and Hans-Henrik Holm (eds), *And Now What? International Politics after the Cold War*, Aarhus: Politica, 1998, pp. 103–24.

Pentland, Charles, *International Theory and the European Community*, London: Faber, 1973.

Peterson, John, 'Decision-Making in the EU: Towards a Framework for Analysis', *Journal of European Public Policy*, Vol. 2, no. 1, 1995.

Peterson, Nikolaj, ' "Game, Set and Match". Denmark and the European Union from Maastricht to Edinburgh', in Teija Tiilikainen and Ib Damgaard Petersen (eds), *The Nordic Countries and the EC*, Copenhagen: Copenhagen Political Studies Press, 1993.

Picht, Robert and Wessels, Wolfgang (eds), *Motor für Europa?*, Bonn: Europa Union Verlag, 1990.

Pierson, Paul, 'The Path to European Integration: An Historical Institutionalist Analysis', *Comparative Political Studies*, no. 29, 1996.

Pinder, John, *European Community. The Building of a Union*, Oxford: Oxford University Press, 1991.

Pollack, Mark A., 'Creeping Competence: The Expanding Agenda of the European Community', *Journal of Public Policy*, no. 29, 1994.

Pollack, Mark A., 'The New Institutionalism and EC Governance: The

Promise and Limits of Institutional Analysis', *Governance: An International Journal of Policy and Administration*, Vol. 9, no. 4, October 1996.

Posen, Barry R. *The Sources of Military Doctrine: France, Britain and Germany Between the World Wars*, Ithaca, N.Y.: Cornell University Press, 1984.

Putnam, Robert, 'Diplomacy and Domestic Politics. The Logic of Two-Level Games', *International Organization*, Vol. 42, Summer 1988.

Rapkin, David P. (ed.), *World Leadership and Hegemony*, Boulder and London: Lynne Rienner Publishers, 1990.

Réau, Elisabeth du, *L'Idée d'Europe au XXe Siècle*, Paris: Edition Complexe, 1996.

Riker, William H., *Federalism. Origin. Operation. Significance*, Boston & Toronto: Little Brown & Company, 1964.

Riou, Gaston, *S'Unir ou Mourir*, Paris: Valois, 1929.

Rosecrance, Richard, 'Regionalism and the Post-Cold War Era', *International Journal*, Vol. XLVI, no. 3, Summer 1991.

Ross, George, *Jacques Delors and European Integration*, Cambridge: Polity Press, 1995.

Ruyt, Jean de, *L'Acte Unique Européen*, Brussels: Editions de l'Université de Bruxelles, 1989.

Sandholz, Wayne, 'Choosing Union: Monetary Politics and Maastricht', *International Organization*, Vol. 47, no. 1, Winter 1993.

Sandholz, Wayne and Zysman, John, 'Recasting the European Bargain', *World Politics*, Vol. XLII, no. 1, 1992.

Sbragia, Alberta M., 'Thinking about the European Future: The Uses of Comparison', in Alberta M. Sbragia (ed.), *Euro-Politics. Institutions and Policymaking in the 'New' European Community*, Washington D.C.: The Brookings Institution, 1992.

Schelling, Thomas C., *The Strategy of Conflict*, New York/Oxford: Galaxy Books, 1963.

Schmidt, Helmut, *Die Deutschen und ihre Nachbarn*, Berlin: Siedler Verlag, 1990.

Schroeder, Paul, 'Historical Reality vs Neo-Realist Theory', *International Security*, Vol. 19/1, Summer 1994.

Simonean, Haig, *The Privileged Partnership*, Oxford: Clarendon, 1985.

Skjalm, Karsten, *Det Europæiske Valutasamarbejdes Politiske Økonomi*, Aarhus: Institut for Statskundskab, Aarhus Universitet, 1995.

Snidal, Duncan, 'The Limits of Hegemonic Stability Theory', *International Organization*, Vol. 39, no. 4, Autumn 1985.

Snidal, Duncan, 'Relative Gains and the Pattern of International Cooperation', *American Political Science Review*, Vol. 85, September 1991.

Sperling, James, 'A Unified Germany, a Single European Economic Space, and the Prospects for the Atlantic Economy', in Carl F. Lankowski (ed.), *Germany and the European Community*, New York: St. Martin's Press, 1993.

Stirk, Peter M.R. (ed.), *Mitteleuropa. History and Prospects*, Edinburgh: Edinburgh University Press, 1994.

Story, Jonathan and Carmoy, Guy de, 'France and Europe', in Jonathan Story (ed.), *The New Europe: Politics, Government and Economy Since 1945*, Oxford: Blackwell, 1993.

Story, Jonathan and Cecco, Marcello de, 'The Politics and Diplomacy of Monetary Union: 1985–1991', in Jonathan Story (ed.), *The New Europe. Politics. Government and Economy Since 1945*, Oxford: Blackwell, 1993.

Stürmer Michael, 'Deutsche Interessen', in Karl Kaiser and Hanns W. Maull (eds), *Deutschlands Neue Aussenpolitik. Band 1. Grundlagen*, Munich: R. Oldenburg Verlag, 1995.

Sum, Ngai-Ling, 'The NICs and Competing Strategies of East Asian Regionalism', in Andrew Gamble and Anthony Payne (eds), *Regionalism and World Order*, London: Macmillan, 1996.

Taras, Raymond and Zeringue, Marshal, 'Grand Strategy in a Post-Bipolar World: Interpreting the Final Soviet Response', *Review of International Studies*, Vol. 18, 1992.

Taylor, Paul, *The Limits of European Integration*, London: Croom Helm, 1983.

Taylor, Paul, 'The European Community and the State: Assumptions, Theories and Propositions', *Review of International Studies*, Vol. 17, 1991.

Teltschik, Horst, *329 Tage*, Bonn: Siedler Verlag, 1992.

Thatcher, Margaret, *The Downing Street Years*, London: HarperCollins, 1993.

Toynbee, Arnold J., *A Study of History*, London: D.C. Somerville, 1960 (1934).

Tranholm-Mikkelsen, Jeppe, 'Neo-Functionalism: Obstinate or Obsolete? A Reappraisal in the Light of the New Dynamism of the EC', *Millennium*, Vol. 20/1, 1991.

Treue, Wilhelm, *Die Geschichte von Deutschland*, Stuttgart: Alfred Kröner Verlag, 1978.

Vedrine, Hubert, *Les Mondes de François Mitterrand*, Paris: Fayard, 1996.

Wæver, Ole, *Introduktion til International Politik*, Copenhagen: Institut for Statskundskab, 1992.

Wæver, Ole, *Introduktion til Studiet af International Politik*, Copenhagen: Forlaget Politiske Studier, 1992.

Wæver, Ole, 'Hvordan det hele alligevel kan gå galt', in Gottlieb and Jensen (eds), *Tyskland i Europa*, Copenhagen: SNU, 1995.

Wallace, Helen and Wallace, William, *Flying Together in a Larger and More Diverse European Union*, The Hague: Netherlands Scientific Council for Government Policy, Working Documents 87, 1995.

Wallace, Helen and Wallace, William, *Policy-Making in the European Union*, Oxford: Oxford University Press, 1996.

Wallace, William, *The Transformation of Western Europe*, London: Pinter, 1989.

Walt, Stephen M., *The Origins of Alliances*, Ithaca: Cornell University Press, 1987.

Waltz, Kenneth, *Man, the State and War*, New York: Columbia University Press, 1959 (1954).

Waltz, Kenneth, *Theory of International Politics*, New York: Random House, 1979.

Watson, Adam, *International Society*, London: Routledge, 1992.

Westlake, Martin, *The Council of the European Union*, London: Cartermill, 1995.

Wiener, Jarrod, 'Hegemonic Leadership: Naked Emperor or the Worship of False Gods?', *European Journal of International Relations*, Vol. 1, no. 2, 1995.

Willis, Roy F., *France, Germany and the New Europe 1945– 1963*, Stanford: Stanford University Press, 1965.

Wolfers, Arnold, *Discord and Collaboration*, Baltimore: The Johns Hopkins Press, 1962.

Young, Oran, 'Political Leadership and Regime Formation: On the Development of Institutions in International Society', *International Organization*, Vol. 45, no. 3, Summer 1991.

Zürn, Michael, 'The Challenge of Globalization and Individualization. A View from Europe', in Hans-Henrik Holm and Georg Sørensen (eds), *Whose World Order? Uneven Globalization and the End of the Cold War*, Boulder: Westview, 1995.

Primary sources

Europe 1990, speech to be given by Dr W. Dekker at the Centre for European Policy Studies in Brussels, on the occasion of the presentation of the programme *Europe 1990 – An Agenda For Action.*

'Wir gewinnen mit Europa'. Grundsatzrede auf dem 3. Parteitag der CDU in Düsseldorf am 27 Oktober 1992, in Helmut Kohl, *Der Kurs der CDU. Reden und Beiträge des Bundesvorsitzenden 1973–1993*, Stuttgart: Deutsche Verlags-Anstalt, 1993, pp. 430ff.

Europa-Archiv, various issues
Frankfurter Allgemeine Zeitung
Agence Europe
Le Monde
Reuter Library Report
Dialog. Reuters. 1168757
Reuter Newswire
Guardian
Financial Times
Independent
Daily Telegraph
The Times
Sunday Telegraph

Index